NewsTalk I

NewsTalk I

State-of-the-Art Conversations with Today's Print Journalists

SHIRLEY BIAGI

California State University, Sacramento

Wadsworth Publishing Company
Belmont, California
A Division of Wadsworth, Inc.

Senior Editor: Rebecca Hayden
Editorial Associate: Naomi Brown
Production Editor: Gary Mcdonald
Print Buyer: Karen Hunt
Designer: Paula Shuhert
Copy Editor: Sally Schuman
Compositor: Omegatype Typography, Inc.
Cover: Paula Shuhert

Printed in the United States of America   19
1 2 3 4 5 6 7 8 9 10—90 89 88 87

ISBN 0-534-06714-X

Library of Congress Cataloging-in-Publication Data

Biagi, Shirley.
  Newstalk I.

  (Wadsworth media interview series)
  Includes index.
  1. Journalists—United States—Interviews. I. Title.
II. Series.
PN4871.B5   1986   070'.92'2   86-9253
ISBN 0-534-06714-X

For Jan Haag

FOREWORD

NewsTalk I is the first in a series of interviews with American journalists about what they do. Through *NewsTalk I*, 12 recognized print journalists from all over the United States can be like "guest speakers," talking with you at your convenience.

Prominent, as well as lesser-known but well-regarded, journalists are included to enhance the scope of each book. *NewsTalk I* includes big names at big newspapers as well as well-respected reporters at newspapers with medium-sized and small circulations. Some suggested Perspectives precede each interview, and following each interview is a sample of the journalist's writing. An Overview of Ideas and Issues to help compare and contrast the interviewees begins on page 209.

NewsTalk departs from the traditional media text to offer the variety, depth, breadth and practical advice that can come only from people working as journalists every day. The goal of this series is to produce a dialogue that is provocative, substantial, timely and important.

PREFACE

The 12 people in this book are all award-winning journalists. Four of them have won Pulitzer Prizes. They also have won the George Polk Award, two Nieman Fellowships, the Ford Foundation Fellowship, the Associated Press Managing Editors Award, the Edward P. Mott Award, the Sportswriter of the Year Award, the Fourth Estate Award, and more than three dozen state and local reporting prizes.

Prizes do not necessarily make good journalists, and some people argue that prizes are not always given to the best journalists. But the profession has in some way honored all of these people for doing their jobs well. They are good representatives of the profession.

The conversations, each of which lasted several hours, have been edited to offer the most significant observations from each reporter's experience. Each person came to the profession differently and stayed for different reasons. Most of them worked on a school paper—either in high school or college—and most of them say they knew very early that they were going to be writers.

Geographically these journalists represent newspapers throughout the United States—from *Newsday* on Long Island to *The Dallas Morning News* to the *Los Angeles Times*. Some of the reporters work where they grew up. Others work 3,000 miles or more from home—a Nevadan works in Washington, D.C., a New Englander works in California, an Italian works in New York.

Eleven of them were born in the United States, one was born in Europe. Some are married, some are not. Some have children, some do not. Some of them finished college, some of them didn't. Some majored in journalism, others didn't. The sexes are evenly represented. None is less than 30 years old. Two are over 65.

They have worked for large, small and medium-sized newspapers. They write columns, reviews, news, features and books. One works for a wire service. Two of them work in broadcast as well as print. After reading these interviews, it would be difficult to conclude that the press is either monolithic or singularly ideological.

That is the message of this collection, and it has been the challenge of putting it together. These conversations took place in locations as different as the people they represent—over lemonade in the humid shade of a 30-foot oak tree in a Philadelphia backyard, a cup of coffee in the press wing of the White House, a Coca-Cola in an empty coffee shop in Jackson, Mississippi, and a cocktail in New York's Algonquin Hotel. This collection gives the reader the benefit of personal and practical information that has taken these reporters 12 professional lifetimes to gather.

Acknowledgments This collection could not have been put together without the selfless time and attention of the 12 people featured in this book who sat and talked with me, often for several hours, sometimes over several days. To them, a deep thank you.

Becky Hayden has been centrally important to me because she believed in the idea for the Wadsworth Media Interview Series before anyone else did. The other people at Wadsworth who have helped me beyond what any author should expect are: Gary Mcdonald, Robert Kauser, Paula Shuhert and Naomi Brown.

For special help with this book I would like to thank Harlene Beattie, Joel Brinkley, Roy Peter Clark, Stuart Dim, Kris Gilger, Frank McCulloch, Harry Silberman, Wendee Wieking and Richard Zahler. For her energetic company and flawless transcription, I owe a big thank you to Jan Haag.

I am also grateful to the reviewers who offered their suggestions and enthusiasm: Giles M. Fowler, Iowa State University; Thomas B. Littlewood, University of Illinois–Urbana; Pat G. McNeely, University of South Carolina; Tommy Miller, *Houston Chronicle*; Ricky D. Pullen, California State University–Fullerton; Sharon Sexton, Temple University; and Stanley Soffin, Michigan State University.

Shirley Biagi

Contents

11

Helen Thomas, United Press International 181

12

Roger Ebert, *Sun-Times* 193

NewsTalk I

"If I don't have a byline pretty often—two, three times a week—I start getting withdrawal pains."

RHETA GRIMSLEY JOHNSON

Rheta Grimsley Johnson writes about her family and her neighborhood—whether she's living off the coast of Georgia on St. Simons Island, where she started a newspaper with her husband, or near the Mississippi Delta towns she has covered for the Memphis *Commercial-Appeal* since 1980. At *The Commercial-Appeal* she writes features and a column. One of those columns, about her father, was included in a series of articles for which she won the American Society of Newspaper Editors' award for commentary in 1982:

> His life's patterns would make poor lyrics for a country song. For he was straight and clean-shaven, rarely drunk and less often in love. . . .
>
> To have had any more than a 30-year mortgage and Saturdays off would have confused him. And the only confusion he allowed in his life centered on the tint knob on his color TV. . . .
>
> When he was betrayed, 25 years into his career, it was more than being passed over for a promised promotion. It was like an unfaithful spouse, an errant child, the ultimate treason. The shine was gone from his 25-year silver tray. The company had forgotten its own. He'd been bitten by his own dog. . . .
>
> It was a turn of events my father had never considered.*

Since college she has been married to Jimmy Johnson, a cartoonist who has just syndicated a comic strip. "I steal the best of Jimmy," she says. "You live with somebody that long, they're bound to make a column

---

* *"Bitten by His Own Dog,"* The Commercial-Appeal, *May 19, 1982.*

or two. He's paying me back, though. I'm literally seeing myself in the funny papers."

Rheta Johnson, 33, has absorbed her Southern environment the way a magnolia absorbs water. She is a storyteller in the tradition of America's many Southern storytellers. But she says that the same proportion of good writers exists in the South as anywhere else. "There's a tendency to think that anybody with a typewriter down here is a genius because of some of the geniuses that have come from here. They think everybody who holds a pen or gets behind a typewriter is Flannery O'Connor. And that's not true."

Several times she and Jimmy have faced newspapers that wouldn't hire a husband and wife together. At one point, the policy against hiring spouses at a Jackson, Mississippi, newspaper forced her to look for work in the Greenville, Mississippi, bureau of the Memphis *Commercial-Appeal* while her husband stayed in Jackson. Rheta Johnson lived 125 miles from her husband so she could work. When she gave this interview, she and Jimmy were headed for Memphis together. She finally was going to work in what she calls "the big house"—the *Commercial-Appeal* in Memphis. ❖

from Rheta Grimsley Johnson
- The role a reporter plays in community journalism
- The difficulties of starting your own newspaper
- The importance of a commitment to succeed

BEGINNINGS

I always wanted to be a reporter, never wanted to be anything else. There's no one in my family who was in journalism. My father was a meat cutter and my mother a housewife and my grandparents were all peanut farmers in Georgia.

I worked on school papers from the time I was in the eighth grade. I almost didn't graduate from college because I spent all my time at the college newspaper. It was the only thing that mattered to me. I like to write stories, and it seemed like a way to make a living, writing stories.

I was born in Georgia, but I grew up in Montgomery, Alabama. I went to college at Auburn University, thinking I would major in English. Then someone told me, "In English they can teach you the words, but in journalism we can teach you how to comfort the afflicted and afflict the comfortable." It's an old slogan on several newspapers. But I loved that. I thought, journalism it is. So I majored in journalism and minored in English.

I was editor of the college newspaper my senior year. At Auburn, editor was an elected position, student-wide. Somebody ran for Homecoming queen, somebody ran for newspaper editor, which is ludicrous, but that's the way it was.

THE FIRST BYLINE

The first story I wrote for the paper, I must have checked my byline on the inside of that paper 23 times. I kept sneaking peeks at it to make sure that it didn't go away. The first story was about traffic tickets. More students had been getting traffic tickets than in the past—some mundane, 10-paragraph story. But I was hooked. It was like heroin, I guess. I was an addict. I'm still not good on long-range projects. If I don't have a byline pretty often—two, three times a week—I start getting withdrawal pains.

Right out of school, my husband and I started a newspaper on St. Simons Island, off the coast of Georgia. We had honeymooned there, and we had looked around and said, "There's not a newspaper on this island."

I had worked summers and Christmas for a small paper in a little town called Opelika, Alabama, at the *Opelika-Auburn News*. And the editor of the *Opelika-Auburn News* liked our idea for starting a paper on St. Simons.

He gave us $2,000, some old equipment and a pat on the back and said, "Go see what you can do." I had not graduated. But I thought $2,000 would never pass my way again. It seemed like an awful lot of money. So I left Auburn in the summer of '75 and we went to St. Simons. A third journalism graduate went with us. We were down there only two weeks before we put out our first issue.

We had to do all the selling of ads, all the reporting, all the writing. We usually averaged only 10 pages, which doesn't sound like much, but we had to fill every inch. We all took pictures and processed film. I did the typesetting on borrowed equipment one night a week. We stayed up two nights a week, all night long, pasting up the paper. Then we had to roll 7,000 papers and throw them to every house on the island. We used an old Volkswagen van to deliver papers for a couple weeks, then it blew up and we used our Pinto.

We had to drive 100 miles just to get the paper printed because the nearest paper saw us as competition, possibly because they didn't know what a shoestring operation it was. But I got this real trial by fire. I think it shaped my attitudes.

We literally wore ourselves out. We lost money real fast. We paid ourselves some weeks, but mostly what we'd do was pay our Pinto payment, just try to survive as best we could, and pay our rent. We had swap-outs with all the seafood restaurants—they could have an ad if we could have some shrimp or clam chowder. It took me about three years after that before I could look at a shrimp again.

We stayed only 10 months, 26 issues. Our last issue was on Christmas Day, 1975. Christmas Day we were sitting in the middle of the floor, rolling newspapers. This was also the first year I was married, and it was like there was no honeymoon. It was the hardest thing I've ever done in journalism. It made everything else, including wire-service work, seem downright easy.

WE MOVE TO THE *MONROE JOURNAL*

Then came our first trouble finding a paper that would hire us both. At this time Jimmy was reporting. And we ended up at a weekly newspaper in Monroeville, Alabama, at the *Monroe Journal*. This was 1976. Monroeville is Harper Lee's hometown, the town described in *To Kill a Mockingbird*.

I liked the fact that Harper Lee had lived there because one of my favorite books has always been *To Kill a Mockingbird*. I felt that if somebody like Harper Lee could grow up here, it wasn't going to hurt to work a year in this town.

Monroeville was in the middle of nowhere—southwest Alabama—but it had one of the best weeklies I've ever seen anywhere. The newspaper was family-owned. The father was the publisher, the son was the editor, his wife was the ad director, and they always hired two additional reporters to do all the legwork. That's what Jimmy and I were hired to do. We split all the wedding announcements, all the community news—so-and-so visited Aunt so-and-so in Mineola last Sunday—and the livestock report.

We shot football games at night in stadiums so small that there were no lights. I remember, on some of the fields, they would line up the cars and turn on the lights to play ball. We're talking country here. If people liked a story you did, sometimes they'd bring in a jar of pickled preserves and vegetables. It was very unspoiled community journalism.

THE *OPELIKA-AUBURN NEWS* IS NEXT

Then after a year I decided to go back and get my degree. Jimmy had already graduated. So I went back to Auburn in 1977 and took 20 hours in one quarter and graduated. Then we both went back to work at the *Opelika-Auburn News* for a couple of years. I did news and feature stories, and I got to write a column every now and then. I was the photographer, too.

The best thing about the *Opelika-Auburn News* was that I got to try my hand for the first time at commentary and found that I liked it. Even now I report a lot and do columns, too, and I don't see how people sit in their offices and, just based on what they read in other parts of the paper, come up with good, invigorating column copy. I can't do it. Maybe deeper thinkers than I are able to, but I have to be out there where it's happening.

It probably all goes back to working for papers so small that you had to do a little of everything. You had to write institutional editorials.

You had to fill up the op-ed page. You had to fill up the front page. I just never quit.

In Opelika, I didn't even follow the rules. I'd cover the county commission meeting on Monday morning, and then I'd go back and hand in an op-ed column that said they were all lunatics. Then I expected to go back to the next meeting and be treated civil.

WORKING AT THE *AUBURN BULLETIN*

I once had this editor who said that he would go on down the road to another newspaper for another dollar and hamburger a week. That's about what I did. I went to a paper called the *Auburn Bulletin*. It was a twice-a-week paper, which is sort of like taking a step down, except they offered to let me be managing editor, which sounded great at the time.

Another reason I left the *Opelika-Auburn News* is because it sold out to the Thomson newspaper chain. The day they ran a big K-Mart ad on the editorial page, I knew I was going somewhere.

At the *Bulletin,* again, I did everything from a little bit of typesetting to running an occasional [newspaper] route. I've never, ever had the luck or maybe the ability to cover the big stuff. No one flood or earthquake or volcanic eruption has made my career. There's been nothing, no big turning point like that.

The *Bulletin* had—this is the God's truth—1,500 circulation. It was on the skids when I went there, but it didn't matter to me. I still thought every story had to be the best. I just cared. I sweat blood over every word.

And the papers were competitive. There was this old-fashioned kind of newspaper competitiveness that was exhilarating. I can remember the rack man at the *Auburn Bulletin* showed me—this was terrible—how to put Super Glue on a dime and drop it in the competitor's rack. It would gum up the works for the rest of the day, and they wouldn't sell any papers. I don't remember doing it, but I liked having that knowledge.

I stayed there for 11 months. The circulation went up a little bit. I thought we improved the product. But I had to do everything. I was making $225 a week, and that was after several raises. And I didn't have any staff. We had to use interns because you only had to pay them $50 a week. We were without a sportswriter at all for a month, and I was having to depend on stringers in a community where sports is the most important thing. Auburn football is just like religion.

It was a joke that I was being called managing editor. The chain that I was working for had no respect for women whatsoever, and I knew that there was never any chance of going from there to another one of their papers in any capacity except a reporter. I knew it was just corporate bait that I was called managing editor. So I left without having another job.

ON TO JACKSON, MISSISSIPPI

Then Jimmy decided to try what he'd always wanted to try, and that was editorial cartooning. They had an opening in Jackson, Mississippi, of all places. We moved here thinking, sure, I'll be able to get on. I had won several Alabama Press Association awards by that time. Wrong. They had a very stern nepotism policy at the *Jackson Daily News*. They would not bend the rules about couples even though Jimmy would be doing cartoons and have absolutely nothing to do with editing or the news operation. They wouldn't even look at my resume. This was 1978.

I took a PR job for a state agency. It was like going to a great day-care center in the sky every day. It was a big multi-story building, and Jimmy would drop me off on his way to go to the newspaper. I was just heartbroken. I wouldn't even watch "Lou Grant" on TV. It was like I was being held hostage. I couldn't do what I wanted to do.

WORKING FOR OLD RELIABLE

I applied to every paper within a 50-mile radius. I was just miserable, I was bitter, I was heartbroken. It's really a wonder that Jimmy survived it. All I'd ever wanted to do was be a reporter, and everybody was telling me that I couldn't. So finally I worked up the guts—and I'd never worked for a large paper at all—to write *The* [Memphis] *Commercial-Appeal*. People called *The Commercial-Appeal* the "Old Reliable" or the "Delta Bible." It was 200 miles away from me, but I thought maybe I could commute between here and Memphis. I was desperate.

A very kind night editor wrote me back. He said the commute was too long and it wouldn't work out, I'd be unhappy. Well, I wrote him right back—which is very unlike me. I'm very shy and I have to overcome it in my work every day. I said, "Listen, I'm being told I can't work here [in Jackson] because I'm married. Now you're telling me I can't work 200 miles away because I'm married. Please let me come talk to you." So he wrote back and said, "OK. OK."

I went to Memphis, and about a week after that the Greenville, Mississippi, bureau job came open. They offered it to me and I snapped it up. I packed up my grandmother's quilt and a few books and found a place to live in Greenville, which is 125 miles away from Jackson. It was expensive. We were renting here [in Jackson], and I had to rent a place there. I probably paid *The Commercial-Appeal* to work for the first couple of years, doing all the commuting.

I didn't fit any mold. I was this married woman, almost 30, trying to break into journalism. Even though I'd been doing it for eight years, it seemed like I was starting over, and I did. The bureau jobs were usually given to people right out of college, who'd never done police beat, court reporting, county commission, any of these things I'd spent years doing. But I didn't care. I was damn happy in that Greenville bureau. It was the happiest I've ever been in my life.

I was back seeing my byline, and this time it wasn't in a paper that nobody got. This time it was in *The Commercial-Appeal.* To me, that was big time. The circulation was about 170,000 weekdays, and it doubled on Sunday. I did the same kind of things that were my bread and butter at papers I'd had to fill up single-handedly. They served me well.

I'd cover federal court, and if it was a slow day, I'd do a story on a woman who had a doll collection. I had no preconceived ideas about what important stories I was supposed to be doing because I'd never done any important stories. I usually had a story every day. I just had the time of my life.

A BRIEF MOVE TO UPI

I'd been there seven months—I tell you, I never stay anywhere long—when there was an opening in Jackson at UPI. I didn't want to take it because nobody gets to go out to cover much, sitting there taking chicken reports from the livestock agency over the phone. But I had to consider my family and my husband. I went to work for UPI in July of '81. I stayed at UPI eight months. In the eight months I was there, we had three different bureau managers.

I'd come in at 2 in the afternoon and work until 10:30 or 11 at night. Every story you write for the wire service, you write three different ways—one's for a.m. papers, one's for p.m. papers and one's for broadcast. It's excellent training, and it makes you fast. You'd see an idea, and you'd call the person on the phone, get a few quotes and write it up. Rip-and-read artists all over the region would be reading your story before your fingers got cold.

BACK TO *THE COMMERCIAL-APPEAL*

I didn't like wire-service work. I called *The Commercial-Appeal* and said, "Please, please take me back. You were right. I don't like wire-service work. I'll take any bureau you've got." I still didn't have the courage or the confidence to ask to go into the big house, to go straight to Memphis. The Tupelo, Mississippi, bureau happened to be open. It was farther than Greenville—170 miles from Jackson. I commuted again on weekends. I got my quilt and my books again and I hit the road.

I couldn't help it. It was like an obsession, and I had to do it. Jimmy was very understanding, but it was even sadder this time, because there was this indefinite feeling that this could go on forever—we're never going to be able to live in the same town and have a normal life. Yet, the other urge was stronger. I had to be back at a newspaper.

I wasn't in Tupelo that long. They called me into Memphis to write editorials, and I did that for four or five months. Then I came back to Jackson. They [*The Commercial-Appeal*] said, "You can do what you do for us from Jackson. You can travel. You can be a regional reporter and you can live at home." I've been back for two-and-a-half years, and I've done a little bit of everything, from covering Bear Bryant's funeral to floods to tornadoes to politics. I started doing a regular column, a commentary that runs in our Sunday magazine. It's also carried by the Scripps-Howard news service. I've enjoyed that a lot.

Last summer I got to go to the Democratic Convention and the Olympics. The best part of that was I drove to L.A. and drove back, and I did sort of a—for lack of a better name—search-for-America series. I did 22 pieces [called "America's Faces"] on Americans who, for some reason or another, had a story that was particularly interesting to me. It's like a dream assignment—just take your time and find what you can.

I was gone all summer. I spent a month at the Olympics and a couple of weeks covering the convention. Some people I had planned to the minute. Others I would just happen upon, or I would go by the office of a newspaper friend in Oklahoma and ask if he had any ideas, and he'd steer me in one direction and I'd end up in another. There was a dentist off the coast of Connecticut. A UPI buddy told me about him and said he'd never had a chance to do the story, but he thought it would be a good one for my sort of feature.

The dentist was handicapped. He had no control over the bottom half of his body, and his office was on a sailboat. He would go from island to island, treating patients. They called him Painless Pete. The patients would line up on the pier on the day he was supposed to get there. If the winds were favorable, he would dock at the appointed time and they would go in. He was free on the water. He couldn't get around on land, but on that sailboat, everything was small and contained and he could manage his trade. It was just amazing to me.

If I came to any conclusions from traveling last summer, it was that the regions are still very distinct, that this homogeneous America you hear so much about is not true. We have interstates and Ramada Inns at each exit now, but that doesn't mean the regions don't have some real birthmarks. The South, possibly because so much of it is rural, has managed to hold onto its identity a little better, I think, than a lot of other places.

SOUTHERN STEREOTYPES

There's an easygoing ambiance in Southern history in both the black and white communities, which are still very separate. I mean, we all eat in McDonald's together now and everybody thinks that means there's a New South, but there's no such thing as a New South, in my opinion. The old attitudes are dying out as some of the older people die, but a lot of them are still around.

The only recreation that's free in this town is a place called Ross Barnett Reservoir. It's a big man-made lake. And blacks sit on the banks and watch the white people on their sailboats on the Ross Barnett Reservoir. I don't see how that constitutes a New South. I'm really on a soapbox now. I think not enough people point this out in stories and columns. We latch onto certain lines and we get carried away with them and start believing them. Sometimes I feel that all of us, not just in the South, but all journalists, repeat phrases about Lebanon or a hostage crisis, the same phrases again and again.

The New South, to me, is the biggest myth of all. There are more black officeholders in Mississippi—I think I'm right on this—than in any other state in the nation. Now that is important and that's certainly a change for the better, but this is also the state with the largest black population. I mean, we latch on to singular statistics to prove a case that's not true. It's just formula stuff.

COVERING THE SOUTH

The South is steeped in religious values that have permeated every part of our society. The shopping centers are still closed on Sunday here. Religion is not a private matter of the heart in the South. It's part of everything, public and private. I think you have to recognize that and you have to write about it.

I'd also say that every story you're covering in the South, no matter how far apart it seems from having a racial angle, you should look for one. You don't need to belabor it in your story, necessarily, but nine times out of 10, it's there.

There are so many things said between the lines here. There's not open race baiting in political campaigns. But there are code words now. There was a race between a black man and a white man in a congressional district that included part of the Mississippi Delta. And the white candidate actually put out a campaign poster that had a picture of his opponent. He wanted everybody who might be unaware that his opponent was black to be sure and know this so the white voters would get out and vote, because white voters can be complacent unless they know they're threatened by a black candidate. The white candidate won.

WHAT MAKES A GOOD REPORTER

If I am a good reporter—and I'm a better writer than I am a reporter, but I think I'm a fair reporter—it's not because I'm aggressive. I'm not aggressive. I'm shy. Sometimes I think people talk to me because they're filling in the silence. They don't see me as pressing because I'm not. So they talk more easily. And reporting is about getting people to talk.

Reporters can be shy but I think they have to see a story everywhere. The old saying, "There are no slow days, just slow reporters" is real true. If you sit around waiting for either major inspiration or some wonderful story to break in front of your nose, you're not going to get anywhere.

If my career has been successful—and it's been successful beyond my wildest dreams, just to be working for *The Commercial-Appeal*—it's been because I tried to approach each story like it was important and not like I was treading water until the real thing came along. If you have an attitude that each story matters, I think that makes a good reporter.

You also must see the overall. To me, legislative reporters start writing for legislators and other legislative reporters, and they forget the simple things that make good reading, and that's what it's supposed to be about. There is the matter of record that newspapers are supposed to provide, but more and more, I think, to survive newspapers are going to have to be readable and be something people are going to be interested in.

ETHICAL DILEMMAS

In Opelika, a bunch of little socialites who were producing the community follies invited me to lunch and said, "Bring your camera." They were using some kind of public funds to put on this show. They didn't have anything against blacks being in the performance, exactly, except that would have eliminated the use of the country club where they had the after-rehearsal party, because the country club didn't admit blacks. If you ate their free lunch, they thought tuna fish and potato chips would keep you from saying that.

I was right out of school, and I remembered things like—you don't take free meals. And thank God, because it turned out to be a big story, a good story. If I'd had their free lunch, I would have still written the story but I wouldn't have felt as good about it.

It seems like a small thing. But the game gets bigger and the players remain the same. I get aggravated because I do what some people perceive as softball journalism now, mostly features and not that much news. People think that the same rules don't apply, but they do.

If somebody says they've got the biggest hog in three states, you can't take their word for that. It's still a case of, if your mother says she loves you, check it out. All those things still apply. You have to be even more careful when you get into feature writing.

HOW TO BE A BETTER INTERVIEWER

I resent a little bit that feature writing is maligned. It has been abused a lot. People who couldn't cut it in hard news reporting a lot of times would drift over to writing features. But the same skills apply. And you have to be a better interviewer.

If I ever try to push, it's almost over. I think it's my personality. I'm a little bit awkward verbally but, if I ever start trying too hard, they clam up, they withdraw. I guess it's because it's artificially me, it's not natural.

I find that the fewer notes you can get by with, the better. Of course, that's not always possible, especially when you're after a direct quote. But the columns I do are usually about other people, and that's an easy situation to go into without a notebook or a tape recorder. You can get their essence and that's what you use anyway, not a lot of direct quotes.

HOW TO BECOME A BETTER WRITER

I write because it's all I can do, and it's the way I make my living, and probably because I liked to read when I was little. I feel like I know the South better and it comes easier here, but a good writer can write anywhere. It doesn't come from the earth and up through our veins.

One thing that I've done to improve my writing is to use fewer quotes. Just because a person says something doesn't mean you have to use it as a direct quote. I would cram a story full of quotes, things that I could have written a lot better. I try to be more selective about them now, and I think that's really helped my writing.

You do your best, you want it to sound good, you want it to have rhythm, and you want the right words in there. I don't like to read my stories once they're in print at all. You think of the right word later. And it tortures me.

HOW I WRITE

If writing is good, it falls from the sky. I don't know how that happens. It's a mystery to me, and I don't like it because I have no control over it.

I have little superstitious things I do, like a ballplayer. I always have a Coca-Cola, and I always have a pencil in my left ear, and I always go to the bathroom first. I never depart from this. Then I sit down and when things are flowing it's like it's coming out of my fingers and not my head at all. It just seems sinfully easy.

I make up for it at other times. If it's not coming easily, it's like having a baby, which I've never had, but I'm assuming that's what it feels like. It's just hard labor. Sometimes editors, I'm sure, are tempted to take it by Caesarean.

I do minimal rewriting on the things that are good. I go back every now and then and think of a better verb that would be stronger or more colorful. The flowing from the fingers is 10 percent of the time. Ninety percent of the time is tortuous. I do a lot of rewriting, and I have to have my lead firmly in mind before I can do the rest. I'm real religious about that.

My ending is always real important to me. I feel like I'm rewarding the reader for getting all the way through a piece. Next to the first sentence, I feel the ending's the most important thing you're going to give them.

With writing, like anything else, I go through some terrible slumps, and I'm not a very self-confident person anyway. I agonize a lot over what I've written, or what I haven't written, or how I've written it. I wish I didn't care so much because my personal life would be a lot better, and it would give my husband a little relief. It's just the way I am. I agonize over everything I write, even if it's not a big story or if it's just a daily column.

Sometimes one exercise that helps me is to take a writer you like—for instance, my big one's Raymond Chandler because I like his rhythms and I like his short sentences—and read some of his writing. Then I put a piece of paper in the typewriter and copy straight from the book, like you were in typing class. You get a real feel for a rhythm or a tone. That helps me sometimes when I'm in a slump for several weeks and I get real desperate. It's amazing how that works. You'd be amazed how they type differently. Flannery O'Connor types very differently from Raymond Chandler. She types real smooth. It's probably just another superstition.

HOW I ORGANIZE

I'm very disorganized. I can't ever find notes or reference files or books. I work mainly out of my house or a motel room, and I never can find everything I need. I can't find phone numbers. It hurts me a lot. I'm not offering it as a way to be at all. No telling how many stories I've missed because I couldn't find the number to call and check on something. It's just the way I am.

I'm the same way in writing. I'm pretty disorganized. It falls together somehow, but it's not because I outline in my head or anything. What helps me most is knowing what I want to say. The only organization I lay claim to is to try to put in one thesis sentence what the story or situation is about. This is rarely ever the lead, but it's the idea behind the story—why did I waste my day doing this story? That helps.

I thumb through my notes real fast and a quote will jump out. I was more a slave to my notes than I realized when I started this "America's Faces" series. I lost three notebooks. I was devastated. I thought, there's no way I can write these stories without notes. I did have to do a lot of backtracking and calling and getting figures again, but as far as the essence of what I'd experienced, I retained more of that than I thought I did.

When I take notes, I write down things like "red blouse," things that are not necessarily what the person is saying so much as how someone looks or what the room looks like or what the wall looks like, what kind of watch someone has on—details, three-fourths of which I don't use. I like to write right away because so much of what I do is just mental images, and they fade.

JOURNALISM AS A PROFESSION

As a college kid, I felt that journalism was one of the last pure professions left. I'm talking about newspapers. I don't know enough about TV to say. It was a profession—informing and teaching. In the morning you'd go in, do a certain job, and then see the results—if not immediately, pretty soon. You'd come home, and your clothes would be wrinkled, and you'd have done an honest day's work, and you'd be sweaty, and you'd have accomplished something.

Maybe I've overdosed on the work ethic because even now I feel ashamed of what my grandfather would think if he knew how easy my job is at times. Yet, when I was in the bureaus, cranking out a story a day, I felt I was worthwhile.

Every now and then you'd talk to somebody who'd never, ever been interviewed for anything, never seen his name in the paper. And he would stand there and say, "*The Commercial-Appeal?*" and be impressed in the right kind of ways. That's heady stuff, to represent a newspaper that is an actual part of these people's lives and is their primary form of community.

It's not that way, of course, as much now. Even people in the Mississippi sticks have a big satellite dish in their yards. They've got tarpaper shacks, but they've all got satellite dishes. And they all get a lot of their news from television.

The profession itself now is not as pure as when I went into it. We have more meetings now than a huge corporation. And we have advisers coming in and telling us how to select front page stories—Oh, God, I'm going to get fired. It's not like it was. I wish I had been born earlier, I really do.

WHAT I WANT TO DO

I think I'll always report and write. Editing doesn't interest me at all. Down here there's still more sexual discrimination. You don't see as many women in newspaper management, but that seems to be a problem everywhere.

As impressed as I was by people like Turner Catledge and Tom Wicker, who left the South and made names for themselves in northeast journalism, I was impressed by Ralph McGill, who stayed in Atlanta. He was the editor of the Atlanta *Constitution* and he was courageous at a time when it was hard to be courageous—during all the civil rights business.

I think it's largely due to his leadership that Atlanta never had the racial tension and problems that places like Birmingham and Montgomery and Mississippi had. I admire him because he stayed in his region. He didn't feel that you had to go somewhere else to be a good journalist or to be the best journalist you could be.

A lot of the editors in the South prefer to hire people from out of the South. They want to hire Indiana graduates and Missouri graduates. I think there's too much of that. I don't think Southerners are the only people who can write about the South, but I think we have a leg up. Maybe it sounds small-minded, but I have an advantage here because I understand this region. I was born in Georgia, grew up in Alabama, Florida and Mississippi. I'm sure there's the same proportion of good writers here that are anywhere else.

PERSONAL LIFE

I think about my writing a lot. My parents have gotten so they hate to see me coming because they know it's going to end up in a column somewhere down the road.

I have few friends because I'm always somewhere else. If I'm not commuting, I'm traveling. I know few of the reporters at *The Commercial-Appeal* very well, and I don't feel close to anybody in the newsroom. My friends are ones who really take a lot of crap, who don't mind me not answering their letters or their phone calls for days. Something perverse in them makes them stick with me.

My job *is* my personal life. We've always lived to work instead of the other way around. When I have a good day at the paper, then we all have a pleasant evening at home. When I don't, we have a miserable time. It's terrible. It's a real failing, it's a personality defect, and it's caused me much grief.

And I have no children yet. I've been married 11 years. I'd like to have children, but at one time we'd have had to build a nursery halfway between two towns.

My work is a disease, a progressive disease, meaning it gets worse and worse. The tireder I get, the more obsessed I am with trying to do better. I'm not doing my best work this year at all. I'm in a real slump. That only makes me more desperate to do something decent. It's a lot harder to worry than it is to work. And I think this year has been spent worrying.

Dentist longs to treat patients in port

Peter Eckerson, dentist and Viking, sails in search of freedom and distant shores

by Rheta Grimsley Johnson

FISHERS ISLAND, N.Y.—No one waits on the pier today.

Fishers Island is floating on the cool edge of autumn, and a soft rain is turning this green dollop of land into a misty Eden.

Sometimes, though, they do come and wait. They stand on the sagging wooden dock with their cheeks puffed from pain, looking for the boat that brings relief.

The pennant flying from the shrouds of "Mistress" is a white tooth on a field of dark blue. Dentist Peter Eckerson is her captain. He relies on a favorable wind to make landfall in time for his Saturday appointments.

His office is the boat—an X-ray machine, the ubiquitous chair, a gleaming sink, the whole works.

It is dark below deck, except for an intense spotlight trained on a patient's mouth. The warm hues of teak and the doctor's seamanly calm ease the hurt—with the help of Novocain, of course.

They call him "Painless Pete."

The patients come in a steady current, making the leap from land to water and climbing down into the boat's dark throat for treatment.

"I get lots of elderly and handicapped patients," Pete says. People with limitations trust a man who acknowledges none.

For the disabled there is an advantage to a nautical dentist. Sometimes a handicapped patient is lowered down the hatch in a bosun's chair, a seat normally used for hoisting a workman up the mast. For all his patients, it's easier to visit the dock than to catch a boat to the Connecticut mainland.

Pete is 50, divorced, a red-bearded

Rheta Johnson talks about this story on p. 11.

Reprinted by permission of The Commercial-Appeal *(Memphis).*

Viking with eyes the color of old denim. He is quiet, perhaps too used to talking to people who can't talk back. His hands and arms are agile and strong, his legs useless. An irreversible inflammation of his spinal cord gradually sapped them.

He doesn't talk much about it.

But it is a strain as he pulls himself up the companionway at the end of the day. A wet wind is slapping the cover over the cockpit and making a pleasant sound. It's not rain on a tin roof, but it's close.

Exhausted, he sits back with the first gin and tonic. Darkness and cigarette ashes are dropping all around him. Painless Pete speaks of dentists and of his past.

Weariness ebbs. Enthusiasm flows. He sounds like a man in love.

"I'm a sailor who practices dentistry, not a dentist who sails," he says with a smile, reminiscing that Humphrey Bogart said the same about sailing and acting. And though he likes his work he needs something more, something to feed the yearnings that growl inside him.

Peter Eckerson is an adventurer, that endangered American species, still plotting his course by the stars and aspiring to them.

His motives are noble and selfish. Dentistry helps support his sailing; he provides a service by landing at an island with no resident dentist.

"Mostly I just can't see spending the rest of my life in an office at 46 North Main, you know?"

He has a prosperous, conventional practice at that address on Long Island; he works there five days a week. The Fishers shuttle is once a week during the warm months.

The weekend expeditions cost him. He must hire a crew of at least one and a part-time hygienist. It's a lot of trouble to hoist sail and make a five-hour cruise to pull a few teeth.

This is a means to an end, though. That end, like a welcome shore, may be in sight. Pete wants to practice solely from his boat, perhaps cruising Europe. In a couple of years, he should be able to do that.

Like most men with an idea, Pete has doubts and bad days. When word first got around about the 37-foot cutter-rigged boat he had made in Taiwan in 1979, other dentists started calling him day and night to find out exactly how he equipped it.

There were, it seemed, plenty of other people who yearned to cast off from routine.

But Pete, plenty peeved when he thought of all the expense, trials and errors he'd endured, just stopped talking. Let others plan their own escapes.

Only two other dentists he knows of operate from boats, but he doesn't really count them because they use motorboats.

It hasn't been easy. He says of his former wife: "She thinks I'm crazy." Not really. The two remain friends.

Yet it isn't up to Pete really. Something within him dictates his travels, a force akin to that which drove earlier adventurers across the Appalachians, over the Plains and through the Donner Pass.

His trips include not only the weekenders, but annual ventures to the Caribbean. And they are all but mental shakedown cruises, preparing him to cruise Europe under the power of bicuspids and sail.

"It takes courage to do something like this, I guess," he says, staring vacantly. "There are a lot of people who would change their lives if they could."

Pete needs a wheelchair to get about on land. On the sea he is agile and free.

Christopher Johns

"In journalism, hard work is 80 percent of the game. It has to do with those classic values of being enterprising, resourceful, working hard and not watching the clock."

PETER RINEARSON

The corner window in Peter Rinearson's second-story home office sketches the blueness of Puget Sound. For three years, Rinearson has spent most of his time here filling two bookcases, two four-drawer filing cabinets and 16 binders with information about Boeing Aircraft. The project, "Making It Fly," won him a Pulitzer Prize at *The Seattle Times* in 1984 for a series of eight stories about the creation of the Boeing 757. Now he's writing a book.

Between the Boeing newspaper series and the Boeing book, he wrote another book about a computer program for writers. *Word Processing Power with Microsoft Word* is more than 300 pages of suggestions about how to use the software to make writing easier. Just to the left of the window in his home office are an IBM AT computer and a laser printer to help retrieve what's in the filing cabinets and the binders.

The six binders hold complete transcripts of more than 80 interviews about Boeing. Programmed into the computer are 15,000 listings of key words from those interviews, which Rinearson can retrieve as he writes. "For example, say that I'm writing and I remember that there was a good quote about the 757 door, but I don't remember it exactly. I can pull up on the computer all the times someone mentioned doors, check the quote and then drop it into my story. With the computer, I never lose anything."

Rinearson is a walking information-retrieval system. He can sit down at the computer and within two minutes show you the 140 times someone told him something about the doors on a Boeing 757. He can reach into the bookcase and pull out the article he just clipped from yesterday's *New York Times* about Japanese/American trade. Or he can walk to the back of the room and retrieve the book *Wind, Sand, and Stars* by Antoine de St. Exupéry to explain the role of technology:

> The man who assumes that there is an essential difference between the sloop and the airplane lacks historic perspective. Every machine will gradually take on this patina and lose its identity in its function.

```
1=0·········1·········2·········3·········4·········5·········6·········7·····┐
   ESTN ramp agent & 57 door    Johnstone    10/24/82    5
 ↑ B response to door           Johnstone    10/24/82    6

2=[····|····1·········2·········3·········4·········5·········6·········]·····┐
```

Boeing first encountered the door problem last July 8, when Nancy
Ballard, a 115-pound Eastern gate agent at Seattle-Tacoma Airport, had
enormous difficulty getting open a 757 door in a test at Boeing Field.

"This young girl damn near got herself a hernia trying to open
the damn door," said Johnstone, now retired from Eastern. In fact,
Ballard came away from the test with a muscle bruise the size of a
baseball on one arm, where she had repeatedly leaned for leverage
while trying to push the door open.

This is a sample search from Rinearson's file of 15,000
listings. His computer index shows a quote about the
Eastern (ESTN) Airlines ramp agent's difficulty with the
757 door (arrow). This listing represents a quote from
Mr. Johnstone, which is stored in the computer memory for
Rinearson to insert into his copy when he needs it. Rinearson
uses this quote in the story that appears on pp. 36–57.

Rinearson, who was 29 years old when he won the Pulitzer, wrote the
series without the computer, and he blanches when you make too much
of the technology. "A tool should be transparent," he says. But he estimates
that using the computer for the book saved him at least six months. "A
computer takes less time for the same reason an automobile takes less
time than a bicycle. Time is the thing which is, to me, most important.
If someone came to you and said, 'I can give you a gift of several months
over the next three years,' that would be very valuable to you."

He attended the University of Washington and has worked for *The
Seattle Times* since 1976. He went from covering city government to covering
state government to covering defense to writing about Boeing. Rinearson,
31, usually works at home. He checks in at the *Times* for his mail and for
messages, but he is at his *Times* desk even less now than when he was
covering Boeing in 1984. The *Times* has assigned him to cover countries
that border the Pacific—the Pacific Rim. "It's an awfully trendy term right
now," he says, "but the Rim is a symbol, not just a geographic area. It
symbolizes the Third World, developing nations, the changing international relations between countries. It's like being told, 'Your beat is the
world.' " ❖

from Peter Rinearson

- How to handle public relations people
- How to use technology to write and report
- How to make a familiar subject seem new to your readers

BEGINNINGS

Does the fifth grade count? In fifth grade, I published a little mimeographed newspaper at Maywood Elementary School in Bothell, Washington, called the *Maywood Report*. My lead story one issue was about a fellow who had fallen into the wastebasket. So I remember standing out in the hallway calling out "Tim Bendokas Falls in Wastebasket," which was the headline. That was the end of my journalism career for quite some time.

My junior year in high school, I lost the election for student body president by 14 votes, and the next day, the newspaper adviser offered me the editorial page editorship of the school paper. I guess that was my consolation prize. Eventually I became editor.

ONE CLASS SHORT

I went to the University of Washington. My major was journalism, but I'm one class short of graduation. I have as many political science credits as journalism. If I were to take the missing class, I think I have my choice of poly sci or journalism as a degree.

I became very involved in the [University of Washington] *Daily*. My first year was my year of being a good student. I did very well, close to a 4.0. My second year, I got five credits for the whole school year because I was at the *Daily*. Constantly. By the end of the second year, I was managing editor.

The editor was a guy named David Horsey, who became editor after having been the political cartoonist. He didn't know anything about journalism, and I was 19 and didn't know anything about life. He's now the political cartoonist for the *Seattle P-I* [Post-Intelligencer].

Horsey and I were living together by my third year of school. Neither of us had traveled anywhere. So we came up with a journalism project. We were going to travel around the country together interviewing editors. Monday we went into the director of the school of communications who promised us $200. Friday morning we left.

We interviewed people at *The Denver Post*, the *St. Louis Dispatch*, *The Washington Post*, the Washington *Star*, the *National Observer*, *The New York Times*. When we got back to Seattle, we'd been gone 20 days. Four days later we left for the Associated Press Managing Editors convention where we spent another four days.

When we came back, we put the interviews out as a book, which we called *The Media Lords*. We sent copies to all the editors and got some college credit out of it. This was 1974.

The winter quarter I didn't go to school at all. I was totally broke. I had charged the trip all on my MasterCard. That summer, we both got jobs on newspapers from editors we had met at the APME meeting. One was the *Wenatchee World* in eastern Washington—that's where I went. Dave got a job on the Tacoma newspaper. This was the summer of '75.

I came back to Seattle and got a job as editor of the *Snohamish Valley News*. This was a $120-a-week job while I was going to school, except I wanted Horsey to work with me. The only way the publisher would agree to this was if we would split the salary. So we each worked for $60 a week.

I was an intern at *The Seattle Times* the following summer, and at the end of the summer they asked me to stay on part-time, which I did while going to school. By the winter of '77, I was covering the state legislature as an intern, working weekends at the *Times*. I went to Washington, D.C., in the winter of '78 on a Sears Congressional Internship, assigned to a congressional staff. Then I came back to *The Seattle Times*. I still had a class to finish. I have not finished it to this day.

TWO IMPORTANT GOALS

I covered federal courts for a while, some general assignment, city hall and the mayor. I set myself some goals. The first thing you have to know how to do as a reporter is to write quickly, high production. In 1980, I had 450 bylines for the year because I made it a point to do a lot of stories. I was doing three and four legislative and city hall stories a day.

Then about 1981, I decided that the time had come to try to write well. I was very deliberate. In the legislature, I would do my quick stories, a lot of them, but I would also try to explain an issue to people so they would understand the world a little better. Product liability was one story. I spent a lot of time trying to explain why industry wanted more relaxed product-liability laws. Talk about a dry issue.

Toward the end of 1981, I was becoming very interested in nuclear war. Reagan was going to pour money into defense. What's this going to mean to Washington state? I put in a proposal to do a story about nuclear war and strategic thinking, and it was approved. The editor said, "OK, you've got about four months. Go do what you want."

One story for the defense series was about survivalism. A photographer named Chris Johns and I spent eight days in Oregon's Rogue River area, sort of the world capital of survivalism. I bought a tape recorder, which I didn't have before, a very small one. It's unintimidating, a very important part of interviewing. I find it to be less obtrusive than a notebook. Once you set that thing down, it almost disappears. It fits in a shirt pocket. It's very unimposing technology.

When I came back, I spent a couple of weeks writing that story. I wouldn't let a paragraph go until I really liked it. Part of this was working on a computer screen. For me, a computer screen is important to writing well because it gives you an opportunity to try things in a million different directions. You almost don't have to write well as long as you can recognize relatively good writing when you read it. As a reader, you see that the paragraph works out pretty well.

Then I helped write the rest of the series, called "Defense in Washington." There were several reporters contributing, but I did a good share of it. I spent a long time trying to write well. Long hours. I probably never worked any less than 60 hours a week.

Then a friend told me that physicians from all over the world were going to meet at a conference in Europe. Physicians for Social Responsibility was the U.S. group, and two Seattle physicians were going. I wrote this memo—why I should go to Europe for six weeks to cover the peace movement.

I felt there was one chance in a hundred they'd send me. On Monday morning, they said, "You're going." I left on Friday. I went to eight countries. What this experience did was whet my appetite for writing about the big picture. It was a long way from covering the parochial issues of the Seattle city council to covering the issue of survival of the human race, to put it in its grandest terms. I was becoming intrigued by the way various things in the world interacted with each other.

The series was five parts. It was long, probably 10,000 words. I wrote it carefully. I was working hard at my writing, reading a lot. I spent a lot of time reading Tom Wolfe, John McPhee, Truman Capote.

MOVE TO THE AEROSPACE BEAT

About this time, I remember thinking, if the aerospace beat ever were to open at *The Seattle Times*—which it never will, because the guy who's been doing it has been doing it for 40 years—that is one job you could do in Seattle where you could make a bid at being the best in that field. Seattle is the world capital of aviation. You could make a mark by writing something nationally significant. It's also the one subject you could look at here from a global standpoint.

Suddenly, in the spring of 1982, the aerospace guy decided to retire. So I put in my proposal. I said, "I want to cover the beat from an international and national perspective. I want to go to the European air shows. I want to be able to travel as I need to. I want to be able to look at the subject as a global story." It seemed to be exactly what the *Times* wanted, so they gave me the job and I started in June or July of 1982. I had never had any exposure to aerospace before that.

COVERING BOEING

Boeing is an interesting company, full of fascinating people—60,000 of them. But I didn't know anyone at Boeing. Sixty thousand of my readers work at Boeing, but you can't run little ads in the *Times* that say, "If you know anything about laminar flow, call me."

I did know what a plane was, but I didn't know that the little wings at the back of the plane are called the tail. I thought they were called the little wings. I had it all wrong. Terminology is the key.

I was sitting around one day lamenting that I really didn't know how to get inside Boeing to meet some people. I had just finished reading *The Soul of a New Machine* by Tracy Kidder, a very good book about the creation of a computer. I was talking to a fellow named Ross Anderson and he said, "You oughta do a *Soul of a New Machine* about the 757."

I remember thinking instantly, "That is a great idea. I'll spend six weeks, I'll talk to someone who's a salesman and someone who's an engineer and I'll try to explain the logistics of putting together an airplane, how this works. And I'll meet some people. I don't think anyone in the community knows what goes into making an airplane. I certainly don't." Then I was talking to Chris Johns, the photographer, and he said, "You can call it 'Making It Fly,' " which, of course, symbolizes not only making an airplane but taking a venture and making it succeed.

So I called some people at Boeing and told them I was going to spend three weeks reporting this thing and three weeks writing it. I talked to public relations and they were helpful, but this was not something they were accustomed to doing.

I said, "Who's the father of the 757?" And they said, "Well, there are probably several people who think they're the father of the 757." All these people had some claim on the paternity of the airplane. We made this list on a legal pad, about one-and-a-half pages long. I suggested areas of responsibility, and they suggested names. Then I just started booking appointments.

One reason there hadn't been a lot written about Boeing is that it's difficult as a journalist to get yourself in a position where you can learn things. That, I'm sure, is by design. Boeing is a closed environment. An employee can be subject to discipline for talking to the press without public relations present.

But I just overwhelmed public relations. I needed so much of their time. Every time I did an interview, three or four names came out of it. Pretty soon, I was calling people at night. I became something of a pain. My aspirations had been far too modest. After about three weeks, the subject matter was so incredibly interesting, I was intellectually completely engrossed.

It was mid-November that I started talking to them: Start November 15, get done, work over the Christmas holidays, finish writing in early January, and we'll publish it at the end of January and go on to something else. By December 1, I knew I was writing a book. There was no way I could tell the story in *The Seattle Times* the way I wanted to tell it.

I doubt I'll ever work that hard again. It was just absolutely nuts. I worked seven days a week. Typically, I'd go to bed around 1 o'clock in the morning and get up around 7:30, be at work about 8:30. I did this for months—writing, researching, transcribing. I taped all the 80 to 100 Boeing interviews. Time with these people was often very limited, so I couldn't take notes. I'd engage them in conversation and then later I'd transcribe the tape.

THE IMPORTANCE OF TERMINOLOGY

Terminology exists because it's a shorthand way of expressing things. Those terms exist because they're very efficient ways to talk about something. I can talk about seat-mile costs in three words, for example. If you're in the industry, you know exactly what seat-mile costs are—the total cost to an airline of flying one seat one mile.

Whenever I heard a term, I made sure I understood what it meant and then I'd incorporate it right into my vocabulary. I also tried to approach my interviews logically, so that by the time I got to person C, I'd already been through A and B, and A and B helped me understand what C was going to say.

So here I am coming in to interview you. I've been told I have an hour of your time and an hour's difficult to get. But I have a number of things going for me when I walk in the room. First of all, I'm not going to ask you to spend that hour explaining the fundamentals of what you do. I understand that. I know some of your terminology, and because I know some of your terminology you're going to be more comfortable with me because I'm now part of your fraternity—very important. I'm not as much of an outsider.

Because I know the terminology, you can talk to me more as a colleague. Not only are you going to be more comfortable, but our time is going to be more efficient. On top of that, I'm going to tape record, and we're going to talk as fast as you want, and you can digress as many times as you want, but we're just talking back and forth.

When I went back to interview someone a second time, even if it was three days later, I had transcribed the first tape. If I had to be up all night to do it, I transcribed it, read it several times. I'd thought about and compared it to other things I'd found out. When I went back, I had a fairly complete command of the previous interview.

Here's another little tip. A company like Boeing is very customer-service oriented. Their customers are extremely important to them. They only have 300 in the world. So I would get ahold of an airline that might buy a 757. If you interview Frank Borman [president of Eastern Airlines] and then you call Boeing and say, "I'm working on this angle with Frank Borman," this is a customer. At this point Boeing wants to be cooperative. It's evidently in their customer's interest because their customer's cooperating, and they're going to try to accommodate their customer.

PUBLIC RELATIONS OBSTACLES

Very often the trick is just to get through the public relations screening. Public relations finally said, "Just go ahead and contact who you want. Don't bother us anymore." They were very useful and helpful at times, but they have different interests. Very often the executive's interests and the journalist's interests are very similar, and public relations has a different agenda. At least this was true at Boeing.

I'd do the first interview with someone, and then I'd ask, "When can we do a follow-up interview?" In one instance I said, "I'd really like to spend four or five hours with you." The guy said, "Well, that would be interesting, but the only time I could do that would be on Saturday." So he and I agreed that on Saturday we'd come back to the Boeing plant, but the PR guy wasn't going to come in and spend his Saturday.

The reality is that it didn't hurt Boeing at all to have that happen because I wasn't out to do a hatchet job. I wasn't being soft on them or putting an arm around them, but my pursuit was not for filth. If it's there, I want to find it, but I'm just trying to see what's going on.

HOW TO GET THE ANSWERS

If I ask you a difficult or embarrassing question, and you give me a sufficiently complete answer to the question, a lot of that embarrassment will disappear because I will come to understand why you did what you did. Very often with embarrassing information, what makes it embarrassing is that it's presented out of context.

In "Making It Fly," I published a lot of things that Boeing considered embarrassing. I wanted to write about chicken testing, where they fire live birds into airplane parts. Public relations told me, "You can't ask questions on that." That did not stop me at all. When the PR guy left to go to the bathroom, I would start talking about it.

I did an interview with the vice president of Eastern Airlines about chicken tests. He said, "Oh, yeah, I've seen chicken tests in Toulouse, France, and I've seen chicken tests for Airbus Industrie," and he described them. Well, that's something I can use at Boeing.

But when I presented that in my story, I didn't say, "Boeing loads live birds up and kills them by firing them into planes." I didn't let it go at that. I put it in context—what they're trying to accomplish, why the bird must be alive, how it affects safety.

If I had done a story saying, "This is chicken testing and this is how it works," I'm sure Boeing would have had animal preservation people up in arms. But I presented it in context. It loses some of its controversial nature, however, which may bother some journalists who are trying to find controversy.

There are journalists who believe a good story is a controversial story, and I love a good controversial story. I write as many as I can find. But I am not going to take situations which are not inherently controversial and make them controversial. That's a dishonest journalistic practice which is common. I don't have a lot of use for that. I just portray the world as it really exists.

A FORTUNATE PUBLICATION DELAY

What happened was *The Seattle Times* and the *Seattle P-I* were negotiating a joint operating agreement [JOA—for the two newspapers to publish together]. This is absolutely key, I think, to the way the series turned out. The agreement was being held up by the courts.

I was talking about a lot of pages of *The Seattle Times* for this series. So what they said was, "Look. The JOA is going to be approved soon. When it is, we're going to have a lot more space and we're going to want some showy things to do at the beginning. This will probably be early February. We'll run it when the JOA's approved."

So I was in this peculiar situation where I didn't have to be done, but I knew that any day a court decision could come down. When it did, the series had to be done. So my fear was that tomorrow the series had to be done.

This fear went on for weeks, for months, throughout the spring. Because they weren't in a position to publish it until the JOA was approved, I continued to work. I was engrossed and I wasn't going to let go. If I wasn't sleeping or eating, I was working on the series.

As it happened, the JOA was not approved until June. A week or so after that, the series ran. I was reporting right up to the end. I remember I was interviewing people at the Paris Air Show and calling my editor daily, saying, "OK, part four, 15th paragraph, take that out, change it to this." When I came back from the air show, the series had just started to run. It ran for eight consecutive days [beginning June 19, 1983].

If, in fact, the story had been published in January, it would have been a fine series, it would have been a lot shorter, it would have been a lot different, and it wouldn't have won a Pulitzer Prize. It didn't have the dimension then, it didn't have the reporting.

The series is a basic celebration of American industry. As a journalist, you sort of wonder about that because we're so accustomed to thinking of good journalism as being investigative. I've done my share of that kind of reporting, but this was something different. It fit into my interest in explaining the world to people.

USING A TAPE RECORDER

In many instances, it's not until I transcribe an interview that I understand what was said. When you're taking notes, you get a sentence or two and maybe you miss a sentence. Your mind is tuning back and forth between what you're writing and what you're hearing.

Very often things are said during an interview that I don't have the background to understand. Several months later, I have accumulated the background. So when I go back and read that transcript, suddenly it's: "Where was this? I thought I knew what was going on, but now I really understand what this guy was talking about." I'll come upon this gem which was completely unperceived to me at the time the person said it. I have it because I captured it on tape, because I transcribed it and set up a system to let me get to it rapidly.

USING TECHNOLOGY TO REPORT AND WRITE

Ideally, a tool should be transparent. You're not conscious of the pen in your hand, particularly. You're not conscious of the steering wheel when you drive. And after you learn to type pretty well, you're not conscious of the typewriter either. You're writing.

The same thing's true with a computer. Once you become accustomed to it and learn how it works, it's just something you use to do your job better. I write better on a computer than I'd be able to write without a computer. And I get more work done on the computer than I'd get done on a typewriter. A tape recorder also can make you a better writer because it can let you be much more discerning about what words you're going to use.

As a general rule, what a computer will let you do is have more months in any given year. Maybe you're able to do 18 months of work in 12 months. For me, that's the same as being given six months.

TIME-SAVING TIPS FOR JOURNALISTS

A computer is a word processor, that's its obvious use. The second use is for database management. You can use a computer to keep track of a large amount of material for you. That's where technology is useful— collecting information, cataloging. I have 15,000 records about Boeing entered in the database.

For example, I'm writing the book and I want to know about how carpets are cut for the 757. If I ask for that information, the computer will give me a list of every one of those 15,000 items that happens to contain a discussion of carpets. I can see where I did those interviews. It also tells me who I interviewed and the date and the page in the transcript.

The third thing a computer can do is make secretarial and clerical duties much more manageable. Journalists do not typically have secretaries. For instance, I'm back from Japan now and I would like to write a letter to about 30 people I interviewed to thank them. I wouldn't do this in the U.S., but things operate a little differently culturally in Japan. If I had a secretary, I could do it. Or if I have a computer, I can do it.

Another nice trick is Post-It notes. Say you're writing about a city budget, for instance, and you're interested in police matters. So you make a pass through your document and slap one of those Post-It notes and write "police" on it, if you want, instead of circling or underlining. Then you can go back when you're done with the police budget and make another pass-through, for example, and slap the Post-It notes down for health services.

WHAT MAKES A GOOD REPORTER

The person who has a B average and does great work on the college newspaper and has a summer internship and maybe a real passion for journalism will have a much better chance of getting work, and will probably do a better job, than a straight-A student with no experience. Unless you go out and get that experience, you don't really know whether you like journalism.

A certain passion is required to really do a good job, and if people don't show that passion in college, I don't know why editors would necessarily want to hire them. There's a place for passion early in a career.

That doesn't mean you have to be a workaholic. I sound like I am because of the way I worked on "Making It Fly" and the way I'm working on the book version—I'm consumed by it. There are occasions when that's very appropriate, but I don't think it has to consume one's life. I do think that if young journalists throw themselves into it with some passion, they're going to learn whether they like the business or not.

The other thing is, I've watched a lot of interns come and go at *The Seattle Times*, and 90 percent of the interns have the same comment to me—"They keep us so busy doing mundane things that we can never do any good journalism. They don't trust us with good stories." I say, "Don't complain about it. You shouldn't be here talking about it. You should be doing a story."

What they're saying is true, but that's exactly what an editor ought to be doing at that point. What always amazes me is that it's only the one in 10 or fewer who go out and do some work.

People get on a paper like *The Seattle Times*, they're out of college and suddenly they're making $400 a week, isn't this great? And they have a great time. They go home at 5 o'clock every night, just like they've been at the paper for 15 years. The comparatively rare person will be in there doing the routine work but within two or three weeks will come in on their own, doing good stories and turning stuff in. In journalism, hard work is about 80 percent of the game. It has to do with those classic values of being enterprising, resourceful, working hard and not watching the clock.

Sometimes people only see as far as they can reach. I don't think you should kill yourself your whole life, but I think there are times when it is appropriate to work very hard. It's appropriate to work very hard when you're trying to get a job out of college. It's appropriate to work very hard when you're on a big project that's exciting. Maybe that's simple advice, but no one does it. I can't believe it.

REPORTERS AND WRITERS

There are people who are better writers than reporters, and there are people who are better reporters than writers. I don't believe that people necessarily have to resign themselves to the fact that they are writers or they are reporters. To cast it in that black/white way makes it sound like fate, which I don't accept.

I was a much better reporter than I was a writer at first because I didn't work on the writing as much. It was harder for me naturally. Writing for me is hard work. I can write a formula news story without thinking about it, as can anyone who's been a writer for five years, but for me trying to write well is hard work.

I don't enjoy writing particularly. I really enjoy having written, and I enjoy reporting a great deal. But if I get a sentence I like or a paragraph I like, I can enjoy on a momentary basis the pleasure of having succeeded in that sentence or that paragraph. Then I have to focus on the next task—writing the next sentence—which is not something I particularly enjoy.

NEW GOALS TO REACH

I'm getting much more interested in ideas and the big picture. The newspaper series is a rather straightforward story—the creation of a plane. That's the first level. The book has the luxury of going to a second level, which is to examine the personalities which are involved. It is the story of the airplane, but there's a much greater sense of humanity. That's possible because you've got 125,000 words instead of 25,000 words—an extra 100,000 words to play around with.

The third level, which to me is the most important, is that I've taken the airplane and the people and I've used them to symbolize or dramatize something that is bigger than the airplane or the people involved, which is the functioning of the industrial process.

When you look at an industrial venture the size of a jetliner, many things that at first may look unrelated are tied together. The rise of the personal computer has a lot to do with automation, has a lot to do with dissent between labor and management, has a lot to do with Japanese productivity, the balance of trade, and on and on it goes. You can tie this web together. I've worked on my writing and my speed. Now I'm really trying to push myself to make some kind of contribution.

REPORTING IN JAPAN

In Japan, if you visit someone, you give them a gift. This poses a very interesting question for a U.S. journalist. Do you take your source gifts or not? Different journalists in Japan answer that question in different ways. Some say to accept them, some say absolutely not, some say we don't give any but we accept them if they're of nominal value, or we accept them publicly and then return them privately through public

Peter Rinearson

relations departments. Others say, on their expense accounts they have to figure out ways to list the gifts because sometimes they have to give them. Life is different in Japan, very wonderful in its own way.

Very often, people bluster into another culture with this attitude of "I'm gonna be me"—the great American attitude of individualism. I am, probably to my detriment, an individual. But there's something to be said for moderating. As a journalist you learn when to pound on the table and when to be polite, when to joke. When you move into another culture, your persona may require a little bit of adjustment.

ETHICAL DILEMMAS

I won't try to make any comments on the classical ethical questions, but there is something I think about a lot and I've never really articulated it very well.

I was mentioning Chris Johns, the photographer. He was doing a story on the Frazier River in Canada. And I went up there last fall, and we took a helicopter ride together and sat over the Frazier River at this bridge. He'd been waiting for six, seven months for the clouds to be just right.

He knew what he wanted, and he waited for months to get it. We got up very early, and we sat up there in that helicopter, hovering in one place for an hour and a half, and all he did was shoot photographs. He took a photo and said, "I think I just got it."

Now, when someone opens the *National Geographic* and sees the bridge and the spires, they're going to see something that is actually more dramatic and impressive than anything I saw. They're seeing the most concentrated moment, the strongest expression of what the experience was. That makes it a good photograph, a journalistically sound photograph. That's what hard work is.

As a writer, you're also trying to find the strongest expression of reality. You're trying to find the wittiest phrase with which to end the article. As a journalist, what concerns me is to what extent you're doing violence to reality by concentrating it. In pursuit of good writing and compelling prose, you pull quotes together, you juxtapose ideas, you take something he said this month with something he said last month and bring them together for contrast, and it reads pretty damn well. All the quotes are accurate, every word is what was said. But in the end, to what extent is there distortion as a result of your desire to create something that is compelling?

If you take this thing far enough, you get to the point where people are fabricating quotes, where people are saying things that you wish they'd said or saying something poetic when they're not poets. I don't believe you have to have "ums" and "ahs" in what someone says. But when you take things that people have said five minutes apart and you run them together, do you put them in the same paragraph or separate paragraphs? Do you tell the reader that, "Five minutes later he said . . . "?

As long as I'm thinking about these questions as I'm writing, I think I make reasonable judgments on a case-by-case basis. But it's these shades of gray that I wrestle with all the time.

WHAT MAKES GOOD WRITING

Very often the things that are absolutely the most difficult to write are the things that are the easiest to read because they seem so effortless. I wrote a section about how the door on a 757 works. I spent a whole evening trying to write those three or four or five paragraphs so that when you read them you wouldn't notice them. Other people could do it much faster than I can. But I did it. I stuck with it until I got those paragraphs, until I finally came up with a combination that reads right.

For example, one of the columnists at the *Times* was reading over the opening to "Making It Fly " and he said, "You have too many short words here—of, and, the." And it was true. I played around with that sentence and, sure enough, by restructuring the sentence, I didn't have so many two- and three-letter words in a row. It was like an obstacle, a little wall that I had erected for the reader.

In my book version of "Making It Fly," I call the 757 the five-seven. I do that for a couple of reasons. One is that in the industry, that's what it's called. If you are an insider, you will rarely talk about the 757. You will talk about the five-seven. By calling it the five-seven, I'm using the language of the industry. It brings the reader in and makes the reader feel on the inside.

You also don't want to repeat words. And in a book that repeats 757 as much as this one does, if I have to name the plane three times I can call it "airplane" once, "plane" once, and then call it "five-seven." The fourth time, I have to call it "757." Five-seven also lets me avoid numerals. People do not like to read numerals.

TWO GOOD STORIES A YEAR

Pick some journalists who are just starting on a paper somewhere and their editor wants them to do four or five stories a day. They hear me saying you should be spending hours crafting paragraphs, and they'll think, "Is that guy nuts? What ivory tower is he in?"

I'm not saying that. But I think you owe it to yourself as a journalist to write a couple of stories a year that are well written. Figure you're going to spend a weekend or two on each one and, a couple of times a year, prove to yourself that you can really write something well.

Look at every sentence. Don't let a sentence go until it's just the way you want it. If people do that, they'll become better writers. And, in a couple of years if they're looking for a better job, they'll have some nice clips.

Designing the 757

by Peter Rinearson

Boeing's newest jetliner, silvery metal with the blue numerals 757 emblazoned on its tail, turned heads like a celebrity as it taxied into Montreal's Dorval International Airport last September.

It came to rest at an Eastern Airlines gate where top Boeing officials were waiting to give the airline's president, Frank Borman, his first ride in the airplane he had helped launch with a $900 million order four years earlier.

A gate agent stepped up to the 757's door, popped out a butterfly-shaped handle and turned it clockwise. Grasping the door firmly, while the top brass of Boeing and Eastern looked on, she pushed and pulled.

The 323-pound door moved only a few inches. It wouldn't budge beyond that. Try as she might, she couldn't get it open.

"See?" said Paul Johnstone, then Eastern's senior vice president for operations.

Johnstone chuckled later and

This is an edited version of one of the eight stories in the "Making It Fly" series that won the Pulitzer Prize in 1984. Peter Rinearson talks about this story on pgs. 26–30.

Reprinted by permission of The Seattle Times.

explained that he had purposely chosen a small woman to open the heavy door— or try to—so Boeing executives could see first-hand that something was wrong. "I mousetrapped 'em," he said.

Although the 757 passenger door met elaborate engineering criteria and reliability tests, in Eastern's view the airplane at Dorval International was a flawed product.

The airline was to take delivery of the first airplane in December, just three months away, and it wanted a door every gate agent, regardless of his or her weight or strength, could open.

The 757 door took about 70 pounds of strength to open, twice as much as a 727 door. There were several reasons, including that it weighed more because the 757 sits higher off the ground and the door must contain a longer escape slide for emergency evacuation.

Boeing hadn't ignored the question of how much strength was necessary to open the door, said Jim Johnson, 757 director of engineering. On the contrary, engineers had calculated everything from the door's weight to the viscosity of its oil to the effects of friction on the door's bearings and rollers.

D. P. Tingwall, chief project engineer for engineering computing, said door loads were examined by computer and the design of cam parts was modified on the basis of the computer's findings.

And yet an error was made.

"We didn't give proper consideration to a small-framed woman with light weight," Boeing's Johnson said. A small person didn't have enough leverage to move the door, he said.

Boeing first encountered the door problem last July 8, when Nancy Ballard, a 115-pound Eastern gate agent at Seattle-Tacoma Airport, had enormous difficulty opening a 757 door in a test at Boeing Field.

"This young girl damn near got herself a hernia trying to open the damn door," said Johnstone, now retired from Eastern. In fact, Ballard came away from the test with a muscle bruise the size of a baseball on one arm, where she had repeatedly leaned for leverage while trying to push the door open.

"I was able to open the door, but believe me, it was a strain," she said.

It took a dozen engineers eight 56-hour weeks to solve the problem by designing a dual-spring mechanism, but the solution hadn't yet been installed when Johnstone sprung his mousetrap in Montreal. . . .

After its stop in Montreal last September, the 757 flew on to England with a load of Eastern and Boeing officials.

On the way, a duck hit one of the cockpit's No. 2 windows, not an unusual incident.

"It's usually not a big deal," said Les Berven, an FAA pilot who was co-piloting the flight. "All it did was just to make him into jelly and he slid down the side of the window."

The window didn't break—but then Boeing knew it wouldn't because the window had gone through a series of "chicken tests."

Boeing is a little touchy about the subject of chicken tests, and points out they are required by the FAA. Here's what happens:

A live 4-pound chicken is anesthetized and placed in a flimsy plastic bag to reduce aerodynamic drag. The bagged bird is put in a compressed-air gun.

The bird is fired at the jetliner window at 360 knots and the window must withstand the impact. It is said to be a very messy test.

The inch-thick glass, which includes two layers of plastic, needn't come out unscathed. But it must not puncture. The test is repeated under various circumstances—the window is cooled by liquid nitrogen, or the chicken is fired into the center of the window or at its edge.

"We give Boeing an option," Berven joked. "They can either use a 4-pound chicken at 200 miles an hour or a 200-pound chicken at 4 miles an hour."

The British government requires that the metal above the windows also must pass the chicken test. This was the test the 757 failed. It had not been conducted on the 767, which has no British customers.

The 757 failure meant both airplanes had to be modified, since the metal overheads are structurally identical. Sixteen 767 cabs already had been completed, and had to be cut apart so reinforcing metal could be installed.

Mort Ehrlich, an Eastern Airlines senior vice president, said he watched Airbus Industrie conduct chicken tests in Toulouse, France.

"A few of us who were there uttered the classic remark about how hard it is to be a chicken in Toulouse," he said. "I guess the same is true in Seattle."

The Washington Post

"A lot of people believe that you can make anybody a reporter and that it's hard to make somebody a writer. I think exactly the opposite is true."

LOU CANNON

Lou Cannon came to Washington to work for *The Washington Post* two years before Richard Nixon resigned as president in 1972. But Cannon's work in California prepared him best to cover the Ronald Reagan presidency that began eight years later.

Cannon smokes cigars at his metal desk in the middle of *The Washington Post* newsroom, a desk piled with *National Journal* and *Congressional Quarterly*. Several boxes argue for space near Cannon's feet. Tacked haphazardly above the desk is a snapshot of Ronald Reagan in a cowboy hat standing next to an open-shirted Cannon.

Cannon, 53, is senior White House correspondent for the *Post,* but he also writes a weekly newspaper column on Washington politics and does a weekly radio commentary on National Public Radio.

Cannon attended the University of Nevada, Reno, and San Francisco State before he was drafted into the Army in 1954. When he got out of the Army, he didn't return to school. Instead, he drove a laundry truck to support his family. Then in 1957 he saw an ad in the paper for a newspaper reporter, and he took the job for $55 a week.

"At the end of the first week, I found out that some of the other reporters were getting mileage, and I was really irate. So I stormed into the editor and said, 'This isn't fair.' And he said, 'You're right. You'll get mileage.' Mileage was a dollar a week."

Cannon learned as he worked. "I think it's very good to have covered a state legislature," he says. "The reporter who comes to Washington really ought to have some background in covering some kind of legislative body, a big state legislature being ideal. I was fortunate to have covered the city council, boards of supervisors, the legislature and Congress. It seems to me the legislature's a great crucible. You've got all kinds of virtue, vice and corruption, nobility and complex problems wrapped up together."

As a Sacramento-based reporter for the *San Jose Mercury,* Cannon first started writing about Ronald Reagan when Reagan was governor of

California. In 1969, Cannon wrote *Ronnie and Jesse: A Political Odyssey,* the story of Reagan's 1966 campaign for governor against Democrat Jesse Unruh. Cannon has written three books since, including a book about reporting and a second book about Ronald Reagan.

Cannon learned the risk of making political predictions when he speculated in his 1982 Reagan book that the president would not run for a second term. Cannon was, however, one of the first people to report that Reagan was going to run again because, he says, "that's what you ought to do if you're a reporter."

Cannon feels that being a biographer makes him a better reporter. "I have a sneaking suspicion that it helps me being a biographer. It means that I take a little longer range view of things, even though I'm very competitive. I know that things will come out eventually. But I do like the stories to come out on our deadline with me writing them." ❖

SPECIAL PERSPECTIVES

from Lou Cannon

- Whether the White House sets the news agenda for reporters
- The relationship between reporters and public officials
- The role a free press plays in American government

BEGINNINGS

I've had an interest in journalism since I was about 10 years old. I used to play football on this little farm of my uncle's, then I would go in and write stories about those games. I always wanted to write, and I always wanted to report.

I can still remember standing on the steps at Reno High School when I was a sophomore, and the journalism teacher was saying, "You better learn to type, Louie, because you're gonna spend your life in the news business." I did learn to type.

I was editor of my high school paper, and I wrote a column for the local newspaper, and I wrote sports. Afterward I went in the Army, and I drove a truck, and I did things that are important. It's important, I think, that a reporter get a broad view of life. When I got out of the Army, I couldn't afford to go back in the news business. I had kids.

I remember in 1957, sitting somewhere in the hills of San Mateo in my laundry truck eating lunch. And there was an ad in the San Francisco *Examiner* for a reporter at a weekly, the *Lafayette Sun*. I went over and took this test that the publisher gave. It was a scrambled news story test, where you'd give people a bunch of facts in random order and ask the person to compose those into a news story.

I'm not a good test taker, but that kind of test is absolutely devised for me because I'm fast and I know what makes a good news story. I was very good, and the publisher was a real cheapskate. He saw this as an opportunity to get somebody for nothing. I was making $110 a week driving a truck—which would be the equivalent of $350 today—and my salary was $55 a week at the newspaper.

I worked for this group of papers called the Concord, Pleasant Hill and Walnut Creek *Sun,* and you did everything. You went to all the council meetings, and you rewrote stolen stories from other newspapers. From there I went to Newark, California, where I was editor of a weekly which is now gone called the *Newark Sun.* Then I went to the *Merced Sun-Star.* First I covered the police beat, and I covered education for a while. When the sports editor quit in a huff, I was sports editor.

I also covered the county supervisors in Merced. I've won a lot of awards since. I've got a prestigious job, and I get paid very well. But I was as proud of a story I did in Merced as I was of anything I've ever done. I found out one of the supervisors had a sister in the electrical business. They were remodeling the county hospital, and I guess they were trying to throw the work her way. They put out a series of small bids that got around the law [for open bidding], and we printed stories about it. The supervisors denounced the paper and said open bidding would cost them a lot of money. Of course, it didn't. They put the job out to bid, and it saved them thousands of dollars.

There's a lot of joy in small-town journalism. I obviously wouldn't have been happy staying in Merced forever, but I really enjoyed working there. I enjoyed local investigative journalism.

Then I went to the *San Jose Mercury,* where I was a copy editor. In 1965, they wanted a full-time person in Sacramento, and I went up there and filed two stories the first day. I worked for four years in Sacramento for the *San Jose Mercury,* and I wrote my book on Reagan [*Ronnie and Jesse*], which was a big turning point in my life. Then I came back to work for Ridder newspapers in Washington, D.C. For three years, I covered the Congress and the California election. I went to Vietnam and Cambodia. I really didn't want to go to work at the [Washington] *Post.* I didn't want to work for a big paper.

I always thought I wasn't a General Motors kind of person—that's what I used to say. I turned the *Post* down once, and they came back and Walter Ridder said to me, "Take the job. They're not going to come to you a third time." I did, and the *Post* proved just right for me.

WORKING FOR *THE WASHINGTON POST*

You hear a lot of stories. The *Post* gets described from the outside as sort of a big snake pit, sort of fratricidal. The truth of the matter is, it's a paper that is really wonderful for reporters. If you can produce, there are great people here to work for. [*Washington Post* Editor] Ben Bradlee is the kind of editor who always backs his reporters, and it was a great thing for me to do.

I'm senior White House correspondent at the *Post*. My column grows out of the beat, rather than the other way around. They're usually a little kind to me on Thursdays when I have to write the column.

If there's a major story, like during the hostage crisis, I report and then I write the column very late at night. I've done that many times. The column runs Monday. And every Monday morning I do a commentary in the form of a Q and A for Morning Edition, National Public Radio.

WHAT MAKES A GOOD REPORTER

I'm tempted to say the most important thing for a good reporter is a high energy level. Obviously, you also need some kind of intelligence. It helps to be gutsy or at least brassy. You've got to be curious, you've got to want to know how things come out.

There's a lot of what [Columbia University Journalism Professor Emeritus] Fred Friendly always said, that some people like to explain things. Some people want to tell you how their ice machine works or how their lawn grows. Depending on the type of people they are, they can be very entertaining or bores. But I think that whatever that sense is—of wanting to explain how things work to others—that's a great part of the journalist's makeup.

A lot of people believe that you can make anybody a reporter and that it's hard to make somebody a writer. I think exactly the opposite is true. You can't make somebody an Ernest Hemingway or some great creative writer or novelist, but you can teach most people who are not dyslexic to write simple, declarative sentences that newspaper readers can understand. That task is not beyond lots of people.

What you cannot teach people is reporting, which seems to me to be partly instinctive. Some people have all the qualities I have listed— they are curious, energetic, intelligent and courageous—yet, for some reason, they don't get stories. Without making too much of a mystique about it, it seems to me there really is a special kind of quality that is called for in reporting, some distillation of all those things.

There are lots of different kinds of reporters. I. F. Stone showed what you can do just by reading government documents. I have always spent a lot of time cultivating the people that I write about. I do that at the White House, I did that in Merced, I did that in Sacramento. It's no mysterious thing. I know the secretaries. I know the people who are relatively anonymous. And I talk to them.

SOME QUALITIES I HAVE THAT HELP

I suppose I'm a caring person. I'm interested in things coming out well. I'm interested in process, how something gets done in government and politics—that has always interested me. Reporting seemed to me to be a way to get into life and into government.

I'm a little bit shy. I'm a lot less shy now, but I was very shy when I started. I can still remember knocking on doors of a family that just lost their kid. There are people who do not have the brass to do that or never will, and many reporting situations don't require that. But I think that the process of reporting overcomes the shyness. If it doesn't, I suspect the person really isn't cut out to be a reporter.

I'm kind of anti-ideological, and I always try to find what's moving the person that I'm talking to or writing about. That's really helped me as a reporter because people who are very far to the right or very far to the left or very confused feel that I'm not hostile to them because of some ideological precept that I hold. I think I'm fair-minded. That helps, too. I'm also very competitive. I mean, I want to beat *The New York Times*.

WATCH FOR MISTAKES

The fact that you know, the date that you know, is invariably the one you don't know. You have to look it up. If you have a good memory—I have a very good memory and that's a help in reporting—you learn to trust it only for certain things. I trust it for feelings and for attitudes and for conversations much more than I trust it for dates. Dates can be looked up.

To be wrong, inaccurate, is something that troubles everybody here. But even with a couple layers of editors and a copy desk, you make mistakes. You're writing under high speed every day. You're writing under deadline pressure, which is something you learn early to live with, and you're going to make a certain number of mistakes.

That is not an excuse for sloppiness. I'm sloppy in my dress, but not in my writing. There is nothing dramatic about it. It's making an extra phone call, it's calling a library to see if you have the date right.

JOURNALISM AND POLITICS

A journalist must be willing, occasionally, to be embarrassed and often, which is much worse, to be accused, attacked and under fire for having—like some of the right-wingers believe—a vendetta against [President Reagan's Director of Communications] Pat Buchanan. They wrote a letter [to the *Post*] saying that either these people who are leaking to me should be barred from the newsroom or I should be barred from coverage, with a fine disregard for the First Amendment. One is always pleased to get their attention that way.

On the other hand, it also bothers me that they would think that. I mean, every politician is a partisan and the press is not. Most politicians have no idea what the hell we really are about. They really do think we have some ax to grind when we write. You could convince the tide to recede by talking to it better than you could convince them differently. I don't even try. I always say—as Bradlee said—government and politics are two honorable professions. They're not the same.

HOW THE PUBLIC PERCEIVES JOURNALISTS

I don't think people really understand what the press does, day by day, and I'm not sure that it's important that they do. There is a school of thought, which I partially subscribe to, which says that we do not do a good job of explaining our own processes—that we do not describe to people how it is we go about putting out a newspaper. We're very critical of the way business and labor organizations as well as government hide or veil their procedures, and yet we do the same. There's some truth to that.

On the other hand, I don't find that most of the criticism we get is criticism that would be changed by explaining a day-in-the-life-of Lou Cannon or Ben Bradlee or anyone else. Most of the criticism is from people who really do not accept the notion of a free press. Most people in government really would like newspapers to write stories about how wonderful they are. Many corporations do not want a press that's free to report what's going on in the country. I think that people who go into the news business ought to know that.

THE ORIGIN OF A FREE PRESS

The founders [founding fathers] had a lot of different proposals before them. They had a contentious, critical, often inaccurate press, and they were very wise to write a blanket protection for the press because they knew that people in those days threw printers, publishers and reporters in jail. They closed the presses down. That's what people would like to do now. They would like to silence the press with libel suits.

They're having some luck, but they're not going to succeed at *The Washington Post*. They're not going to succeed at *The New York Times*, and they're not going to succeed at a lot of places. I guess the bigger problem is that there just are not enough people who are really committed to freedom, including a lot of people who spout it. Sometimes I think they understand only too well, and they don't like what we're doing.

HOW TO REPORT IN WASHINGTON

There are so many different kinds of reporting in Washington. Some people report just government agencies, some people do nothing but Congress. The general advice would be to learn about Congress and how it works, to make some sources and friends on the Hill, to watch a committee in operation, to try to understand the difference between what is publicly and privately happening.

I've learned that there are very few real secrets here, and there are no secrets once they get up to Capitol Hill. Sooner or later—the fear that every president has is true—that if you brief Congress that the CIA is involved in mining ships in Nicaragua harbors [the information] will get out.

Another thing I've learned is that the good people are really busy here. You should make the effort to find out when people are accessible. I mean, some people jog early in the morning. There's a Congressman I wanted to see recently who I knew was very, very busy and might or might not return my calls, but I got his schedule and went over to where he was speaking in town and talked to him afterwards. If people are very, very busy, you have to learn the ways to see them. When do they go to work? When do they take phone calls?

The other thing I've learned is you have to do more cross-referencing in Washington than you do anyplace else. That's where Washington is very different. There is almost no issue where there isn't something happening in more than one place on the same day.

If you're covering, let's say, the MX [missile]. This administration has, throughout its five years of bungling its MX approach, had several fights on its hands at one time. The struggle to get authorization for what is now going to be 50 missiles overlapped the earlier struggle to get a release of some funds to allow the building of some first missiles. Usually there is someone—a lobbyist, a Congressman who is working on a committee—who isn't dealing with the issue in March but will have to deal with it in July. There are usually different checkpoints.

I broke the Sandra Day O'Connor appointment [to the U.S. Supreme Court]. That's a story that only three, four or five people knew. But there are very few stories like that. On 90 percent of the stories, there is a range of experts and if you check them, somebody will usually have heard something. That's the relevant thing in Washington. In Merced, there might be only one person who would know anything. In Washington, information is diffused.

REPORTING TECHNIQUES

I don't believe that reporting is an exercise in methodology, of trying to induce people to do something they don't want to do or techniques to get people to say something, like the cross-examining a lawyer would use to get an admission. That isn't the way I report. Any reporting should be congruent with the person's own personality and approach to life. It's not some skill you learn, like hitting a golf ball, that's outside your life.

I'm a fast writer and I know certain shortcuts in writing, and there are certain techniques I use, like I try to get as many home phone numbers as I can of people who are hard to get that I would want to use in an emergency. But when I question people, I don't have a dual agenda. I don't act one way to get some kind of a response.

Today I want to find out whether [Nevada Senator] Paul Laxalt is going to run again. I'm not going to call up people and say, "Hey, I haven't talked to you in a long time, let's get together," and then slip in a Laxalt question. I'm just going to call up people and say, "This is what I'm doing. Can you help me out?" I will give them my theory and let them respond to that.

The only thing that I suppose I ever do with someone who doesn't want to talk, if I'm able to reach them, is to say—which is the oldest thing in the book—"Look, there's no way for your story to be told unless you're willing to talk about it. There may be all kinds of reasons you're not going to tell me your side of the story—you may be too crushed, you may be under orders not to." That may be a technique, but it's also a simple truth.

I think what I do that's special is trying to understand people, whether they are telling the truth and what their perspective is. I don't think I'm an extraordinary questioner or interviewer. I know the right questions to ask, but I don't make a fetish of methodology.

I do not think there is a mystery about being a reporter. A reporter's got to do a lot of things—you have to make relationships, you have to understand what somebody's telling you. There are a lot of people who will not tell you something completely, but they will give you enough clues. You have to be able to do a little detective work.

COVERING THE PRESIDENT'S CANCER

I guess on every story there are little mysteries. The questions, "What did you know and when did you know it?" are the basic questions that are usually valid. Take the most recent story on [President Reagan's] skin cancer operation.

The question was when did they know what he had and what did they do about it? It became pretty evident to me by just reading and talking to people that something had happened on Thursday. We now know what did happen on Thursday, which was that they got a preliminary report on the biopsy that said it was cancerous. Then the question became, what did they do about it?

One person in Nancy Reagan's office lied, just lied to another reporter, said that Reagan didn't have cancer. [Press Secretary Larry] Speakes put out a statement that didn't refer to a biopsy but said this had been tested for infection, which was true but beside the point. I think you could tell from what Speakes said that he knew more.

By talking to people, it was quickly evident what had happened, which was that Nancy Reagan had directed people not to talk, not to give out the correct information. She totally controlled this, and different officials, given this edict, did different things with it. Some of them lied outright, others tried to keep their credibility, as Speakes did, not by lying, but by not telling you anything. It was interesting.

This happens on story after story. It's interesting, not because the nose cancer is particularly important, but because it shows you who is in control of the White House.

HOW TO GATHER INFORMATION

When I'm tracking down information like this, my first instinct is to read whatever is on the record so I know what's been said and what hasn't been said. The next thing is that a reporter, like a scientist, needs a working hypothesis. Now, I don't think reporting is a science. I don't think political science exists. I don't think those things are science. They're arts. But artists need working hypotheses, too.

Then you start calling people. The trick is—the trick probably is that there isn't any trick—that you let yourself be guided by what you find out. You must be willing to discard your working premise if it proves to be wrong. That doesn't mean you were wrong to have it. In fact, it's probably indispensable that you have it because your questioning is going to be too unfocused if you're calling without some idea in mind about what happened.

In the Reagan cancer story, my working hypothesis was that Nancy had run the show, that Nancy had pulled the plug on Speakes, that Nancy was in charge. All of which turned out to be right. But I don't think that the fact that it turned out to be right is very important.

THE WHITE HOUSE AS AN ORGANISM

You are a more informed questioner if, when questioning somebody, you have some idea of what you're doing. You tend to engage them more. If they think you're wrong, they'll try, sometimes, to tell you that. But as somebody said—I can't remember if it was Helen Thomas or who—the White House is not a person. The White House is an abstraction, a codified word for the collective, like Moscow or Peking or Washington. When the White House does something, somebody has made a decision to do it.

The White House is a collective entity in the sense that there is a line of the day, there is a message that they're trying to get across. There is an organism there, but different people are in every administration.

THE WHITE HOUSE PAPER BLIZZARD

The hardest thing to fight is that you're just overwhelmed with official bullshit. With any White House, the paper flow is so great. The amount of official news, both real news and propaganda and all shades of stuff in between, is so much that it's sometimes hard to fight through the blizzard of what you have to report to get to what you ought to report.

There's just an enormous amount of news that has to be reported and there are only so many hours in the day. This is a much greater problem for the wires, which have to report all the news. It's a much greater problem for some of the smaller bureaus that either do cover national news or have pretensions of covering national news and have a limited staff to do it.

We don't have as many people as we ought to have, but we have enough people that we're able to divide and farm out some of the official news stories and that gives us more time to report on what's really happening. We have all kinds of people who specialize in one subject or another—education, religion or finance, for example.

You can't deal with the paper blizzard simply by ignoring it. For instance, the White House press office put out a statement by the president on the 40th anniversary of the bombing of Hiroshima. It repeated offers that the Soviets had already rejected. It was designed totally for public relations effect. Well, what do you do with it?

Do you ignore it? I don't think that as a newspaper we could ignore it. I argued all day, in fact, that we shouldn't ignore it. And late in the day, they came to me and said, "Would you write an eight- or 10-inch piece on this thing?" which would be 350, 400 words. And I did. I pointed out the little things that made it more a detective story, so that it wasn't exactly what the White House said.

I wrote a small story that put it in perspective, but the lead was still what they [the White House press office] would have wanted, which was that the president observed this anniversary by saying whatever he said. That was a piece of official news, and that [kind of story] takes a certain amount of time and background to write because every day the subject is different, and that's just time-consuming. Yet it can't be ignored.

WHAT THE WHITE HOUSE SAYS IS NEWS

If the White House says it's news, is it news? Sometimes yes and sometimes no. The White House, first of all, rarely says that something's news. They're not dolts. Nobody would put out something and say, "This is your news story of the day."

They have an idea what people will go for. And some days they're right and some days they're wrong. But no president can control the events of the world, no White House can. For instance, the June agenda of the White House was tax reform. They unveiled it on May 28, and they did a good job on the unveiling from their standpoint. Then along came the hostage crisis, and it just drove everything else off the screen.

The next time you have a crisis like that, exactly the same thing will happen because we're in the news business. So you had 17 days in which the news was really dictated by the hijackers. Then you had another unplanned event, which was the president's colon cancer. And you had another several days in which that was the news. Within that context, everybody tried to dictate what the news should be.

The question is how you're used. If by used somebody means using you as the transmission to get their point across, that's what people hold press conferences for, whether they're terrorists with hoods over their faces or presidents. That's why they want you there. They would not invite you to press conferences if you were not going to write about them or put their pictures on television.

When Reagan was recovering from the colon cancer operation, which was handled with a great deal of candor, the events were not determined by the White House. But they did try to create a definite impression the week he was in the hospital—the release of the smiling Reagan, the release of certain quotes, jokes and one-liners to show a portrait of this rather virile man who looked death in the face and once more was going about his business.

The impression the American people got was calculated, but also was largely real. The basic fact is, Reagan made a remarkable recovery. They painted the lily a little bit. But if Reagan had, heaven forbid, died or become incapacitated, all the candor in the world and all the clever ideas in the world wouldn't have done a thing. What I'm saying is that the objective reality—in our Soviet friends' words—tends to govern much more than we think.

Reporters like to think that we put things in perspective, that we have taken stories and put them in context. The White House likes to think how smart they've been. But basic underlying realities are what people pick up. These guys, in my book, can't hold a candle to the

Nixon people for thinking up events or holding media events. Well, Nixon left office with a Gallup poll of 28 percent.

Nixon's now been in a full court press for well over a year rehabilitating his image. He's spoken, he's been in *Time*, he's given interviews, he's even given interviews to two groups of people from *The Washington Post*. But his approval rating's almost exactly what it was when he left office. Almost exactly. Because people made a fundamental judgment.

What I'm saying is that what governs things are not the little tricks they play to make the president look good or the things we do to counter it. What governs in the long run is basic reality.

PUBLIC RELATIONS PEOPLE AND THE PRESS

I once spoke before a group of public relations people and they were asking me for advice. I said, "The most important thing you can do when you deal with the press is tell the truth, answer the questions." After this, a guy came up to me and said, "You've given me a whole new insight into the way to deal with the press." Maybe he graduated from remedial lying school or something.

ETHICAL DILEMMAS

When I was a young editor, I remember writing and running a story about a teenage suicide and printing the note the person left. It was a personal note to his girlfriend or something. I wouldn't print the note now. I was 25 years old at the time.

It was harder for me to talk to the parents—and I did—of kids who had been drowned and pulled out of ditches in Merced than it is for me to talk to anybody in the government about whatever they do, no matter how badly I think they're doing it, and no matter how adversarial the relationship is.

But I don't think that the ethical dilemmas that come from covering the White House are different from those that come from covering the city council. Maybe there are some. Theoretically, there is one.

You do get into national security issues. Every administration, it seems, has used national security. That was the constructed defense in Watergate. In the last [hostage] crisis, for instance, we knew that one hostage was an employee of the National Security Agency, and we held it because that information would have jeopardized his life.

I think that was the right thing to do. I don't think we should be compelled by the government to do it—that's another whole issue. On our own, we ought not to run the names of people when that jeopardizes their lives. We ought not to give away a secret. You run into that maybe more in the White House. In national public affairs reporting, where you get into foreign policy considerations, you do get into that dimension.

Now, someone might argue that when we [*The Washington Post*] ran a story about the first space shuttle to be used for military purposes, we were disclosing classified information. Sure, they had classified it, but this information had appeared in technical publications, and we know the Soviets read those. I don't believe the government should decide what we print. Had that information not appeared anywhere before, we would not have run it, I'm sure.

We have obviously had cases at this paper and at other papers of reporters who make things up, who don't tell the truth, and I think there is probably value in studying aberrational behavior in newspapers, as there is in the government or the military or anywhere else. But if you exclude the reporter who, for whatever psychological reasons, lies or makes up something, the real ethical questions involve two things.

First of all, it involves confidences. You really do have to get a lot of confidences, and there's the question of how you deal with them. People will tell you something off the record, which you're obliged not to print. Some people want you to print it, they just don't want their name attached.

Other people are really telling you something they don't want to see in print and that they don't want you to repeat to your editors, and you have to sort out that jungle. You have to figure out what that person is telling you and why. A lot of times people will say, "If you can get this from some other source, you can use it." And you go out and you try to get it from another source.

The other problem is reporters who are always sweet and nice to you and then do you in. I mean, I am a friendly person, and if I'm calling the press secretary or the national security adviser or their secretaries, I'm calling them as Lou Cannon of *The Washington Post*. I'm obviously not calling them to go out to tea. I'm calling because I want information in a story, and if they tell me anything, they should expect to have it in the newspaper.

But some people are not sophisticated in government or are not sophisticated in the ways of the press. They normally take friendliness at face value. A reporter can do everything right, do everything that is morally justifiable, but if what he's trying to do is to make the person look bad without telling him what he's doing, that's an ethical question.

I don't think there are very many people who are surprised when they see themselves in print. But some people have no idea how they look in print, just like there are people who have no idea how they look or how they sound to others. They will be surprised.

The great ethical dilemmas and situations of my life involve my private life. I don't feel that I'm under any pressure or compulsion from editors or competitors to print something that I don't believe is right, to put a story in the paper that isn't true. I feel enough security in what I'm doing that if I have to hold a confidence and we get beat sometimes, that's fine. In the long run, we do better professionally because of that.

THE RESULTS OF WHAT I DO

The personal integrity of a reporter is the most important thing he's got. I like to think that the people I've covered or that I've written about feel that I have that.

Sometimes I feel that what I do makes a difference. I wrote the story about how Reagan had approved an investigation of his own people for reportedly leaking information that involved national security when, in fact, people in the administration had given us that information. Do I make a difference every day of my life? No. But in the long run, I think my columns about Reagan have contributed to an understanding of Ronald Reagan, and I think that's important.

Aides acknowledge confusion about Reagan's skin cancer

'But I did not lie and I told the truth,' Speakes says

By Lou Cannon

White House officials acknowledged yesterday that they had issued confusing statements about the skin cancer that was removed from President Reagan's nose last Tuesday, but insisted that no deliberate attempt had been made to deceive the public.

Answering questions at an unusually acrimonious briefing, White House

---

Lou Cannon talks about this story on pgs. 47–48.
Lou Cannon, "Aides Acknowledge Confusion About Reagan's Skin Cancer," courtesy of The Washington Post.

spokesman Larry Speakes said the information given reporters was incomplete and sometimes "confusing," but said he had been truthful in his responses.

"You pulled an iron curtain down on the truth," senior White House correspondent Helen Thomas of United Press International said.

"Exactly right," Speakes replied. "But I did not lie and I told the truth."

Informed sources said that the "curtain" Thomas referred to had been drawn at the order of Nancy Reagan, who last Thursday instructed White House chief of staff Donald T. Regan,

Speakes and her own aides to limit the information about the growth removed from the president's nose.

These sources said that it is not clear how much Mrs. Reagan knew about the medical findings at the time but pointed out that a preliminary report received at the White House on Thursday indicated that the growth was cancerous. A more complete report was received Monday.

The president disclosed at a meeting with reporters Monday that the removed growth was "the most common and least dangerous" type of skin cancer and would not require further treatment. He said he had not known until the weekend at Camp David that the growth was even being tested for cancer.

Speakes said in an interview yesterday that "once the president had the full facts on the biopsy he was anxious to explain it himself and wanted to do it in an opening statement, but decided instead to wait for a question." Reagan would have volunteered the statement if he had not been asked, Speakes said.

Reagan's comments Monday raised questions among reporters about the credibility of Speakes and especially of Jennefer Hirshberg, Mrs. Reagan's press secretary.

During an angry confrontation yesterday morning with Sam Donaldson of ABC News, Speakes maintained that he had told the truth and said, "You want to call me a liar? You want to?"

"I haven't called you a liar," Donaldson replied. "Questions of your credibility have been raised."

Speakes told reporters last Thursday that a biopsy to check for cancer would be routinely performed. Later in the day a statement was issued from the press office, without Speakes' name on it, saying that the tissue "was submitted for routine studies for inspection and it was determined that no further treatment is necessary." The statement did not mention either a biopsy or that the cancer was found.

On Friday, Speakes declined to answer questions about the biopsy, but Hirshberg told UPI that Mrs. Reagan had said that no biopsy had been performed. A White House official acknowledged that another member of Mrs. Reagan's staff told a reporter the same day that the removed growth was not cancerous. On Monday, Hirshberg told *The Washington Post* that neither of the Reagans knew of the biopsy until they were told the results over the weekend. She was unavailable for comment yesterday.

Privately, White House officials said that Speakes had walked a tightrope between the desire of Mrs. Reagan to have as little information released as possible and his recognition that reporters are intensely interested in any medical treatment of Reagan since the removal of a cancerous tumor from the president's colon last month.

"Everything is different now," one official said. "People will be interested if the president has a cold."

Recognizing this, both Speakes and chief of staff Regan were said to have recommended full disclosure of the facts about the removal of the growth from the president's nose. Their counsel went unheeded, said one source, who said Mrs. Reagan was concerned that confirming removal of even a minor cancerous growth could lead to "scare stories" about the president.

One official said that aides' response to questions about the growth on the president's nose had "taken the luster off" the performance of the White House in the days after the removal of the president's colon cancer. After the colon operation, White House officials and Reagan's physicians disclosed more information than had ever been made available after surgery on a president.

An official said yesterday that this candor gave credibility to the White House effort to dramatize Reagan's recovery through release of a carefully timed series of photographs and other well-orchestrated events.

Withholding information after the far more minor nose surgery produced an opposite effect. One official, reflecting on the past week with misgivings, said "it should provide a lesson learned" for the Reagan presidency.

"I tend to write about the very rich or the very poor because they're the most interesting."

MARYLN SCHWARTZ

Maryln Schwartz, less than five feet tall, is dwarfed by the computer terminal on wheels next to her desk. Newspapers and files piled 10 inches high near her feet and in her bookshelves dwarf her more.

Schwartz worked briefly at two newspapers in Mobile, Alabama, before she came to *The Dallas Morning News* in 1969, where she was assigned to write obituaries. She says she was so desperate to get off obituaries that she took an impossible assignment—to cover the Duchess of Windsor when she came to town.

Schwartz figured she could never get a personal interview with the Duchess, so instead she did what she has done best ever since—she stood back and watched. The result was a story about a woman unaccustomed to being alone, who carried no money with her, and how she survived her visit to Texas. The story ran on Page 1, and Schwartz left the obituary desk.

Now she covers stories as well as writes a column, but she winces when you call her a gossip columnist. She writes a column, she says, but it is not gossip. Speaking in her slow Alabama accent, Schwartz says she is constantly surprised by how rich people in Dallas spend their money. These people provide her with never-ending story ideas. There were, for instance, the high school sophomores who drove Porsches and Mercedes to school. And the sixth graders who hired a limousine to go to a Valentine's dance. And the man who spent half a million dollars on a party for his two daughters but said it really wasn't *that* extravagant because it was only $250,000 apiece.

"When I write about Texas characters, people say to me, 'These people are going to absolutely kill you when they read this story,'" says Schwartz. "Well, they send me flowers."

Schwartz, 41, has written about what rich women give their hair-dressers for Christmas, but she also covered the 1984 Democratic Convention in San Francisco. She has won four Penney-Missouri Awards from the University of Missouri, as well as 16 other statewide awards for feature writing from the Texas Associated Press and United Press International.

"I don't want to write a story that people have already read somewhere else," she says. "I want them to read something I wrote and then, six months later, say, 'Oh, I remember. Maryln Schwartz said that.'" ❖

from Maryln Schwartz

- Why feature writing is important
- How to look for a story that's distinctive
- The reporter as observer

Beginnings

I think that I've always written, but I never understood that I was going to. I put out a school newspaper in the third grade. It was fun to write a newspaper. I designed the paper and wrote school gossip. I never thought I could write.

Then in high school I took this creative writing course, and I found that I could write. There was a job at the local newspaper when I was a senior in high school called Teen Editor at *The Mobile* [Alabama] *Press Register,* where I did five interviews of different, outstanding seniors and then a Sunday gossip-talk thing. I liked talking to people and finding out things about them.

Then I went to the University of Georgia and worked in the summers and for a while at *The Mobile Press Register.* I majored in English. Journalism was something I loved doing, but it never really occurred to me that this was a very serious thing. This was in the mid-'60s.

HIRED BY *THE DALLAS MORNING NEWS*

When I graduated, I went to Houston and Dallas because they were places I'd never been before and I didn't know anybody. I liked Dallas a lot. I was 21, and it was lonely for about two or three months until I really met people, but I loved *The Dallas Morning News* and I loved what I was doing.

I always intended to stay here just four or five years and maybe try New York. But the paper was growing and I was growing and I like Texas a lot. It's a wonderful news state. Politics are very big here. Wild and interesting. Sports are big. Medicine. It seemed like big stories were constantly coming out of Texas.

MAKING SOMETHING OUT OF NOTHING

I started here writing obits. I think I learned a lot from that. I wanted to get off those obits so badly that I would do anything. I would answer the phone and they'd ask for other reporters, and I'd say, "They're not here, but I'll take the information." There was no pressure. That's a good way to begin because you learn how to make something out of nothing.

For example, when the Duchess of Windsor came in, it was a Sunday. She was going to the Neiman-Marcus Greenhouse, which is a beauty spa. It was supposed to be just see her at the plane, take her picture and write a few lines, because it was a Sunday story and they knew I couldn't get an interview. They sent me because they knew nobody else was going to get a story anyway, so then I could do cutlines [captions under photos].

And I watched her, which I like to do. Stanley Marcus picked her up with her entourage. And she said that she had never been away without the Duke. She had to use the telephone and she had no money, so she turned around and borrowed a dime for the telephone. Then she was very thirsty and there was no snack bar, and everybody fished around and gave her money to buy a Coke. And then she went to the ladies' room, and she came out and whispered in someone's ear, and they gave her a dime. I did a story about this woman who had never had to use money and who didn't even carry money. Ever. It turned out be a Page 1 story that the wire services picked up.

Then there was the time when the circus was here and the gorilla got sick. It was a silly little story, but it turned out to be funny because they couldn't find anybody who would treat a gorilla. You really do learn to go and look, and I think that's something that reporters don't do anymore. Everybody expects to be given something. You can't start out with the big story.

That's how you learn about people, too, because it's important to know whether people are lying or not. A lot of people don't lie, but their perception of the truth is distorted by how they feel. The only way you can really learn that is to go through lots and lots of experiences of talking to people so you get an instinct that works. So many times I've gone along with people. I thought, "I like these people and it's just so right." Then you check into little things and they're not true.

CHECKING ON CLINT EASTWOOD

I was doing a story about a woman in real estate who's very flamboyant. I was writing about her as the typical Texas tall-tale woman. And she talked about going on "The Dating Game" at one point and dating Clint Eastwood. She said this had happened 10 or 12 years before.

Well, I had just happened to read something in a newspaper or a magazine a couple of weeks before that talked about Clint Eastwood and his 20-year marriage. And he couldn't possibly have been on "The Dating Game" if he was married. So I called her and I was going to give her the benefit of the doubt because she could say, 10 or 12 years later, maybe it wasn't Clint Eastwood. Maybe it was somebody else.

She insisted it was Clint Eastwood. I said, "Carolyn, I have to tell you. I'm going to have to check into this. And this is going in the newspaper. You could give me an explanation now. It would be a lot better." She kept insisting. She would not change her story. Of course, I called "The Dating Game" people, and they said Clint Eastwood had never been on the show. But I might not have caught that if I hadn't read about it.

THE HYATT (AND MARYLN) MAKES A MISTAKE

I'll tell you a good example of checking that was just bizarre. The Hyatt Hotel had a new maitre d' in charge of the wine cellar. They called and said, "Maryln, this is somebody you might want for your column." He took care of the wine cellars for the royal family. They advertised him like that. The Hyatt, you'd figure, would check people out. So I interviewed this man and he obviously knew his wines. He was telling such delightful stories, and I got such a wonderful column out of it. I guess he figured, who would see it in Dallas?

But my stories go out on the wire and a lot of papers use it, and they used it in London. So these reporters were calling from London. The guy was a fake. He'd never worked for the royal family, he'd never done any of that. Well, I just thought, "Why didn't I call Buckingham Palace?" And I said, "I would have, except that the Hyatt presented him as legitimate."

I'd written it in a column, and so it was, what to do? We had a big debate, and I said, "Look, it's my mistake. I did it. I'm going to write a column and explain—I did this, this guy really took me in. Can you believe it?" I'd much rather have it out in the open than one day have it come back and haunt me.

DON'T JUMP TO CONCLUSIONS

I also think reporters sometimes jump to conclusions about people. We have a reporter here who did an interview with someone who'd been going through the whole day doing interview after interview with a run in her stocking. I don't think she's a sloppy person. She was apologizing for it and saying, "This is how bad the day has been and I'm embarrassed by it."

But the reporter wrote about her like she was a slob who walked around with a run in her stocking. The reporter was just trying to be cute, and I think a lot of times people write about other people to make themselves look good, rather than the other person. You've got to be sure of what you're saying because you're taking somebody's life in your hands.

I learned that myself last year when I had a story written about me in *Time* magazine. The story was all wrong. It was a very important thing to me. The story said something silly like, "She doesn't have a mortgage." Well, I *do* have a mortgage. They said I was covering the singles scene, and I'm not. They wanted copies of 12 stories and maybe four of them were about people who were single but that's not covering the singles scene.

I think they wanted to peg everyone, and so they did. But if *Time* does that, you can see how other people do. I think it's real important to understand the people you're writing about, to know instinctively when something's right or not. Don't call someone hysterical if they're not. It could be that they're just a nice person who's scared to death. That's why I always try to make people feel at ease, and then I talk to quite a few people to make sure that my perceptions are right. You have to check and check and check.

FAULTS OF THE PRESS

Particularly with features, I sometimes feel like it's like eating too much cotton candy—everything is the same and it's fluff. Like cotton candy—you eat a little bit of it and you feel your teeth are going to rot. On television they say, "And coming up next we're having the Queen of Jordan and Crystal Gayle." I mean, are we going to have Mother Teresa reading the news the next day?

I'm not just picking on television. I think newspapers do it, too. They get too cutesy, and we copy each other. They just pick people up and make them celebrities for a day and then drop them. Everybody just grabs and picks the story clean and leaves, and everybody has the same story.

Every time you turn on television, you see the same people doing the same things, writing the same things. It's like I'm watching everyone just glorifying all of these rock stars for doing "We Are the World." I think that's wonderful. I mean, they're raising money. I've just watched more and more reporters interviewing these people, saying "Isn't this wonderful—look at what they gave."

And I'm thinking, "What did they give? They gave four hours of their time when they were getting all this publicity. Let's not build them up into great heroes." I think that maybe the little lady in Mobile, Alabama, who lives on the farm who gave $200 that really hurt her was doing more. I don't think we point out those things.

WHAT MAKES A GOOD REPORTER

A good reporter has the ability to listen, to sort things out and to get them straight, to take good notes and to be fair. I don't think people are very fair today. I think they're more worried about their image and their reputation and creating a splash, and I think they're careless.

Yet, what's wonderful is you still find some people who consistently come up with good stories that are original and different, and they do them well. You come up with reporters who are fair and accurate and do a good job and editors who insist on you going back and not panicking and grabbing something first, but having it right.

COVERING TEXAS

When I write about Texas characters, people say to me, "These people are going to absolutely kill you when they read this story." Well, they send me flowers. Because what I try to do is not to write them as Maryln Schwartz feels about them. I write about them as they are.

There was the Carolyn Farb interview. She was married to a man for six years, and she got a $22 million divorce settlement, even though she'd had a prenuptial agreement that she would only get $2 million. She was not giving any interviews, and I kept after her. Finally I convinced her that she should talk to me. I just stayed with her for two days, and she poured her heart out to me. The interview was wonderful, and it was in *The Washington Post* and all the big papers. People kept saying, "How could she say that to you? Why did she say that?"

One thing she told me was that she thought she really earned this money. People thought it was just six years [of her life], but that was ridiculous. She took an ordinary little mansion and she turned it into a showplace. When her husband wanted his pineapple pie from the bakery, she just didn't send a maid for it. She went and she got it herself.

And he wanted to sing and he was someone who wasn't very glamorous, but she went out and hired a recording studio and backup singers and an orchestra and made an album.

She never even ate Japanese food because he didn't like Japanese food. He didn't like chicken, and she banished chicken from the house. And she suffered, and she deserved it [the money]. She did this for women everywhere.

I tell you she was bizarre in a lot of ways, but I ended up liking her. She is what she is, and I know that when I wrote that story, I wrote her. I was not making a fool of her because it would have been easy to do. But I don't believe you should say, "Look at this ridiculous woman." I think you write what they are and you let the reader say, "Isn't she ridiculous?" She's shrewd. She's got $22 million. That makes her a very powerful woman.

NORTH DALLAS STORIES

I do stories called "Only in North Dallas" [Dallas's wealthy neighborhood]. I always promise I am never going to write another North Dallas story ever again. And then something else comes up, like the drugstore that sells diamonds. There is a drugstore that sells diamonds and rubies right next to the Pepto Bismol.

I tell people you have to understand two things. One, you're dealing with some of the richest, most powerful people in this country, and, second, they're not fools. They're not fools at all. They're doing this for a reason, and you have to find out that reason. You have to understand that a million dollars for them might be $500 for us. I'm not saying it's right and that I approve, but it is not up to me to approve.

There are 5-year-olds with mink coats. I did a column about going to a party, and the youngest woman was the only one in a full-length fur. She was 8 years old, and her mother referred to it as her "starter coat."

Then there were the third-graders who had a Dolly Parton look-alike birthday party. There were all these little 8- or 9-year-olds who came dressed like Dolly Parton. It just goes on and on. At one point, I decided, that is enough. I can't write this anymore. I've got to put it all in perspective.

So I'm doing a long, serious story about growing up with the best of everything. Most people say they could not raise a child in Dallas because, while there's materialism everywhere, it's outrageous here.

I know the North Dallas people who are very rich, I know the West Dallas people who are very poor, and just kind of middle-class people in between. I think what you have to do is go out and talk to people and see what's going on and feel what they're feeling.

A WEDDING WITH THE OKLAHOMA SYMPHONY

There was a Texas-size wedding where I heard the family hired the Oklahoma Symphony to play in the choir section, and I thought it might be worth going. Well, it was one of these bizarre weddings where the groom's cake was a chocolate replica of the family's condominium complex. They did have the Oklahoma Symphony, and as you walked in, the symphony was playing the theme from "Dallas."

The bride had on a $20,000 dress. When they kissed, the orchestra struck into the theme from "Rocky." When the minister was blessing them, his diamond Rolex watch, a gift from the groom's father, was flashing. So he talked all about the father during the sermon. And the father said, "I want this to be a fairy tale for my son, and to him, a fairy tale is having a horse and buggy like [Prince] Charles and [Lady] Diana to drive from the church to the hotel."

They wouldn't let him put the horse and buggy on the toll road, so they went to the toll road and had a uniformed guard stand there, throwing in quarters for every single guest that went on the toll road. There were 2,000 guests, and they had an entourage of 18 Rolls Royces, and I'm driving my Honda.

When you finished reading the story, you could gag and laugh. But there wasn't one thing in that story that was making fun of them because that's how they felt.

THE VERY RICH AND THE VERY POOR

I tend to write about the very rich or the very poor because they're the most interesting. I did a story about a Mexican maid who was smuggled in. We usually read about the immigrants in the fields. Yet so many of these people are living in the most affluent houses in the city—tucked away, no friends, no one to visit, without a language. She has been here for a long time.

She was smuggled in, and she'd worked for people who were worried about her being clean. She was taking care of their children, and one night her employer went out. She was living in their house, and she had tried on one of the woman's dresses, and the woman came home and found her and threw out the dress. The maid was saying, "This woman leaves me with her children, yet she thinks that my putting on her dress is dirty."

ETHICAL DILEMMAS

Ardeshir Zahedi, who was the Ambassador to the United States from Iran, was in Houston for a party. It was about nine years ago, before the bad stuff had come up with Iran. I had written a story something like, he wasn't the handsomest, he wasn't the wittiest, he wasn't the most charming man in the room, but every eye was on him the whole evening because he was the richest. I told how he went around giving away things.

About two weeks later, I got a call from a catering service saying that they had a delivery for me, and they wanted to know if I would be home because it was perishable. And they delivered this kilo of caviar. Now this is worth about $500 nine years ago, which was a lot of money and a lot of caviar. And it was from Ardeshir Zahedi, thanking me for the story, which was not flattering.

Well, I can't accept $500 worth of caviar. I called the caterer, and they said it's perishable, you can't return caviar. And everybody said, "Forget it. Keep it." And I said, "I don't want to keep that much. I don't like it, and I don't think it's right. One day, something could come up and it's going to look like I've been getting this stuff from him."

So I finally sold it to a local caterer and gave the money to the cancer society and wrote him a note telling him that I did that. Of course, right after that, everything went crazy with Iran, and he was in a lot of trouble.

KNOW WHAT NOT TO WRITE

I also think that a lot of times it's more important to know what not to write than what to write. I don't think that's hiding a story. As a reporter you run across things that are very, very serious and are very personal. A lot of them have nothing to do with what you're writing about.

It's a constant nightmare—wanting to make sure if I'm really going to rake something up that I'm right, and I'm not just doing it because it's going to make me a heroine for two days. That's another thing I've learned. You have the big story today and then tomorrow it's "What have you written?"

If I'm writing about a high school principal, and he has a jail record, and he has embezzled, and he's running for a big office, that's important. But if I find out that his son is a homosexual who has tried to kill himself and he's in a home somewhere, I don't think there's any need to write that. People will write about it because it's interesting, people are going to read it. But that has nothing to do with a man who is running for public office. It's knowing when to do that and when not to.

The only things I have not used are things that have nothing to do with what I'm writing about. If I'm doing a personality profile, and these people know I'm writing it and they come across as drunks or idiots or they say terrible things, they knew what I was doing and I'm going to write it. Because most people are what they are because they want to be. I may not admire someone and I may think they're making fools of themselves, but they don't.

A lot of times people have come to me and said, "You're going to ruin my life if you print this." And I have to sit and think. Most of the time I'm not going to ruin their lives. They've ruined their lives and they're mad at me for finding out.

HOW I WORK

I write three columns a week, but I don't have a schedule. I know when my deadlines are, and sometimes they come easy and sometimes they don't. I wrote a column this morning in three hours, but to me, that was not fast.

I consider myself a good writer, but I don't like to check things. The hardest thing I have to do is go back and check those little details. I just like to write it and get it out, but I know that the basics are important. If I say a "myriad," she [the editor] says a myriad is over a thousand, not a smaller amount. Those are little things, but they're important.

THE IMPORTANCE OF EDITORS

I think everybody needs an editor. That's essential. You need an editor for two reasons. You need an editor to help stimulate you and to see that you're on the right track, and you need an editor to read something.

They don't rewrite you. A good reporter doesn't need rewriting, but you need an editor to read something and say, "You're not saying what you think you're saying. It's in your head. Talk it out." Or you need an editor to say, "There are two words in the third paragraph that change the meaning of your story. Think about it."

Sometimes, with an editor, I'll sit down and we will spend 20 minutes talking about one word. I need that give-and-take, and I also need someone to say, "You said this came in 1941 and that wasn't invented until 1945." You can't catch everything.

FIND YOUR OWN STORIES

I try to never follow the pack. I either want the story first, or I want a different look at it. I try to reach stories before everybody's talking about them. I don't want to write a story that people have already read somewhere else. I want them to read something I write and then, six

Maryln Schwartz

months later, say, "Oh, I remember. Maryln Schwartz said that." I think it's important to pick up trends.

I always find stories wherever I go because I'm always looking. In sports stories, when everybody's worrying about who's getting picked, I go to the people who aren't getting picked and write a story about what it's like to sit there and wait. Or I write a story about somebody who's been in the game for 15 years and they know they can't last much longer. The day they get cut, I do a story on what it's like.

Relationship stories—people go crazy over stories about relationships. I did a story about people who have been engaged for 15 or 20 years. They just don't ever get married. You start asking people, and you talk to marriage counselors and psychiatrists and psychologists. I save things. When people tell me something, I write it down and put it in a file.

Everybody's doing stories about big proms now. One night I stopped at a Howard Johnson's to pick up some ice cream, and I met a friend and we sat down and were talking. There were these two sweet young girls, cute, looking really miserable. We overheard them talking about this prom night. They didn't have dates. They were at Howard Johnson's because they didn't want to run into anybody. So I did a story about famous people who didn't go to their proms and had them talk about what it was like.

NOT JUST WRITING FLUFF

Sometimes I feel what I do makes a difference. Yeah, I do. I never used to. I don't think that I'm so important that I can change the world. I don't mean that. But I don't think that I'm just writing fluff. I think that I use humor a lot. I really try to say something.

People aren't going to waste their time reading something unless they get something out of it. It doesn't have to be a great, major thing, but sometimes it's just good to know that other people feel the same way or that other people have been through the same things or that something is going on and you're not crazy.

WORK EARLY AND HARD

I still think that some of the best stories come from small things. I went to the [1984] Democratic Convention, and there were at least 2,000 or 3,000 reporters there. There were only four people who got an interview with [Vice Presidential Nominee Geraldine Ferraro's husband] John Zaccaro. I was one of them because I've never depended on other people. Two of them were the wire services, and one was a San Francisco newspaper that was set up ahead of time. And I got him.

What I did was, when I got there, I knew that the nominee was going to be either Ferraro or [San Francisco Mayor] Dianne Feinstein. Before I did anything, I checked into my room, I called Dianne Feinstein's husband when nobody cared to get him, and did an interview. And I got Zaccaro and did a preliminary interview. Then, when Ferraro got named, and they weren't giving interviews to anybody, I just spent one day following him around from place to place. I grabbed three minutes here, four minutes there, five minutes there. When you put the whole day together, I had about 45 minutes, plus I had my preliminary interview, plus I saw how he was responding and reacting. I got a really good story.

KNOW HOW TO FIND A STORY

One of the best stories I got out of the convention was the last night. I heard that Mondale was going to the Washington Square Bar and Grill, which was the media hangout. It's got this huge glass front, but it's a tiny place. I drove there, and there must've been 500 or 600 people outside. Of course, they weren't letting anyone in, but we could look in the window.

And there was Walter Cronkite and Art Buchwald and Andy Rooney at one table and David Brinkley and [former Democratic Party Chairman] Bob Strauss and their party at another table, and Tom Brokaw at another. People were pressed up against the window like they were at the zoo, watching these people eating and talking. I just did a story about how everyone was watching these people eat, and it was like feeding time at the zoo. It was a story saying something about how television people had taken over the celebrity. It was a good wrap-up, when we were tired of everything else.

If someone said, "Get an interview with Mondale because he's going to be there," a lot of reporters would come back and say, "Mondale wasn't there, and I couldn't get in." They might have stayed a minute and looked at Walter Cronkite and left. But that was a story. And you've got to know how to find a story no matter what.

It was a Texas-size wedding

Nothing's too good for Danny Faulkner's bride

by Maryln Schwartz

When Danny Faulkner Jr. married Debbie Jordan Friday night, the bridegroom's father explained, "This wedding and this love story are just like a fairy tale."

A caravan of 18 Rolls Royces lined up outside Park Cities Baptist Church.

Inside, the entire Oklahoma Symphony was playing in the choir section. The musicians burst into a rousing rendition of the theme song from the television show "Dallas" as guests were escorted to their seats.

"We tried to get the Dallas Symphony," said the bridegroom's father, millionaire developer Danny Faulkner Sr. "But they were all booked up."

Faulkner stood in the foyer greeting the more than 2,000 guests as they walked in the door. The bridegroom, 24, stood at his father's side, wearing a white tuxedo designed for him in Italy.

Father and son wore triangular diamond pins with a large initial "F," the insignia of Faulkner's condominium development at Lake Ray Hubbard.

"My son has found a woman who loves him as much as I do," explained the father, with tears in his eyes. "There is nothing too wonderful for her. Tonight she will be Cinderella."

This is an edited version of a longer story about an unusual Texas wedding. Maryln Schwartz talks about this story on p. 65.

Reprinted by permission of The Dallas Morning News.

The original plans were for Debbie and Danny to leave the church in a horse-drawn carriage, just like the wedding of Prince Charles and Princess Diana. This plan had to be abandoned when the reception was scheduled in a North Dallas hotel. A horse-drawn carriage would be too dangerous on the North Dallas Tollway.

Debbie Jordan was a secretary in Phenix City, Ala., three years ago when she came to Dallas to visit her brother, who is also named Danny. The brother introduced her to Danny Faulkner Jr.

"It was love at first sight for me," said Debbie, 25. "But he was dating a different girl every night. It took me six months to get him away from those other women."

The wedding was on the anniversary of their first meeting. They became engaged on the same date one year ago.

The bride's parents, Mr. and Mrs. Haynes Jordan, came from Phenix City to meet their daughter's boyfriend just before the engagement.

They were overwhelmed to learn their prospective son-in-law came from a family that owns 17 Rolls Royces, two helicopters, a Learjet and a hot-air balloon.

Connie Jordan was still awed Friday night as she walked down the aisle in a purple designer dress.

"From the cotton fields to this," she said, "can you believe it? We are simple people. My husband is a retired textile worker, but we started out on the farm in the cotton fields."

. . . The altar of the church had been turned into a lush garden of trees and fresh flowers. Thousands of tiny white lights adorned the trees. Six video cameras were in place to film the event.

By 7:30, the giant church was filled. The orchestra finished playing the theme from the film "Arthur" and began a stirring version of "Here Comes the Bride."

The six bridesmaids and a flower girl wore long, burgundy dresses. Debbie walked down the aisle in a Priscilla of Boston gown with an eight-foot train. Her long black ponytail cascaded from the veil, all the way down her back.

. . . As he addressed the bridal couple, the Rev. Starkes spent five minutes talking about the love and philanthropy of Danny Faulkner Sr. The symphony played the theme from "Chariots of Fire" in the background.

As the happy couple kissed for the first time as man and wife, the orchestra played the theme from "Rocky." The bride and bridegroom joyously raised their arms high in a victory sign.

The reception followed at the Westin Hotel at the Galleria. A uniformed guard stood at the toll road with a sackful of change to pay the toll for each carload of guests as they traveled from the church to the hotel.

On display on the second floor of the hotel was the bride's cake, towering seven feet tall. The bridegroom's cake was a replica of the Faulkner Point condominiums, sculpted in chocolate.

The father of the bridegroom was still teary-eyed, explaining this was a night he wanted to share with all of his friends. He is a man who is known for his generosity. Family members say "well over 100" of the guests at the wedding that night were wearing diamond Rolex watches given to them by Faulkner.

"I know what it's like to be poor," said Faulkner. "Just seven years ago, I was a house painter, nothing more."

He pointed to a man across the room.

"Look, John Smith is here. He was shining shoes for a living when I was painting houses. Now he's painting houses—and look at me."

Then he introduced another man.

"This is the happiest man here tonight," said Faulkner. "He sold one of those rings that are on the bride's fingers."

The bride was wearing two rings. One was a large cluster of diamonds about the size of a large walnut. The other was her engagement ring—11½ carats. Faulkner Sr. wore a 21-carat diamond on his finger.

. . . Looking beautiful and very starry-eyed, Debbie toasted her bridegroom with a glass of Artesia water. He toasted her with a glass of cola. The family does not drink alcoholic beverages or smoke.

Guests were served fruit punch in wine glasses. Artesia water was iced in champagne buckets. A beef-and-seafood buffet was served next to a giant ice sculpture spelling out "Debbie and Danny."

On the cheese and chocolate fondue table was a chocolate Learjet.

At the end of the evening, the happy couple boarded their own Learjet and took off for a honeymoon in Hawaii.

"My boy never smoked, he never cursed, he never took dope, he never sassed his daddy," said Danny Faulkner Sr. "A boy like that just deserves the best."

Sharon Wohlmuth/The Philadelphia Inquirer

"I've always had a very, very strong sense of social justice and idealism. Being a journalist was a way I could really do something about the issues I care about."

HUNTLY COLLINS

Causes have always attracted Huntly Collins. In 1984, she transferred her attention from Portland's urban green to Philadelphia's urban gray. But she still cares.

Huntly Collins, 40, worries about equity. "I grew up alone with my mother, who was a divorcee, in a small farming community outside of Portland," she says. "I worked every summer in the fields and every summer a lot of derelicts from the streets of downtown Portland were bused out to the fields. Migrant families also came.

"I began writing paragraph descriptions of people I would meet. During the school year whenever I'd have an assignment in English, I'd often draw on my summer experiences to fulfill the assignment.

"Simultaneously, I had a godfather who was a reporter and a cameraman at a small newspaper in eastern Oregon. He would take me out on assignments with him. From going out with my godfather, I could tell that being a reporter gave you this great opportunity to go up to absolute strangers and ask questions.

"I think these two factors—my early exposure to injustice in agriculture, and my exposure to my godfather—really were the genesis of my becoming a reporter." In Portland at *The Oregonian*, Collins wrote about school desegregation. The 14-part series won her the Charles Stewart Mott Award in educational journalism. She won more than 10 different local and national awards for her education writing, and then Oregon's recession shifted her interest to the economy.

"The recession made me realize that all the education in the world won't help if there aren't jobs for people and if the economy isn't working." She and two other reporters wrote a 20-part series called "Sorrowful Spring." One story was about unemployed sawmill workers in southern Oregon's vulnerable timber industry. Huntly Collins worries about a reporter's responsibility to the people she covers.

"When I was interviewing these sawmill workers and their families, they were baring their souls to me," Collins says. "They sit in these small, rural towns. And they have no idea that millions of people are going to be reading about their efforts to commit suicide, the details of their lives, because they're unsophisticated people. And they bare their souls to me and I go away and what do I give them? I sometimes feel as if I've used them, and I don't like that."

In 1982 Collins attended Harvard and MIT as a Nieman Fellow to study economics and technology. During her year as a Nieman Fellow, Collins envisioned a new kind of labor reporting. "I wanted to turn the labor beat into the workplace beat, to really cover work, not unions *per se*. Unions are a part of that, but only a small part, an increasingly small part." *The Philadelphia Inquirer* hired her in 1984 to cover business, and she has recently moved to the labor beat. ❖

from Huntly Collins

- How a reporter develops sources on a beat
- The relationship between a reporter and her sources
- Similarities between reporting on business and reporting on labor

BEGINNINGS

There wasn't any sort of precise moment when I decided I wanted to be a journalist. I just fell into it through writing. I'd always loved to write about what was in the "real world" as opposed to making things up.

I began writing for my high school paper when I was a sophomore. What became clear to me was that journalism represented a really powerful tool for making a contribution to society, to right wrongs. I've always had a very, very strong sense of social justice and of idealism. Being a journalist was a way I could really do something about the issues I care about.

As a high school student, the only newspaper job I could get was a weekend job at the *Gresham Outlook* coming in and cleaning up all the old photos they hadn't used and doing some filing, but to me it was great just to be in the place. The editor had gone to the University of Washington, and he taught there. He really encouraged me to go there, plus I had developed a real interest in the Far East and China. Washington, of course, has an excellent Far Eastern studies program.

My idea was to combine journalism and Far Eastern studies. My goal—I had a very specific goal—was to be the first American reporter inside communist China. Somebody else from *The New York Times* actually did that. But that was the goal.

I went to Washington in the fall of 1964 on a scholarship. This was a really major transition for me. It was difficult to leave home, and even more difficult since it had always been me and my mother against the world. I ended up leaving Washington after two months. With much chagrin and kind of a sense of failure, I went back to Portland and worked for the rest of that semester as a retail clerk. I enrolled at Portland State University that winter term. I still wanted to be a journalist, but I decided, I'll get a good liberal arts education and see what happens.

WORKING AT *THE VANGUARD*

I hadn't been there more than a semester when I became real involved with the student newspaper, *The Vanguard*. This would've been '66. It was a very exciting time to be a college journalist because student protest and the war in Vietnam were heating up, and we were writing about all these things in the paper.

I began as a reporter, and became news editor, then managing editor and then editor. I didn't take any formal how-to-write classes. I pretty much learned that on the job.

Then I fell in love my senior year in college and married right before we graduated. This was really pre-women's-liberation days. He [my husband] was destined to become a Methodist minister and wanted to go to seminary after college, and I followed him. I really didn't even think about my career, which is hard to imagine these days. He wanted to work in urban ministry of some kind, and the seminary he chose was in Kansas City.

In Kansas City, there wasn't anything else to do, so I went to graduate school in English and education, and I got a master's degree. I taught high school English for a year while Mike finished up at the seminary. Then we went back to Oregon, where he had his first church.

A WATERGATE SCOOP AT THE *OREGON TIMES*

When I couldn't get a teaching job in Oregon, I decided that I would write for something called the *Oregon Times*, which was a monthly magazine of investigative reporting. It paid something like $40 a story, and it would take two to three months to do one of these stories, so that's what I was earning.

The most interesting and sort of bizarre story I did exposed a small part of the Watergate story. We are a footnote in Woodward and Bernstein's book. Do you remember Donald Segretti?

He was the mole who was going about infiltrating Democratic campaigns. The [Washington] *Post* had just exposed Segretti and his efforts to disrupt Democratic campaigns primarily in the South. My editor had read one of their stories in which they listed the towns that Segretti had visited, and Portland was one of them.

The editor asked me to find out what Segretti had done in Portland, who he had talked to and when he had talked to them—specifically, did he try to disrupt McGovern's or anyone else's campaign in our state? What I tried to do was to reconstruct the primary campaign's organization.

At that point the Watergate burglars had not been connected to Richard Nixon. They were connected to the Committee to Re-elect the President, CREEP, but nobody had been able to make the link to the president. Segretti was an agent of CREEP.

I began reconstructing the primaries in Oregon. I actually went through old volunteer cards for the various campaigns. Very painstaking work, very dull. I was about ready to give up when I went to interview a lawyer who had headed the McGovern campaign during the primary. He had saved every slip of paper that ever came over his desk during the campaign. I sat in his office turning over papers for two days.

Finally I came across this letter from Gary Hart, who was at that time McGovern's national campaign coordinator, saying, "I just thought you'd like to know that Nixon is due in Portland on such-and-such a weekend and he'll be staying at the Benson Hotel."

Well, stars went off when I saw this, because the weekend that Nixon was due in Portland was the same weekend that Segretti was in Portland. I knew when Segretti was there, but I didn't know where he stayed. Like I said, up until this point, Segretti had only been linked to the Committee to Re-elect, not to Nixon himself.

So I immediately went to the files and dug out *The Oregonian* for those days, and the story was all over the front page—Nixon with an entourage of two or three hundred had stayed in Portland at the Benson Hotel. Here we had, now, Segretti and Nixon in the same hotel at the same time.

We knew that certain floors were reserved for Nixon's party alone. I needed to find what floor Segretti was on. If we could do it, we would have ourselves quite a story. So I went to talk to the manager of the Benson Hotel. I did not lie, but I didn't exactly tell him the whole truth, either. I made him think I was just a mushy woman reporter. I said, "Can you tell me, what was Pat wearing?" I said I was reconstructing Nixon's visit to Oregon. All this was leading up to this final question, which was, "Gosh, there were so many famous people here. Do you suppose I could see the register book and see who visited?"

He said, "No."

I said, "Thank you very much," and I exited.

So we decided to go with the story, simply placing Nixon and Segretti in the Benson Hotel at the same time. It was a cover story, and we had a news conference to release it. It was the lead story on all three networks that night from this little magazine. The next day, [Democratic Presidential Candidate] Sargent Shriver was campaigning in Mt.

Holyoke, Massachusetts, holding up a copy of the *Oregon Times* and demanding an answer from the administration.

HIRED BY *THE OREGANIAN* [PORTLAND]

Then my marriage fell apart, and I needed work. So I took a job as press secretary to a woman named Betty Roberts who ran for governor in Oregon. That lasted less than a year. She came in second.

But right after her campaign, I was hired by *The Oregonian.* I was delivering a press release one day, and the political editor said, "Are you interested in a job here? I think you ought to apply." I started where every reporter does—the police beat. Then I became the paper's city hall reporter for two or three years. I was offered the education beat in 1977.

HOW TO COVER EDUCATION

One suggestion would be to spend as much time as you can in classrooms, as opposed to school board meetings. You need to get where the action is, which is the classroom. Another piece of advice is not to jump at the latest gimmick in education and write about it as if it were the best thing since sliced bread. Keep the longer view.

Always ask basic questions, such as "Is this helping kids?" "Are they learning?" "Is this promoting equity in society?" Try to pick a very large issue in society, subject to a lot of debate, and find ways to illustrate that with real, live examples from real, live kids and parents.

I even went to China to cover education. I wasn't the first reporter [see page 75], but I was among the first group of American education writers that went in to look at Chinese schools. In 1980 in China, it was just beginning to be OK to read Western literature again.

COVERING OREGON'S RECESSION

I was starting to get restless. Then a recession hit Oregon in 1981. Because of the state's dependence on the timber industry, it was really devastating. I was talking one day to a Headstart program director who said, "You know, for the first time we're really beginning to see hungry children in these programs." These were largely white working-class areas.

So I proposed that we look at the human face of the recession in Oregon. I took time off from the school beat, and they assigned two other reporters to the story. We spent four months. My task was to go out and interview unemployed sawmill workers and their families and find out how it was affecting their lives. I was just shocked. I had done a lot of traveling at that point. I had been in Nicaragua and China and I had been to southern Africa.

But here I saw, in our own backyard, the kind of thing I had seen in Third World countries. These were middle-class people who had worked hard all their lives for what they had, and all of a sudden, their companies shut down and they weren't likely to reopen. They had no skills, no training, and had never known any other way of life.

I interviewed one man who had been a sawmill worker all his life, and when he lost his job, he went on unemployment for a while. When that ran out, he had to go on welfare, and this was just more than he could take. He didn't believe in gifts from the government, and he tried to commit suicide on the way to the welfare office. He lived to talk about it.

I would sit around kitchen tables with oilcloth tablecloths and talk to families about what was going on. We wrote a 20-part series called "Sorrowful Spring," the story of the recession in Oregon. As a journalist, I had always been most interested in education. Now I was beginning to see there was something even more fundamental and that was economics, jobs.

On that basis, I decided to apply for a Nieman Fellowship so I could study economics, a subject I had always avoided. I don't have a mathematical mind. I'm not interested in a lot of abstractions. A Nieman Fellowship is basically an open-ended ticket to spend a year at Harvard and study whatever you want. You can also take classes at MIT. What I developed out of this year was a vision to develop a different kind of labor reporting.

Historically, labor reporters have focused on unions and contract negotiations and strikes. With the labor movement experiencing a precipitous decline in membership and influence, I believe that labor reporting has got to change to reflect that change.

I went back to Oregon for about three months after my fellowship. Then an offer came from *The Philadelphia Inquirer.*

COVERING BUSINESS IN PHILADELPHIA

I was assigned to cover economic development in the Philadelphia area. Philadelphia, like every other major northeastern industrial city, is going through an enormous transition from heavy manufacturing to service industries. We have tremendous growth in real estate, insurance and banking, business services, and a tremendous decline in manufacturing.

Certainly we can cover the Philadelphia-area economy and Philadelphia business in a way that *The Wall Street Journal* can't because they don't have the staff. Personally, I try to humanize everything I write about. I really try to translate the abstract ideas into flesh and blood.

As an example, I did a long story in the business section on the fact that automation doesn't necessarily lead to the elimination of jobs, but that automation can also increase a company's competitive position to the point where it can actually add new positions. I focused on one specific company and even started the story with one specific individual.

This was a company called La France. They manufacture specialized plates that go on custom cars. They have a work force that's rather old, that was used to the old hand methods. In fact, they have one man there who learned his craft in Italy when he was a child, and he's really regarded as an artist who works in steel.

I focused on how his work changed with the advent of computer-assisted technology. He said he could get things done much more quickly and he could spend more time on the hand operations, creating some new products that he couldn't do with the computer-assisted stuff. It was a story that was replete with a lot of statistics and quotes from economists around the country, but it started with one plant and one man and it took off from there. Otherwise it would have been a very academic-sounding piece.

COVERING LABOR IN PHILADELPHIA

I took the labor beat last October. Philadelphia is where the labor movement was born. The first union was here, the first strike was here, the predecessors of the AFL-CIO began here, the Knights of Labor and other groups. There's a rich history, and I think in part because of that, and because Philadelphia has until recently been a large manufacturing center, the labor movement itself is stronger in Philadelphia than it is in other big cities in the country. Because it's stronger, there's more to cover than just the unions.

Several months after I took over the beat, I learned that three of the building trades in our area—plumbers, carpenters and sheet metal workers—had pooled a portion of their pension fund and invested that money in the construction of a downtown office building.

Typically, most unions have invested their pension funds simply where they can get the highest interest rate. But here were three unions who were being pretty creative, using their pension money to create jobs and to improve the local economy—essentially, a good news story.

In the past, most labor reporters in this community had not been very kind to labor. Many of them were not very interested in some of these changes, maybe operating under some of the old stereotypes that all unions are corrupt. Because of that reputation, a lot of labor leaders in this community were fairly reluctant to talk to the press. I had just started on the beat, and I wanted to do this story that could only be positive. Still I had trouble getting the union leaders to meet with me.

I wanted to meet the head of the plumbers union, Edward F. Keenan. He put me off, like the others, over the phone. His secretary kept telling me, "No, he's not in, and we don't know when he'll be in." Finally, I said to his secretary, "Look, could you just put him on and let him tell me in his own words why he doesn't want to talk to me?" So he came on the phone, and finally he relented and I went out to talk to him. He's huge—he could be a tackle for the Chicago Bears.

He started the conversation by saying, "I don't really want to talk to you. I don't know you, but I don't trust you. I don't trust any newspaper reporter. They've always screwed up."

I spent about 45 minutes just talking to him about who I was, where I came from, what I was interested in, how I saw labor unions today. Finally, he relented and talked to me. I asked him some tough questions, and we had a good meeting. I felt like a door had opened.

At the end of the interview, I got up and shook his hand. I think he was a little surprised. He doesn't have many women shaking hands with him. I went to leave, and there was obviously a rapport there. He said, "Can I take you to your car?" And I said, "No, that's all right, I'll get there." I was driving a 1980 Subaru, and I did not want him to see the foreign car because I knew how he'd react.

He said, "No, no, let me take you to your car." He insisted. So we went to the car. And he looked at me and he looked at the car, and he said, "How long do you plan to cover labor in this city?" And I didn't have the sense to say to him at the time what I should have said—which was, "Well, as long as this piece of Japanese junk gets me around."

It's a problem. It is hard to cover labor in this community if you're driving a foreign car. There's no doubt about it. But I'm not going to let them blackmail me into buying another car. I'll deal with it if it comes up.

It's a tough city. In the past, there is a history of corruption in labor here, especially in the building trades, a history of violence. They're not the easiest folks to deal with, and you've got to be really tough and thick-skinned.

FEAR ON THE BEAT

Sometimes I've been afraid. As an example—this didn't occur while I've been covering the beat—but the Teamsters here are very strong and, as far as I can tell, clean, not connected to the mob. But they use some pretty heavy-handed tactics to get what they want.

They were negotiating a contract with the University of Pennsylvania. I believe they have drivers that work there who deliver things around campus. And the president of the university was sitting down at the negotiating table with the head of the Teamsters. The president was giving the union official a lot of academic rhetoric, and the union official couldn't follow it. He was getting frustrated. So he just reached into his vest and pulled out his gun, set it on the table and said, "Let's talk again." The president signed right away.

LABOR AND THE PRESS

Labor people don't want to talk to the press, unlike the business community, which has something to sell—their product, their company, their approach, their personality. These guys [labor] assume you're out to screw them, and some of them do have something to hide. A whole lot of time has to go into building trust. In all my years of reporting, I've never encountered a situation like it.

I've mostly done it by setting up lunches with people, talking totally off the record. I don't even bring my notepad. I sit down with union presidents and say, "I don't know anything about the garment workers' union here. How long has it been going? What are the issues that you're concerned with today? What do you think of the press?" Basically I tell them what my history is and how I got interested in labor reporting. It's frustrating because there's no immediate payoff.

We're talking about 40 or 50 key unions and hundreds of others. If you were covering the school system, you'd at least go to school board meetings, but if you're covering labor there's no focal point. It just takes a lot of time, a lot of leg work.

WHAT MAKES A GOOD REPORTER

First of all, you need an inquisitive mind and an interest in people. You have to have some sense of justice, some sense of, "This is really wrong" or "This is really right." A lot of reporters don't have that and become terrible cynics. Not only are they the worse for it, but I think the industry is the worse for that.

When I say you have to have a sense of justice, I don't think you have to be an idealogue or be pushing for one particular point of view. You do have to have a real sense of fairness and right and wrong.

WEAKNESSES IN THE PROFESSION

Cynicism is endemic to our profession. It keeps people from writing stories that need to be written because their cynicism immobilizes them. They just don't see any point in writing about something because, of course, it will do no good. Cynical journalists also are pretty lousy human beings to work with.

Also, despite the fact that it's sort of a cliché for the public to critique the press and say, "You're only writing about the bad things," there's some truth in that. Journalism is to blame for not explaining how the things that work are working—schools, for instance. There are schools that are succeeding, and I think the public deserves to know that they are and why they are and what it takes to make a good school. That doesn't mean I don't think we should cover corruption and negative things, but certainly we ought to cover the positive as well as negative things.

Another real fundamental weakness, with some notable exceptions, is that by and large the media does not go after the larger issues until a crisis forces them to. There's too much crisis reporting and not enough in-depth reporting on the issues in advance.

For instance, I don't think there's been any newspaper in this country that's taken a hard look at illiteracy in American society and what it means. That's not the kind of thing that has a lot of action attached to it, but it has enormous consequences.

There's been too little reporting about disarmament, other than institutional stories about talks in Geneva. It's not a sexy issue, yet this is an issue that will decide the future of the human race.

A lot of things are going on in science that certainly have that kind of monumental impact down the road. Bio-engineering, for instance, and what its long-term consequences could be for the race and for society. What I'm saying is that journalism is way too reactive.

ETHICAL DILEMMAS

One dilemma is that we were trained to be fair, to report all sides, and I personally bend over backwards to do that. But sometimes, it's quite clear that what one side may be saying is an absolute falsehood. It doesn't serve the public to be writing something that's a blatant lie.

It comes up in my beat in little ways. Recently the city government in Philadelphia was forced to end all of its summer jobs for kids because one of the city unions objected to the program. The union's reasons on the surface were that the kids had to take make-work jobs, like sweeping streets. The other reason they gave was they weren't paying typically female jobs as much as typically male jobs.

I know enough about what's going on to know that those issues had nothing to do with the dispute. Basically, the union's upset about other issues, but they won't say so publicly. But I have to write a story that says the city says this and the union says this. The story makes it appear that each side has its point of view, when I know what the union is saying is absolutely false. So there I am. I feel uncomfortable in that position.

Real ethical dilemmas also arise regularly about which word to use. Recently a doctor has been on trial in Philadelphia for murder in connection with an abortion. The story called the "fetus" a "baby." That decision to call this a baby sets the tone for the rest of the story. That wasn't my story, another reporter did it, but that's an example of having to make very critical decisions about what kinds of words to use.

All reporters also eventually face the whole dilemma of using unnamed sources. That's a pretty common issue. Up until the time I hit the labor beat, I generally would say, "I don't want to hear it if you can't tell it to me on the record." Since I've been covering labor, it's almost impossible to get stories unless you agree to that. It's something I live with.

MANIPULATION AS A FACTOR IN REPORTING

I've talked to enough reporters to know that the more sensitive reporters feel they are sometimes manipulating people, particularly when they're doing stories about someone's hardship. Sometimes I feel like I am manipulating people for a larger good for the society as a whole. They may be under the impression that somehow their talking to me is going to result in assistance for them, but I know that isn't my point. I'm not a social worker. I don't want to be.

For instance, there was a woman in Pennsylvania who lost her factory job. I'm pretty sure she thought that by talking to me, people would donate things to her. I learned a year later that nothing of the sort had occurred. If anything, she's even worse off now than she had been. My point in writing that was to illustrate the human tragedy. It wasn't ever explicit, but she may not have wanted to talk to me had she known that she would not get any help.

I have felt uncomfortable in other situations. Sometimes you have to lead people on a little bit to get information. For instance, I did a long story on the casino-hotel workers' union in Atlantic City, which is controlled by the mob. A number of top union leaders have been indicted for alleged connections to the father of the mob. It's a union that has enormous power and that doesn't want to talk to the press.

To get them to talk to me, I more or less had to come on saying, "Tell me what you've done for your people. Here you have one of the biggest unions in the country, one of the biggest single units. You've got maids starting at $13,000 a year. Some of the top people have been killed or gone off to jail. Gosh, how have you done all this?" And these people opened up to me. They talked to me about what they had accomplished.

Union leaders would call and say, "When's the story gonna come out?" They thought this was somehow going to clear them. Well, it didn't do that at all. I ended up writing a story which was not very complimentary because I found dissidents within the union who were so terrified of the mob connection that they wouldn't even publicly announce their opposition to the union leaders.

When the story came out, I felt just a little bit of guilt. In a sense, I misled them, but I never would have gotten their side of the story had I not done that. I told their story in a fair way.

WHAT I LIKE ABOUT BEING A JOURNALIST

In some ways, I've always felt like reporting is a strange combination of art and science. Science represents the inquisitive mind, always asking questions and demanding evidence to back up statements, that's the science of it. The art of it is the intuition that leads you to a story and the kind of rapport it takes to get people to open up to you in interviews. That's an art. The writing itself, that's an art.

As a journalist, I have an excuse to talk to anybody and that's wonderful. I sometimes feel like what I do makes a difference, that it has a positive impact on an individual's life or the life of a community, and basically I enjoy the act of creation—of putting something together with words.

Quietly, a challenge to A.C. union leadership begins

by Huntly Collins

ATLANTIC CITY, N.J.—It first appeared in a newspaper here last week. The notice tucked away amid the classified ads asked casino-hotel workers who wanted to elect new leadership for their union to send their names and phone numbers to a post office box in nearby Pleasantville.

At the end of the notice, printed in boldface letters, was the word *confidential*.

This is an edited version of Collins' story about unions in Atlantic City. Huntly Collins talks about this story on p. 84.

Reprinted by permission of The Philadelphia Inquirer.

The want-ad section of a newspaper is not the usual place to launch a campaign to replace union officers. But then, Local 54 of the Hotel Employees and Restaurant Employees International Union, which represents almost all non-gaming employees at Atlantic City's 10 casino-hotels, is not the usual labor union.

With nearly 10,000 members employed in the casino-hotels—including maids, bellhops, cooks, cocktail waitresses, oyster shuckers and others—the union wields considerable power in the casino industry here and collects more than $2 million a year in dues and other fees.

Roy Silbert, who was elected president of Local 54 on Dec. 10, hands out business cards that show his name and title against a miniature Monopoly board.

And despite scattered signs of disaffection, such as the classified ad, and a history of corruption among union officials, Local 54's monopoly on the casino-hotel work force shows few signs of weakening.

Members generally appear pleased with the way the union has represented them, winning substantial wage increases and compiling an impressive success rate in arbitration cases.

In the last regular election for union offices, in 1982, then-president Frank Gerace and his running mates were unopposed.

But some dissidents say the lack of opposition stemmed from fear rather than contentment.

The union shop steward who placed the classified ad said he hoped to head a reform slate challenging the union leadership in June, when Silbert, who was elected to serve the last seven months of Gerace's term after Gerace left the job under court order, will seek a full, three-year term.

Yet the steward asked that his name be withheld, saying he feared retaliation.

"I was thinking of running for president" of the local, said the shop steward, who is weighing rank-and-file support for his candidacy. "Then we started asking, 'What are you going to do when you run up against Nicky?' "

Ever since the first casino-hotel opened here in 1978, Local 54 has been dogged by allegations that its top officers are controlled by Nicodemo "Little Nicky" Scarfo, the reputed head of organized crime in Philadelphia and South Jersey.

The allegations have come from the New Jersey Casino Control Commission, the U.S. attorney's office and the U.S. Senate's Permanent Subcommittee on Investigations. In August, the subcommittee issued a 144-page report saying there was "little doubt" that Local 54 was controlled by organized crime, an assertion strenuously denied by union officials.

In recent years, Local 54 has been shaken by indictments and convictions of top officials on charges ranging from illegal gambling and drug trafficking to extortion and murder. The major cases involved three officials, who are no longer associated with the union:

■ Frank Lentino, a former Local 54 organizer, who was sentenced Jan. 3 to 10 years in federal prison after pleading guilty to an extortion scheme involving former Atlantic City Mayor Michael J. Matthews. Matthews, who pleaded guilty in November to accepting a $10,000 bribe from an undercover FBI agent, received a 15-year sentence.

■ Albert Daidone, former vice president of Local 54, who was convicted last summer of the 1980 murder of John McCullough, president of Local 30 of the Roofers Union in Philadelphia. Daidone was sentenced to life in prison after a jury deadlocked over whether to impose the death penalty.

■ Gerace, former president of Local 54, who was indicted last year on charges of embezzling union funds. Gerace, who was an unindicted co-conspirator in the Matthews case, is awaiting retrial on the embezzlement charges after a mistrial was declared last January.

In recent interviews here, many rank-and-file union members seemed unaware or unconcerned about those cases. And many of those interviewed dismissed as "garbage," "baloney" and "trash" the government allegations that the union is controlled by organized crime.

One union member likened Gerace's battle with the Casino Control Commission with the fight waged by Lech Walesa, the Polish labor leader, against his country's Communist leaders. Gerace, 45, resigned Dec. 10 as president of Local 54 after a 3½-year effort by the casino agency to remove him because of his alleged ties to the Scarfo organization.

"It's just like in Poland," said Jim Gabrysz, 47, a shop steward and bartender who works on the casino floor at Harrah's at Trump Plaza. "I feel the government shouldn't be able to tell us who we can have and can't have as officers of the local."

Gerace is still on the union's payroll as a $48,000-a-year consultant to work with the 5,000 union members who are employed in non-casino jobs in Atlantic City and in hotel and restaurant jobs elsewhere in South Jersey. The union's total membership is nearly 15,000.

Silbert, 40, a former grievance officer and business agent, was Gerace's choice to fill the unexpired portion of his three-year term. Silbert was nominated by the union's executive board and elected, without opposition, at a membership meeting attended by fewer than 1,000 union members.

"Frank and I worked together for so many years that our philosophies have been intertwined," Silbert said in a recent interview at the union's bustling hall on North Texas Avenue. "We have one basic philosophy, that we can get the best wages, benefits and working conditions for the rank and file."

❖   ❖   ❖

. . . Black and Puerto Rican union members also complain that the union

has not followed up on their complaints of mistreatment by casino managers. Despite the wage gains, they say, the union has done little to help them gain promotions from menial jobs.

"I can't understand it," said a black maid as she made up the twin beds in a casino-hotel suite. "You can never move up. I've been making beds and cleaning rooms here for 14 years and I never move up. They also cut your hours. I can't even get eight hours. It's been that way for the last two years."

A Puerto Rican worker who was sweeping the carpet at another hotel said, in halting English: "The union is no help to the people. You got some problems. You go to the union. They say they will help, but they do nothing for the people."

Other workers expressed concern that Gerace and his close associates would continue to control the union.

According to these critics—who asked that their names be withheld, saying they feared retaliation—the spirit of union democracy was violated in Silbert's election, although the balloting technically conformed with the union's bylaws.

The shop steward who is considering challenging Silbert for the local presidency in June said there was no prior public notice that a replacement for Gerace would be elected at the Dec. 10 union meeting. "A lot of us didn't like the way it was done," he said. "This is a group of 50 people running this union."

But other shop stewards and union officers insist that Local 54 is run democratically. Asked about possible opposition in the June election, Silbert sat back in his huge swivel chair, paused and said: "If we do have opposition, we will campaign very, very hard."

Courtesy of Madeleine Blais

"It was outside the vocabulary of my ambition to consider myself a candidate for the Pulitzer Prize."

MADELEINE BLAIS

Madeleine Blais was born in 1947 in Granby, Massachusetts, one of six children. She lived across the street from a public library, which was open on Tuesdays and Fridays, where she says she was able to read "everything I ever wanted to read."

Blais attended Catholic schools, the College of New Rochelle and Columbia University. After working at three New England papers, including *The Boston Globe*, she went to *The Miami Herald* in September 1979, writing features for *Tropic*, the Sunday magazine.

Four months after she joined *Tropic*, *The Miami Herald* nominated her for a Pulitzer Prize. Her editor submitted five articles—four of which she had written as a freelancer for *Tropic* before she was hired.

"I was basically trying to pay the rent. Afterwards, I remember being grateful that those were stories that I'd done mostly as a freelancer. I was really working on my work and not working on a prize." When Blais was awarded the Pulitzer Prize in 1980, the Pulitzer committee gave special mention to her story "Private Zepp Goes to War," about the battle of an 83-year-old man to overturn the dishonorable discharge he had received in 1919.

Blais sometimes spends six months to a year on her stories. Her recent subjects have been people involved in social controversy—a 12-year-old boy who murdered his mother and brother and a 16-year-old boy who was born disfigured.

Blais could find stories like this anywhere in the country, but she says Miami offers a writer almost too much material. "Miami is considered by a lot of people to be the best news city in the United States," she says. "It's got an incredibly volatile combination of old money, new money, drug money and no money.

"Its people combine tourists with drifters with drug dealers with legal immigrants with illegal immigrants, sun customers from the north who long to live here because of the mildness of the winters and sun customers from the north who are fleeing bad business deals and bad affairs of the heart. There are even natives—that's not just alligators. There actually have been people here for 80, 90 years. The diversity creates a very electric type of town."

When this interview was conducted, in *The Miami Herald* cafeteria overlooking the Florida shoreline, Madeleine Blais and her family were getting ready to move to Cambridge, Massachusetts, for a year. Blais had just been awarded a Nieman Fellowship to Harvard. ❖

from Madeleine Blais

- The difference between covering news and covering features
- How to coordinate several kinds of information—court records, interviews and news events—into one story
- How to use research and interviews to reconstruct an event

Beginnings

I've always wanted to be a writer from an early age. When I was in the third grade I had a teacher who asked us, for a civics lesson, did we read the newspaper? And everybody raised their hands. And she said, "What do you read?" And they said comics. And she said, "Anything else?" And the boys all raised their hands and they said they read the sports.

I was the only child whose hand remained raised. So she said, "What do you read?" And I started reciting headlines like, "Estranged Wife Shoots Hubby in Chickopee Tavern." It was one gory headline after another, "Melee Breaks Out at Hockey Rink," "Food Poisoning at Eastern State Exposition." Finally she said that she believed me and I could stop reciting headlines.

I've often wondered why I read the paper at the age of eight. And I think that I really did read the front page news. I was particularly interested in news of the heart—impromptu dramas, like the shootings and riots, the strange events that people really didn't speak of in the presence of children.

My favorite books in high school were *Pride and Prejudice* and *Jane Eyre*, two absolute staples of most schools. To me, Jane Austen was a writer of manners. She wrote about the way people behave and what that says about them. I wanted to be Elizabeth in *Pride and Prejudice,* and I wanted to be Jane and have that wonderful affair with Mr. Rochester.

I also was able to understand that maybe I couldn't have these experiences, *per se,* but maybe I could be the person who writes about them. What I really thought when I was 16 or 17 was that I would be a poet. My poetic strategem was to use the words "honeysuckle" and "bittersweet" just about every other word because I found them to be so pretty and evocative.

Well, obviously what I was creating was not good poetry. Every experience was bittersweet, and there was something about the smell of honeysuckle that permeated whatever was described in each poem. When I realized that was not going to pay the rent, I thought of becoming a novelist. But then I couldn't think of a word to write. So I revised my sights and finally realized that I could combine my love of writing with the practical need to earn a living and get a job on a newspaper.

I think you can divide most journalists into two categories. Most reporters who are good writers will either admit that they wanted to be fiction writers, or they won't. But most did.

In college, I majored in English. I minored in Latin. I also worked on the school newspaper, where I was editor for a year. Then I applied to Columbia University. After getting accepted there and going through their journalism program, I thought I'd go straight to *The New York Times* to a very high-ranking position, which didn't happen.

FIRST NEWSPAPER JOB

In college we were encouraged to be rebellious. That urge to rebel does not sit well beneath the mandate to earn a living, and I had debts from college, so I had to join what we called in those days "the straight press" to earn a living. The *Norwich Bulletin* was my first real newspaper job. I covered everything.

One day the Chamber of Commerce in Norwich got a big block of ice and put it in the center of the town—it was the hottest day of the summer. I covered the contest during which people guessed how long it would take to melt. The winner got a gift certificate to the biggest department store in Norwich. So I covered events of earth-shattering moment.

A VALUABLE MISTAKE AT *THE BOSTON GLOBE*

Then I was a suburban reporter at *The Boston Globe.* One day I was asked to do a weather round-up. You have to call various police stations, and I called up this police station and I found out that two young girls had been hit by a truck along the side of the road, Route 3A.

I reported that the police said this had happened at 3 a.m. One of them had died. I put this in the paper. The girls were 13 years old, and they'd been out walking. This was directly from the police department, with names.

The next day, the family called. They were distraught, not only about what had happened to their daughter, but that *The Boston Globe* would report that this had happened at 3 a.m. What kind of a family did they think this girl came from that she would be out walking along a major highway at 3 a.m.? As it turned out, that was the time that she had died at the hospital.

My editor came up to me and questioned where I got the information. Obviously I hadn't made anything up. I had taken something down correctly, but what the editor said was, "You should have been more sensitive to the fact that this was an odd time of day. That should have immediately raised a red flag.

"In the future, you should develop your own radar for that kind of information because any inaccuracy, however unintentional—as this one was—diminishes what you have done." In this case it added further emotional hardship, so it had a very direct and incredibly unhappy consequence.

So one of the things I tell young reporters is: Don't be afraid to check the spelling of something a hundred times. Don't be afraid to check and re-check facts. Don't think that people think you are stupid. You are doing your job, you're trying to be as accurate as possible, and there's no dishonor in that.

I worked at the *Trenton* [New Jersey] *Times* as a feature writer and did free-lancing after that, and then came down to Miami and have worked at *Tropic* magazine for about seven years.

AN INTEREST IN PSYCHOLOGICAL DILEMMAS

The way I look at the world is that there are fewer accidents than we think there are. The kinds of stories that I'm most interested in are psychological dilemmas, looking at people caught in events that, if you just read the headlines, you think, "What an awful fate to befall someone"—like a recent story about a 12-year-old boy, Kenny White, who killed his mother and his brother.

COVERING KENNY WHITE

I like to delve into the situation from as many points of view as I can. Usually what you find is that a pattern preceded an event that makes some sense out of the event. From a purely philosophical point of view, there should never be an explanation for why a nice-looking, smart 12-year-old boy kills his mother, who was doing her best in many respects, and his younger brother, who was surely a true innocent.

From a theological, moral point of view, there is no explanation, but you can find roots in the rage that precedes some of these events. As a reporter I'm always fascinated by that because I think that those events color the quality of our lives. They are sort of the modern scourge.

The Kenny White story took an enormous amount of reporting. The writing of it is mostly timing—when you present what. The writing is not fancy. In some writing, I've done much greater prose stuntwork. The majority of the work was in the research and in getting people to talk to me.

I had been interested in parricide as a subject. But when I do a story on a sociological topic, I don't like to do it from the general point of view, like "Children Who Kill," a big headline and then maybe an interview with 10 children, 10 families who have been victimized by this crime, 10 psychiatrists. To me, the power of the subject gets diffused, and I don't like that approach to any issue that I care about.

One of my theories is that domestic violence is violence that, in many cases, is occurring on schedule. It is occurring when logically it should. A lot of the violence we see in society is the child's rage postponed, and it comes out in adulthood, generally against people who had no direct bearing in the formation of the rage.

I was interested in what the environmental influences might have been on this child to create a person at the age of 12 capable of this act. I also argue that, although this is a very private story, it becomes public once the act has been committed because society gets involved. I think the state of Florida is paying $50,000 a year for his placement in a private hospital. So the public is implicated, whether we want to be or not, if only through our dollars while we are caring for this child.

AN EVENT FOCUSES A STORY

When the story first broke, I realized I was interested. I happened to be on a leave of absence, so it was four or five months later when I came back to the paper that I first contacted the boy's lawyer.

He said that he would talk to me, but he didn't think his client should because nothing had been decided in this case. So I talked to the lawyer and established my credentials as a reporter who is interested in the subject.

As a feature writer, I can pursue some stories over a long period of time. In this story, I went to all the hearings involving the boy—I think there were four or five from May until October—just so all the lawyers on both sides would see me there. I barely took notes, because I knew that the hearings would never be the point of my story.

When I decided to do the story in May, I did talk to the neighbors, and I realized there was a story worth pursuing. They said things that I found fascinating, like they never saw the family once get in the car together. That seemed to me to be a family that was at odds with itself in some fundamental way, if there was never the kind of joy of being together out and about.

Then in October, I once again contacted the lawyer, and he said, "I will take you to meet the child now." I went to see the boy about 10 times only in October because he left in November.

The events of the day as told from the boy's point of view were practically the first thing we talked about. At the time I talked to him, he was 13. He had done this when he was 12. He described it totally from his point of view, and I knew that would be interesting no matter what. He was angry because "It was a bad day." One of the reasons it was a bad day was because the ice cream man wasn't there when the boy was on his way home from school. That's the kind of detail that I'm not even sure a fiction writer could make up. But what that detail does is show how much Kenny was still a child, yet he had committed an act that is not only an adult act, but a reprehensible adult act.

IMPORTANCE OF THE FIRST INTERVIEW

One of my words of advice would be, if you're planning to interview someone over a period of time, the first interview is always the most important. You should arrive with a certain sense of stamina, and try to stay as long as you can, no matter how overwhelmed you feel emotionally in the face of what you are being told.

I stayed at least two-and-a-half hours, and if I had it to do over, I would have stayed at least five or seven. That's a point when you'd expect the least trust because you don't know each other, but there's some kind of chemistry that often will yield a great deal of information. The freshness of the situation inspires a certain volubility.

When I go back, I'll read my interviews and try to refine things. I'll ask people the same question over and over. Even with this child, the question that I asked over and over was, "Tell me about that day." Each time there might be a fresh accretion, very slow, of new information, a new detail—like when he said, "It was a bad day. My teachers yelled at me." The first time he said that. Then the second time it was, "It was a bad day. My teachers yelled at me, I flunked English, I had dirty clothes in my locker so the gym teacher was mad." I started to get details that I don't think he was withholding before. They just didn't occur to him the first time.

I'm adding little touches, almost like an artist outlining a canvas—in the beginning filling the canvas with broad strokes and then [the artist] suddenly squints at it and decides over time where the details of color go.

The other thing to do with a child like him is to try to get as much of his point of view as possible and then try to get someone else to balance the point of view against. I didn't get to talk to the father until December. The father was actually very good about being able to supply a different perspective from the child's view.

By the following February I had interviewed school people who had been involved with the boy as educators, and as much of the mother's family as I could, which was very few members. They were so distraught that they really didn't want to be part of anything that had to do with this boy being in an article.

When they wouldn't talk to me, I backed off. I don't believe in badgering people. They feel badgered enough by the circumstances they're caught in. As a reporter you realize that what you are doing is not necessarily going to thrill them.

As a journalist, you are limited by what you can find out. You are not creating reality the way a fiction writer might because you are not conveniently supplying a detail because it occurred to you to supply a detail. You can supply it only if you learn it.

RESEARCH IS WRITING

Of all the records I found in that story, the most compelling was the [school] test the boy had taken a month before the crime, where he revealed an incredible obsession with guns, rifles and the wish to shoot. For various reasons, probably just the glut of kids, the preoccupation he revealed [in that test] was overlooked by school officials. The test became public when the boy got arrested. Those are always confidential until a public event makes them public.

When you are doing the research, you are writing. Never think that you're not. Research is not a part to be disparaged in any way. There has to be an incredible amount of editing as you research. Even as you interview someone, you are editing what to ask them, what not to ask them. You are editing from what you hear. I think young reporters should keep that in mind.

QUESTION PEOPLE GENTLY

I was asking mostly very undirected questions. I remember once when I was a young reporter going to a press conference at Logan Airport. Sometimes when celebrities go in and out of a town, there is an impromptu press conference at the airport. Ella Fitzgerald was going to be there because she had just been at Massachusetts General Hospital for a very difficult eye operation, and there was a very strong chance that she might be blinded.

I was there with a bunch of young reporters, and one reporter, who was even younger than I, had written a list of questions. She read from her notebook this question: "How do you feel that you might be going blind?" in a tone of voice that in no way reflected the solemnity of the question, that showed no empathy in her tone because the reporter was so nervous, she was almost rattling the question from a piece of paper. Miss Fitzgerald looked at her with eyes that were very watery from the operation. She basically said, "What kind of question is that?"

Well, in a sense it was the *only* question to ask, but asked too boldly, it was a question that would never be answered. So that with Kenny White, you don't say, certainly not at first, "Why do you think you killed your mother and your brother?" You say, "How was school that day?" You go through a lot of indirect material before you get to the heart of the beast.

Sometimes I don't take notes. All my notes are almost atmospheric—how I experience the person. Sometimes I start to take notes really to make other people comfortable because I think that's what they think I should be doing. If I'm sitting down face-to-face with someone doing Q and A, then I take notes. But if I'm out just doing something, accompanying them someplace, then I don't take notes. I take far fewer notes than most people.

I don't use a tape recorder, just because of the endless time it would take to transcribe. I don't have a secretary and I don't have patience.

Once when I was at journalism school, Gay Talese spoke to the class, and he said he writes up his interviews right away. If that's true, he's doing the right thing, but his work habits are better than mine. I should do that, I do sometimes, but lots of times I don't. I might be more moved to do it when I really think the interview is urgent in some way—when it's urgent that I remember every word and fill in the blanks. That's a feature writer. A reporter who operates on a deadline basis doesn't have that luxury.

HOW I WORK

I'm not very good on deadline, really. My husband says I'm unemployable by most newspapers for most functions because I really almost can't write on a deadline. Some reporters are constitutionally in need of that daily shot of adrenaline, to see their name in the paper every day. There's a kind of verification of their existence that is endowed by the constant presence of their byline in the paper. I don't mind working with long bouts of obscurity.

Because of having a child, I lead a fairly regular life. And because of the kind of latitude I have at the place where I work, mostly I make my own hours, although I generally try to work between 10 [a.m.] and 6 [p.m.]. I do interviews sometimes in the evening, and if something is happening on a weekend and I can't avoid it, I'll work on the weekends.

I sometimes dream about my stories, and I am obsessed with a lot of them. I don't mind being obsessed by them. That's usually a good sign.

So much of writing is mental time. I write when I run, and I write when I go to exercise classes. I always think that *The Miami Herald* should pay all of its reporters to do these things because you really are working. It's kind of like thinking time, like white noise time—white thinking, I don't know what you'd call it.

I write at work more than at home because I have a three-and-a-half-year-old at home who doesn't like it if I am not totally devoted to him. At the end of many days here [at work] I'll get a printout and take it home and go over it after dinner at my leisure, for 10 or 15 minutes, to see if there's some way that I can order things that I hadn't been able to come up with during the day. Especially with long pieces, the order, the sequence is a great deal of the writing.

FIND A WORKING LEAD

I worked on that one piece [Kenny White] for almost three weeks. It was January before I started writing it. The very first paragraph, "There were four shots in all," had been buried in the piece. I had begun with Kenny describing his day, the quote "It was a bad day all around." Then at some point I realized that the paragraph that began, "There were four shots in all . . . " was a better lead, a better topic sentence. So I began with that.

I have to have a working lead when I'm writing something. Any writer, at the end of the process of creating the story, will put aside a working lead for a better one if a better one occurs. But I have to have the illusion [of a lead] at the beginning. Especially with long pieces like this one, even if you don't know your lead but you know your ending, you can begin writing. If you know your ending, then you know your focus.

LEARN TO PRECONCEIVE MATERIAL

One feature writer told me that he felt that the ability to preconceive material is very important when you're a feature writer. I think that my ability to preconceive is stronger than it was five years ago. It's basically to think about the material beforehand and listen to your own conscience and your own intuition. But if something isn't conforming to your preconceived notion, abandon it.

I recently finished a story about the Miami riots in 1980, with portraits of two young people who were victims of the riots. I had a wish for that article that didn't quite materialize. I wished that the two young people had been able to survive even better than they have.

They have done their best, but the boy has suffered some brain damage and it doesn't look as if he's likely to recover fully, and the girl lost a leg at the hip, so she is facing a very severe handicap. As triumphant as she is, in many respects, there are still problems, in terms of physical recovery.

So my wish for them was that I could be able to report that they were in better shape than they were. And I had to just go with what I found out, which was that their lives were filled with struggle, and there was no way to gloss over that.

FRIGHTENINGLY DISORGANIZED

When I'm writing, all the background material is piled up usually in a drawer, which gives me a false sense that it's neatly stored. But what it is, is that it's stuffed into a drawer.

I would call myself extremely disorganized, usually frighteningly so, to the point that I once said to an editor that if they ever went over my notebooks to try to figure out how I come up with my stories, I would be embarrassed.

HOW I WRITE

I write with very few notes. And often when I write, I'll come to a place where I want to quote someone and I'll remember what the person said in my mind, and I'll almost write a paraphrase of it and then go back to my notes and get the exact quote. I'll try to let it flow and then go back and fill in things precisely.

I like to write when it's all done and people say it was good. Then I just love writing. Until that point I'm usually in a state of absolute torture. But I think there is an amnesia that afflicts writers that's not unlike the amnesia that afflicts women right after childbirth. After the baby is born and everything's fine, any pain or discomfort has been completely forgotten until the next pregnancy and then it all comes back.

When you're a writer, the pain, the discomfort and agony of writing is absolutely forgotten when the finished product is pronounced healthy—until the next project. Then all the insecurities reappear, sometimes in a heightened fashion. Any time you start a story, it is a whole new education, just as any time an author writes a book, it is a whole new monster of blank pages coming at you.

Writing is the only task for which I have patience, except maybe once in a while, a little bit with cooking. I was aware for years that it was the one task to which I could apply myself for endless hours. There's nothing else I can do for that long without fidgeting, without going a little bit crazy. So it's obviously my calling. It's the one thing I can do for sustained intervals.

THE IMPORTANCE OF GOOD EDITORS

What you want is an excellent editor, at least one who doesn't interfere with your work if it's good. What you don't want is a bad editor, someone who changes words for the sake of changing words, who isn't paying attention to what you are trying to do. Even if in a draft you're not succeeding, a good editor is able to tell that you're not and tries to help you identify the problem.

A good editor will also encourage almost to the point of being a cheerleader. Sometimes that makes it hard to be an editor because you have to do so much cheerleading and the holding of writers' hands. At times that takes a sublimation of your own ego and your own needs in the face of the writer who generally is hysterical in one way or another about whether what the writer is doing is going to work.

The best editors follow the principle of Hippocrates, the first principle of medicine, "Do no harm." They never try to interfere by dampening your enthusiasm, and to the degree that they interfere, they interfere to encourage you.

I love good editors. I definitely go on the record saying that. The finest and funnest thing is to write something that doesn't need a word changed, not a comma, but that doesn't always happen. If you have readers you can trust, which is what an editor should be ideally—an eminently trustworthy reader of what you do—then you have a helper in your process. I need that, and I think I always will. In my life, there's always room for good editors.

WHAT IT MEANS TO COVER MIAMI

Most of the stories I do could happen anywhere. If they happen, they happen in Miami because that's where I'm writing. But they could happen in any city.

One thing that absolutely differentiates Miami as a place to cover is that Miami is a city that's wide open. It's a place for which its dense foliage is a metaphor in every respect. It's a lush place, it's overripe.

The idea that comes to my mind is somebody reaching up to an overripe tree and picking a piece of fruit. It's a place where reporters are not tripping over each other, like in Washington, which is a place which is considered very prestigious for reporters to work.

Anything I want to do as a reporter here is available to me. The competition is less in some ways, but I hope that when somebody does something good, it's as good here as it would be someplace else.

ETHICAL DILEMMAS

As a writer and as a reporter, you always have to be mindful that what you do may hurt somebody. Then you have to further consider whether the hurting of that person is something you want to do in the face of what you want to communicate.

I have an ethical dilemma coming up. I am writing a story about a boy, 16, who was born in Miami with what you would describe from a layman's point of view as a cleft face. His face was divided to the point where, as a baby, he really was quite monstrous.

His mother gave me a picture of him at birth, and he could be mortified if that picture were in the paper. His mother gave it to me because she knows that the difference between that newborn and what this boy looks like now is the difference of 40 surgeries and an enormous amount of maternal love. She feels that since the boy is approaching the age where he's got to face the world, he also has to face his past.

So she didn't have a dilemma in supplying me with this picture, yet her son is very frightened about the possible repercussions of the picture being in the paper. So there's your dilemma. Who do you listen to—the mother or the child?

The picture of the child is very frightening. It might turn people off to the story. Maybe it would keep readers from reading the piece, and that's a consideration. That's not an ethical consideration exactly, that's a more practical one.

But this is a very dramatic example of whether or not to include information that may or may not be hurtful. The other thought is, this child thinks it could be hurtful. Well, is it really? Is the mother right in thinking that the more open you are, the more this child's interests are served?

If the article is viewed by the reporter as a cruel exposition of what this child has been through, I'm not sure it's worth doing. Is your motive only for the purpose of exposing something egregious and terrible in the history of birth defects, almost from a pornographic point of view, and not showing the healing or the spiritual forces that came into effect to save this child? If shock value is the motive to show the picture, do you want to be that kind of person who would do something purely for shock value? I don't think most reporters want to be that way.

If the boy really felt that this would ruin his life, I wouldn't run it. This is definitely something you would talk over with an editor. I also did tell the boy that if he didn't want the picture in the story, his mother and he should convey this to my editor. We couldn't use it if they didn't authorize its use.

I'm in a conflict of whether to encourage him to allow it to be used. This is a perfect example of the kind of ethical dilemmas I face in feature writing.*

BEING A PULITZER WINNER

The Pulitzer committee considers me a good writer. I don't know if I do. There is a wonderful old saw, which is that you're only as good as your next story. I'm sure I have a vested interest in thinking that what I did in 1980 is not as good as what I'm doing now because once you win a Pulitzer there's a slightly bittersweet feeling every April when you don't win one. I was a finalist in 1981 for feature writing. I have won many other awards. So I suppose that I have to console myself that my work has improved, if only in my eyes and not in the eyes of those stern judges.

I don't know if this is true for most Pulitzer winners, but I didn't feel I deserved it. So I had to go through a lot of angst to somehow reconcile this award with the kind of person I thought of myself as being, which is not someone who was worthy of that.

I was 32 when I won the Pulitzer. And I remember saying to our managing editor at the time, "I'm old enough to win this," basically not thinking I was. If I'd ever thought about winning a Pulitzer, I thought maybe I'd win one when I was 83, when I'd toiled long and hard in the vineyards of American newspapers.

The feature category had just begun, so until that point in my career there wasn't even a category in which I'd even qualify. It was outside the vocabulary of my ambition to consider myself a candidate for the Pulitzer Prize.

You worry that everything else will be an anti-climax, but the reality is that your work is the climax, it's not an award. It would be terribly misleading for anyone to think that an award is the end of a career because many, many fine works don't win Pulitzers, and many not-so-fine works do. To have that [award] be the goal is to really mislead yourself terribly about the true importance of what you're doing now.

WRITE WHAT IS WORTH READING

I love what I do. I think that what I do may make a difference in a sort of slow, stealthy and very hard-to-acknowledge way, which is that I try to

---

* *Author's note: The picture was tastefully published accompanying the article inside the magazine—not on the cover—with the consent of the mother and the boy.*

change attitudes a little bit, and make people spend more time with certain events than they would normally.

Sometimes if you read something in a daily paper, you're not necessarily pondering it. I try to write something that will look at those events that fill the daily paper in a way that makes people ponder them. Ultimately, most reporters have a certain idea of how the world should be run. I think all reporters are reformers.

Part of my role is to write things that are worth reading and to have people, after they've read them, say things to me like the man who read the Kenny White story said to me. "You know, I hated that article on Sunday. My wife and I both felt that we didn't like it, and we weren't really sure why we didn't like it. And we have talked about nothing else all week long. That piece just won't go away." So I think my role probably is to write pieces that won't go away.

The twisting of Kenny White

by Madeleine Blais

There were four shots in all, one accidental, one test shot, and then the shots for the two victims.

Neighbors recollect hearing the gunfire, but they mistook it for something else. They heard the sound and they tamed it.

It was the busy time of day in a nice part of town, the time when mothers call to their children to come in for dinner, when there is the clatter of garage doors opening and closing while bicycles and other equipment are stowed for the night, or that unmistakable thump!—one last toss of the ball into the hoop.

This is an edited version of the 10,000-word story about Kenny White. Madeleine Blais talks about this story on pgs. 93–96. Reprinted by permission of The Miami Herald, Tropic *magazine.*

The report from the gun was automatically, unconsciously processed into the expected reasons for such a sound in such a neighborhood.

Firecrackers.

Or, a car backfiring.

Or, the Jacksons must be working hard on their gazebo.

Kenny White sits on a bench in the windswept courtyard of Youth Hall, dressed in the standard-issue gym shorts and T-shirt, studying his gnawed nails, and trying to summon the exact mood of the day when at the age of 12 he shot and killed his brother and his mother with a Colt Python handgun.

A year has passed.

"Have you," he says, "ever been in a fight?" He appraises his audience, and something about her, something she's wearing perhaps, the look around the eyes, a hesitancy in her manner, makes him shake his head violently and quickly conclude: "No, you probably haven't. As soon as you start to move forward everything goes real fast. Every time you see a face you swing at it. That's the way the day went by, in a blur. . . . "

"It was," says Kenny, "a bad day all around."

"We are not the kind of people to have a tragedy like this," says Richard White, Kenny's father, a small balding man of 48.

He speaks in a quiet, even voice: It has the shy keep-the-peace tone of someone who wants very much to avoid a scolding. The words often have a formal flavor, as in a speech.

"We were a happy family. If there had been alcohol, or drugs, or child abuse, if there had been internal strife, or jealousy, or the belittling of one child versus another, well then what happened might have been if not something you could understand, well at least you could expect it. But there was nothing like that. . . . "

His most startling feature is the near-dazzling blueness of his eyes. It is a handicap of eyes like that, and an unfair burden to their possessor, the way they convey an impression of reflecting more than they absorb, as if their purpose is to be looked at rather than to look. He shakes his head, back and forth, sadly. He says there are two events in his life bonded by mystery and sorrow and he doesn't understand them and never hopes to: why Kenny did what he did and why his own father walked out on his mother when he was 1 year old. . . .

The first media reports were of a model boy, Kenny was called a typical kid, all American. *A little gentleman.* He was very bright: His IQ is 131. The affluence of the family was appealing; the murders had occurred, after all, in the game room, and something about the repeated use of this term in all the stories created an impression of an emporium for kids, a kind of well-equipped arcade. These were people with all the advantages. . . .

"The thing I want to do most of all is . . . a rifel."

"The thing I do best is . . . shoot."

Less than a month before the slayings Kenneth White was asked by the Dade County school system to take a sentence completion test. . . .

"Tardy again, White."

These were the first words to greet Kenneth upon his arrival at school on the day of the murders. . . .

Kenneth's grades that day were a disaster: He got an F in English; no great surprise. He got a D in Math; how he always hated math. That day, as he sat in class trying to puzzle through a problem, he turned to a girl sitting near him: I wish I could kill my mother, he said. She barely paid attention.

He went to science and got the one and only good mark of the day. Not that it mattered. His parents had a favorite saying: You're only as good as your lowest grade. Their other famous saying was: If you mess up once, you have to be an angel for the rest of your life.

And then, on the way home from school, complete betrayal: no ice-cream man.

He couldn't even get an Astro Pop.

The thing about an Astro Pop is it's not ice cream, it's a sucker and it lasts all day.

He took a willow stick and began beating the brush.

Dinner was his responsibility that night. He took out some chicken and put it in the oven but forgot to check the temperature, which was on broil.

It burned. . . .

He went into his parents' room. He looked for his father's Colt Python in its secret place, on a hook, behind the nightstand.

The first shot went off accidently, inside the house, blowing a hole in the floorboards of one of the bedrooms.

Carrying the gun, Kenneth went outside to see if the exterior of the house had been damaged as well.

Then, just to make sure the gun was working OK, he aimed it at a tree: shot number two. A sizable chunk of bark splayed itself across the lawn. . . .

Kenneth was seated on the living room sofa. MASH was on the television. The Colt Python was at Kenneth's side, hidden beneath a pillow.

6:05 p.m. Kevin White enters his home.

Kenneth thought: "Oh no, I'm going to have to abandon the mission."

"Where's Mom?"

"She's not home yet."

"Oh."

"Why don't you go out and play?"

"I don't want to."

"Mommy said it would be OK."

"I don't want to."

He was following his brother. The gun was behind his back.

"Here, would you put this toy away, right there in that closet?"

It was the walk-in type, a utility closet, used to store paint and other household items.

As soon as you start to move forward everything goes real fast. Every time you see a face you swing at it. Kevin obeyed. He walked into the big closet, his back to his brother. Kenneth, coming from behind, lifted the hidden gun; he raised it level with the head of his brother, whose back was still turned.

The third shot of the day.

Kenneth closed the door of the closet and went back to watching MASH.

Over the sound of the set he thought he could detect words mixed in with the sounds of his brother's final breathing: He thought Kevin was urging him to keep up his plan.

6:15: June White walks through the door. . . .

There's one aspect to all this that continues to trouble Kenneth White. He doesn't understand why he didn't kill himself. He really was planning on it. It's just that right then, after the murders, when he tried to bring the gun to his temple, he couldn't. . . .

The clock said 6:15. The calendar said October 19.

Appearing as smart and put-together and in place when she returned from work as she had when she left, June White, burdened with the dry cleaning, saw Kenneth and asked:

"Where's Kevin?"

"I don't know."

"Didn't he come home?"

"Yeah, but he went out."

"What's burning?"

"Dinner."

She put down her purse and started for the game room, looking for Kevin. When she failed to see him, she turned around to re-enter the kitchen.

Her oldest son was waiting for her.

In the instant before he shot her, he recalled something he learned at military school: It is less painful if you shoot someone in the head.

He aimed for her eyes.

She staggered, slumped and fell.

The fourth and final shot.

He felt, he would say later, like the whole world was lifted off his shoulders.

Los Angeles Times

"If Tommy John is pitching and all of a sudden an idea forms in my mind of a good idea for a column about Tommy John, I start to root for Tommy John—not because I'm a big fan of the Dodgers, but because I'm a fan of leads for the column."

JIM MURRAY

When you call the *Los Angeles Times* and ask for Jim Murray, the newsroom gives you his home phone number. Murray has been working at home since the beginning of his career as a sports columnist at the *Times* in 1961. He got the mumps right after he went to work, so he dictated the column over the phone. Today he sends his column by computer.

Murray was raised by his uncles in Hartford, Connecticut. He studied English and history at Trinity College, where he played freshman baseball but didn't make the swimming team. He came to Los Angeles in 1944 and worked for four years reporting and rewriting on the old *Examiner* before he joined the staff of *Time* magazine. He wrote several *Time* cover stories about movie stars, and then he was included in the original meetings with Henry Luce when Luce decided to start *Sports Illustrated*. From *Sports Illustrated*, Murray went to the *Los Angeles Times*.

In 1979, when he was 59, Murray was forced to give up sportswriting for nearly a year because he started to go blind. Red worms appeared in his left eye while he was reporting on the 1979 Super Bowl, and he learned that he was hemorrhaging from a detached retina. Then his right eye developed a cataract.

"I had eight eye operations," he says, sitting on a comfortable brown sofa in the family room of his home in the hills above Los Angeles. "I couldn't really see. I could see light, could see shadows and forms. I'd come out in the morning and I'd grope my way along the wall. When my hands went through, I'd know I had hit a door." Eight operations later, Jim Murray can see well enough to write his column again. He writes on his computer in an office near the family room. While he's writing, an answering machine takes his calls.

In April 1984, Jim Murray's wife, Gerry, died. His tribute to her appeared in his column on the sports page that day. "This is the column I never wanted to write, the story I never wanted to live to tell. I lost my lovely Gerry the other day. I lost the sunshine and roses, all right, the laughter in the other room. I lost the smile that lit up my life." For this column Murray was a finalist in the American Society of Newspaper Editors' 1985 awards competition for commentary.

This was an unusual subject for a sports column, but it would have been inconsistent for Murray to write about anything else. He was grieving and he wanted his readers to know about it. More than most columnists, Murray *is* his column. You can hear in his writing the same clipped East Coast accent mixed with locker-room epithets that you hear when he speaks.

Murray is the most widely read syndicated sportswriter in America. He still travels the country to observe breaking sports stories and to find material for his column, which appears four times a week in the *Los Angeles Times*. His columns have been collected in two books, *Best of Jim Murray* and *Sporting World of Jim Murray*. In 1982 he was awarded the Red Smith Award for meritorious labor in sportswriting. He has been named 14 times as America's Best Sportswriter by the National Association of Sportscasters and Sportswriters. ❖

from Jim Murray

- ■ The difference between writing a column and writing a news story
- ■ Sportswriters as reporters
- ■ The role for women in sportswriting

BEGINNINGS

I played baseball as a kid, you know, the neighborhood games, and I swam. I played sandlot football. Basketball was not a big sport in my neighborhood. We played it in school, but I didn't play it. I played freshman baseball at Trinity. I tried out for the swimming squad, and I didn't make it—not that I was a good swimmer.

We played baseball and football voraciously. I think that's why I gulp my food to this day. You would be out playing and your turn at bat would be coming up and grandmother or somebody would yell out, "Come on in for dinner." So you'd go in for dinner and you'd just wolf the food to get right back out there. Sure, I played sports. I didn't play them well and I didn't really aspire to. I would've liked to have gotten a letter, but I never vagrantly conjured up a career in sports. I didn't hanker for that.

I wanted to be a writer, not necessarily a newspaper writer. I wrote plays. The first play I wrote, when I was 16 or 17, was about a girl in Havana, Cuba, and it ended up with her dying with a tear frozen on each cheek. That's a pretty good trick for a salt tear in Havana, Cuba.

In college, I took English and history. I didn't discount a career in journalism, but I knew I wanted to be a writer. I guess I always thought I'd get a job on a newspaper, just marking time until Broadway called.

When I was young I thought I wanted to write sports, but I had given up on that. I don't know what in the world I wanted to do. I really sort of wanted to be a foreign correspondent. It appeals to every young guy. Glamorous. Joel McRae in a trenchcoat. And it just seemed a Humphrey Bogart type of job.

But the necessity for making a living changed my mind. Absolutely. As soon as I got out of college, I got a job at an a.m. [paper], the *New Haven Register,* and then saved my money and came to L.A. I was only going to come here for a couple years and then go back to a really important city like Philadelphia or New York.

Looking back on some of the stuff I wrote when I was 23 years old, it was a good thing there was an editor there, but you don't think so at the time. You think he's killing something marvelously creative. He was probably just saving the paper.

I came to L.A. because it was about as far away as you could get from Connecticut. Not that I entertained any ideas of becoming a screenwriter here, although that was in the back of my mind, too. I'd write a great play and then they would produce it here. I'm talking about 1943. I came to California the first week of January, 1944.

I MOVE TO TIME, INC.

I worked for a paper in Los Angeles until February '48. Then I went to work for *Time* magazine. I covered everything. Then I covered the movies for three or four years pretty exclusively. I did John Wayne. I did a lot of movie covers, but I also did a lot of cover stories on sports personalities, simply because I knew a lot about sports and there weren't many people in the company who did.

It's really strange how it all came about. I would never be a sports-writer if they hadn't decided to start a sports magazine. [Henry] Luce knew nothing about sports. Nothing whatsoever. But every place he'd go, all over the world, the conversation would veer to the World Cup or the British Open or whatever. He got fascinated and irritated, I guess, and finally said, "Why this all-consuming interest in games?" We said, "Well, that's the way the world is, Harry." He said, "Well, maybe we ought to start a sports magazine."

So when they started up the sports magazine, I was called back to New York the summer of '53. We got together the first dummies, the first real copies of *Sports Illustrated* for Luce's approval. He was in Rome at the time because his wife was the ambassador. When he came home at Christmas that year, he had to make up his mind whether he would start the sports magazine or not. Then when they started it, I was the Los Angeles editor.

HOW SPORTS REPORTING HAS CHANGED

Sports reporting had begun to change when I went to work at the L.A. *Times* in 1961. Television changed it. Let me give you an anecdote to illustrate it. A pitcher named Jim Brosnan came to my house a couple of times. In the course of conversation with him, I mentioned a sportswriter. I said to Broz, "You know this guy?" He said, "No, I don't know him." I said, "Wait a minute, Jim, you pitched for the L.A. Angels for five years." He said, "Yeah." I said, "This guy covered the Angels for five years. You must've seen him in the locker room." He said, "I don't think he was ever in the locker room." I thought that was astonishing.

I later found out that that's the way those guys used to work. They covered the Angels, so they came to the press box five minutes before the game started, they watched the game, and they banged out a story—"His bat flashing in the sun, comma, John Jones yesterday rapped out three hits to defeat the Portland Beavers, period, paragraph. This moved the Angels up into third place in a hotly contested Pacific Coast League race, period, paragraph." Then they locked up the typewriter and they went away. The presumption was that people didn't know the score. They didn't know how it happened. So you did a game story.

You can't do that today. Anybody who's interested in the World Series has already seen it. Can you imagine writing a straight story on a Super Bowl, like who won and how? Maybe for two monks in Siberia. Instead, you'd have to get an angle. You have to go out and find something to write about the Super Bowl.

FOCUS ON PEOPLE

Most people my age would have been at sportswriting, if they were like Red Smith, all their adult lives, but I wasn't. I didn't get into the sports field until *Sports Illustrated* started up [in 1953]. By that time, I'd worked on everything else. And writing is writing. The subject matter is incidental.

OK, so you write about a 7-foot basketball player or you write about the Prime Minister of Belgium. You've still got to write. You've still got to describe the person, you've still got to find out what's interesting about him, you've still got to entertain the reader with your story.

If the writing is bad, it's just as bad if someone's writing about a sports figure or if he's writing about the president of the United States. You may think it's inconsequential if it's bad writing about a baseball game. Still, if it's bad writing, it's bad writing. If it's good writing, it's good writing.

I suppose my training at Time, Inc., taught me one thing—that people are interested in people, they're not interested in things. And that's all journalism is about. *Time* magazine was just high-level gossip. The tremendous increase in Washington coverage is not because people are interested in the budget. It's because they want to know what Nancy Reagan does between the hours of 8 p.m. and 4 a.m., or whatever.

I always took that position. It isn't always possible to write a personality piece, but I always try to. I try to entertain the reader rather than inform him. They can get their information from television or from other places in the paper. I also feel that the column should have a beginning, a middle, and an end—hopefully humorous. These things are not always possible, but I try.

I remember one time, another reporter was covering the missile beat for *Time*. And I was sitting in as bureau chief. The bureau chief was out of town or on vacation. This reporter came in and he had written a long, involved story on the new fuselage for aviation. He described it in great, great detail.

I looked at it and said, "God, John, I can't send this thing out. This thing reads as if it ought to go in a pipefitter's manual. Who the hell cares how many valves there are?" He said, "That's revolutionary." And I said, "You're going to get two guys down in a rocket assembly plant in Huntsville, Alabama, who are gonna get excited over this. The other two million readers are gonna say, 'Oh, shit' and turn the page."

I said, "John, I tell you what you do. Can't you go find some old German scientist with dandruff all over his collar, absent-minded with two different colored socks on—you know, kind of a Sid Caesar guy? Then describe him walking around and quote him in his musical German. Then we'll get into your goddamn fuselage. You can tell all you want to about pipe fittings, but by this time you got the reader in the tent, you got him reading." Again—people are interested in people, and people are very interested in eccentric, out-of-the-ordinary people. Anyway, basically that was my philosophy of journalism.

You look for what makes a person unusual, what makes him interesting, the same things you do in any kind of journalism. For example, the famous story about a pitcher named Two-headed Brousan who watched first base and third base at the same time.

To find these stories, you follow sports. You find out some day that the Houston Astros are coming to town and they have a first baseman who raises rattlesnakes for a living. I'm just using outrageous examples for illustrative purposes. Well, OK, here's a column. Why the hell would anybody raise rattlesnakes? How do they go about it? That's the sort of thing I look for. I look for somebody who's skillful and a champion who has another dimension to him. And hope that he talks to the press.

WHEN SOMEONE WON'T TALK

It's a semi-adversary relationship sometimes. Some athletes realize they need publicity for whatever things they have going for them on the side or that they hope to have going for them. Others like publicity, others realize it's necessary. Then there are others who think it's perfectly natural to get $2 million for bouncing a ball on the floor all night.

Sometimes people avoid seeing me because they're afraid of what I might say. For instance, one time there was a golfer named Gary Player. So I requested an interview with him, and he was kind of wary. He went to a friend of mine, Stan Wood, and he said, "You know, Stan, Mr. Murray wants an interview with me. I understand Mr. Murray misquotes people"—which is usually what they say when you write something that somebody disagrees with. Then you're a guy who misquotes or twists, even if you're not. So I said, "Well, Stan, you can go back and tell Gary, not only do I not misquote people. I don't even quote them, really quote people. I write *about* people."

There's nothing you can say to people who won't talk to you. It would take years to educate them. Sometimes these people find out late in their careers that it's too late. So you just deal with the ones you can deal with.

QUALITIES OF A GOOD REPORTER

A good reporter is curious and energetic. I think you have to be able to put up with rebuffs, to be very persevering. None of these is describing me. I don't consider myself a good reporter. I just don't. I'm more of a writer and an observer than a reporter.

I've reported. I've reported very energetically. I covered murder stories and did business stories where the protagonist wasn't too pleased. I could do it, but I wouldn't regard myself a good reporter. I always figured I was a little too lazy to be a good reporter.

There were certain stories that I didn't want to do. I did a story about technicolor once for *Fortune* magazine, and I'll never forget it. It was so complicated. When you've got to interview the chief of development for the Technicolor Corporation, you don't ask him how the kids are. You get into magenta dyes and three-color processes, things that I not only have no interest in, but I had a terrible time even passing chemistry. It was a fascinating story, but it was a two-week crucifixion.

One reason I have not done more with hockey is because it's difficult. If you don't know a subject, you don't know what to ask, what to talk about. One of the difficulties about soccer and hockey is there's no controversy to it. The essence of sports is competition and controversy.

Baseball, all winter long, you say, "Why did he walk him? Why did he put in a pinch hitter? Why didn't they bring Koufax in? Why did they leave that guy out in center field? Why didn't he bunt?" In football, "Why didn't they try a field goal? Why didn't they forward pass there? They should've left Johnson in at quarterback." People argue all winter long.

What do they argue about in soccer? Why did he make a goal? You can get down and ask Steve Carlton, "Why the hell didn't you throw a curve ball right in the face?" But what do you ask a guy after a soccer game?

HOW I WRITE

To start to write a column, you've got to have an idea. You can't just sit down and write. Usually, what I like to do is have the column in my head the night before. I just let it sit in the mind overnight. Say I had a luncheon interview today. I go interview a guy and come back with my notes and put them away and get on with everything.

When I go to bed, I start thinking. "Well, let's see. Tomorrow I'm going to write about this guy. What am I going to say about him?" I let it kind of germinate overnight. I can't imagine sitting down with no idea in mind. I've had to do that sometimes and I didn't like it at all. If it got to be frequent, I think I'd think about getting out.

I've had friends, for instance, when I had my eye problems. They'd say, "I'll take you to the ballgame any time you want to." So I'd say, "OK, let's go to the ballgame." And it's a 1:30 game, and their idea of going to the ballgame is to get you there at 1:25. That's no damn good to me. If the ballgame starts at 1:30, I've got to go there at 11:30 and interview.

For football games, they'd say, "Well, we're going to the game. If it's one-sided, we'll leave in the fourth quarter." And I say, "Hey, I can't leave in the fourth quarter. I've got to go down to the locker room and get an interview. I've got to get a story." Twenty million people have seen it on television. What the hell can I tell them? I can tell them that the quarterback's in the locker room, crying his heart out, or something like that.

That's just one illustration of the misunderstanding people have about your job. Even with my eye problem, all the doctors thought it was imperative that they correct my eyesight so I could see whether the second baseman made the tag or not, whether Jones was really offside. I didn't care about that. What I want my eyesight for is so that as I get writing I can pick up a book and see what year Ty Cobb batted .402. That's far more important to me than whether the guy really caught the ball or dropped it. I can ask the guy afterwards.

ETHICAL DILEMMAS

I don't think the public has any real perception of journalism whatsoever. In the first place, most people grew up with a different breed of journalist. They grew up with the guy who was probably a little bit underpaid and used his column to augment his income and augment his reputation and to play a role. They conceive of you as a guy who gets free tickets, and this is totally against journalism's new rules.

ROOTING FOR THE COLUMN

You don't go to a sports event to enjoy it. Just the other night when they were introducing the boxers in the ring, I kept thinking to myself, "Oh, my God, they're going to introduce these guys till 8:30 [p.m.], then the fight's going to go 12 rounds and it'll be a waltz and it'll take 15 minutes to argue about getting the [score] cards." Your deadline's 10:30 [p.m.]. So I sit there and hope somebody knocks somebody out. Anybody.

One time somebody asked me if I rooted. I said, "Are you crazy? What do you mean, root? How can I root? You'd be in a straightjacket by Mother's Day if you sat there and rooted." He said, "Well, you must root a little bit."

And I said, "Well, I'll tell ya, I don't root for the Dodgers. But if Tommy John is pitching and all of a sudden an idea forms in my mind of a good idea for a column about Tommy John, I start to root for Tommy John, not because I'm a big fan of the Dodgers but because I'm a fan of leads for the column."

REPORTER AS OBSERVER

Sometimes you learn more about a person by observing him. I ask the same dumb questions everybody asks, but I observe the way the guy answers a question or his mannerisms, because that all has to do with writing about people and describing people, which makes the best kind of reading.

I've often said if I were going to do a piece on Maury Wills, I would never go in and ask Maury Wills these terribly acute questions. I'd go up to the locker room and I might sit over with Don Drysdale and watch Maury Wills when Maury Wills didn't know he was being watched.

I always use Maury as an example, because Maury is the guy who never did anything without a purpose. A lot of ballplayers are very aimless. They come in, they flop around, they scratch and insult each other and tell jokes and spit. Maury came in and, man, boom!—he went right to his letters, and boom!—he'd go to the telephone.

MEMORABLE SPORTS PERSONALITIES

Of all the people I've met, I always sort of revered Ben Hogan, the golfer. He was just fascinating. He was so meticulous. He paid so much attention to detail and was so determined. I loved to watch him play golf because he was so relentless.

Golfers would come out in vermilion slacks and alligator shoes. Hogan wore a pair of gray pants, a white shirt, a white cap on his head, old-fashioned cap with a snap on it. And if the weather got chilly, he put on a black sweater. Of course, golfers basically are meticulous people. They have to be. They're like diamond cutters. They can't leave things lying around that might get in the way of their performance.

If you asked a question, you had to ask it precisely and you got a precise answer. I remember one time when I did a cover story on him. We had a chart on the average length that he would hit a four wood. It was marked down as 240 yards. Hogan says, "Two hundred forty yards? Wait a minute. That doesn't mean anything. It depends on what time of day it is." I said, "What do you mean, Ben?" He said, "Well, the weather gets chilly later in the day. The ball doesn't go as far. What kind of ball are you playing? Are you playing a British ball, playing an American ball? Is the grass wet?" I thought, "Holy God."

Another time, Gary Player hit a shot in the Masters [tournament], and he was bitching about it. He says, "I got this fluffy lie. I hit a seven iron 190 yards. That's a bad lie." So Hogan comes in and I said, "Ben, Player is complaining about the fluffy lies out there." Hogan said, "Well, this time of the year in this part of Georgia, you're going to get fluffy lies because you've got the grass and then you've got a layer of silicon and a layer of lime."

Christ, he was down to the core of the earth in three minutes. I thought, "Holy God, he's got a club for the third layer of subcutaneous gravel!" Anyway, I respected him for that. He was a fascinating guy. On the golf course he went into a catatonic state until he finished his round.

I also like Pete Rose, the baseball player. He fascinates me. Pete is a 43-year-old man going on four. It's written in his face. It isn't put on— he loves baseball, loves what he's doing. He plays the game like the little kid who hated to go have dinner.

The rest of us left it behind. I don't think Pete ever did. He has a boyish temperament that makes his face boyish. As I always said, Pete comes into the game of baseball like a kid coming down the stairs on Christmas morning, looking for the new bike.

Oh, I also loved Joe Louis. Joe was a kindly man, decent person. I don't care what kind of troubles he got into. At bottom, Joe was a very decent man for such a great athlete. He really had a lovable quality about him. And so does Muhammad Ali. I find Ali fascinating. We were friends.

My wife ran into him one time. He was fighting a gorgeous Argentinian who looked like every tango dancer you ever saw. About 6-foot-3. And Ali was just as handsome as he could be. And they were both in white dinner jackets and tuxedo pants at this dinner party at the promoter's house.

And Gerry [Murray's wife] hated fights. She came in and she said, "My God, look at you two. What in the world are you going to go in there and bloody each other for? Two pretty-looking men like you?"

And Ali incorporated it into his act immediately. The next paper I picked up said, "I'm too pretty to fight. I'm too pretty to be here with you, you big ugly...." He may deny it, but I know because he picked up things like that.

WOMEN IN SPORTS

There've been women in sports all through my lifetime and women on the sports pages. Babe Didrikson. There was Fanny Blankers-Koen, Wilma Rudolph. There was Stella Walsh, Eleanor Holm. But there haven't been women sports reporters for a lot of reasons, most of which would get me in terrible trouble with the feminist movement.

I think women tend usually to think that whatever men are doing, they're having a better time. So if that son-of-a-bitch is out there being a sportswriter, there must be something about sportswriting. Whatever you really feel apart from, you're curious about. I think that's part of it. But I suppose girls who grow up following sports have a yen to write about it. It's much more possible today that they would be able to do that.

Copyboys in the old days, they could pick what they would apprentice to. Nine out of 10 of them chose sports. Quite a few people moved through the sports pages to someplace else.

SPORTS ON TELEVISION

On television, the medium does the reporting. The game is all there. The game is more than you could see if you had 20 eyes. It's got instant replay. One of the superfluities of our time is the guy who's telling you what you've just looked at.

Then the sports guy on Channel 4 usually has got two minutes and 11 seconds to give 19 scores. He can't really express any opinion, or if he does, he does it inadequately or clumsily. I don't think on television there's any exact equivalent to what I do.

GIVING UP LOCKER ROOMS

When I go on vacation, I can't stand to hear the sound of a typewriter or a computer machine. I hate it. I like sports all right. I love to watch a good fight or a game, particularly on television, when I don't have to write about it. I loved watching the Masters Golf Tournament, but if I were there, I would probably be walking around, biting my nails, hoping that the guy I had picked for my subject would not hit the ball in the water. When you bring your typewriter or your word processor, it ain't no vacation, as Sparky Anderson would say.

When I retire, I sure as hell won't miss going into locker rooms. Another sportswriter quit after years down in the Coliseum lockers. People in the locker room pretended they didn't know him and wouldn't let him in. So this guy says to me, "See? Ten minutes after you leave your job, you won't be able to get in the locker room." I said, "My friend, ten minutes after I leave my job, the German army with fixed bayonets couldn't get me in a locker room."

ADVICE FOR YOUNG JOURNALISTS

I like my job because I'm a journalist and if you're going to be a journalist, this is what you work for. I put in my time ringing doorbells, interviewing people in jail cells and tracking down reluctant news subjects. Now, I'd probably be very envious of myself if I were a young reporter and I knew somebody who had my job. I would envy his status, his ability to write what he wanted, how he wanted.

When I talk to young people about getting into journalism, I always quote a guy named Tim Turner, who was a very colorful old newspaperman. He had a shaved, bald head 20 years before Yul Brynner. He was a big, tall, lanky, lugubrious man who had ridden with Pancho Villa. He had a very colorful career.

And a young man once said to him, "Mr. Turner, I'm so-and-so. I went to the USC School of Journalism, and I don't know what to do, whether to go into newspapering or advertising or broadcasting or public relations, and I was hoping you could tell me." And Tim says, "Well, son, I'll tell you. Newspapering is kind of like sex—when it's good it's terrific, and when it's bad it's pretty good." That's what I tell young guys. Although I do advise them that if money is their main interest— and it is most people's—to first see if they can develop their talking skills. Really.

To become a journalist of any kind, you learn writing. Kids come up and say, "I know every batting average since 1903 and I know every yard Jim Brown ever gained." And I say, "Hey, look. You've got books you can find that in. You got people to look that up for you. Learn how to write, don't learn about sports. You can find out about sports later."

I think everybody thinks he can write. Everybody who can spell at all thinks he's really a writer, and some of them are. Some very poor spellers are great writers. Hemingway, for example. But not every great speller is a great writer. I think things just don't click together for some people the way they do in a writer's mind, no matter how much you practice or how many courses you take or how much studying you do. I think you're sort of born with it.

Conversely, when people come up and say, "Should I write?" I say, "Hey, look, there ain't no way to stop a writer from writing. They'll write if nobody reads it. It doesn't matter. A real writer has got to write."

IMPORTANCE OF AN AUDIENCE

You would hope somebody reads what you write. It's important to you economically. If they don't read it, then you fail the readership surveys. If I write a good column, I want them to read it. If I write a bad column, I hope they skipped the paper that day.

LIVING WITH DEADLINES

Writing under a deadline is a different kind of job. One time my son was here in the living room and I said, "You have any idea what time it is?" And he says, "No." "Not even within a couple hours?" I said. He says, "No." "Any idea whether it's afternoon or morning?" He says, "Not really." God, what a luxury.

Because, almost all my life, I've had to know what time it is in L.A. even if I'm in Moscow. So you always know what time it is because of deadlines. You live with them. And you get in the habit of knowing what time it is, how much time you have left.

FAMILY LIFE

As for what it does to family life to have the kind of job I do . . . [long pause], I don't want to think about it. Of course, I worked at home all those years. But even though you're here, you're also there, you know? Just imagine if you were the wife living here with all these commotions going on around you.

I wouldn't want to be married to a columnist. I wouldn't want to be married to a movie star, either. I wouldn't want to be married to somebody who had a consuming career. And it's a consuming career. The damn thing comes up every day. Once I likened it to having a tiger by the tail. You can't let go. You just keep letting it whirl you around.

His letters
aren't just
x's and o's

by Jim Murray

SAN FRANCISCO—You look at Bill Walsh, and the last thing you expect him to be is a football coach.

A concert pianist, perhaps. A Latin teacher, a priest. He looks like a guy who might go to the ballet. You figure, Swinburne maybe looked like this.

It's lousy casting for a football coach. Any Hollywood producer would throw you out if you came back with a guy who looked like Walsh for the part. "This is a football picture, not a remake of 'Camille,' " he would yell. "Take this guy back and bring me Bogart."

You know how football coaches are supposed to look. They got this broken nose, a blue beard and gaps in their teeth. Their hair, if they got any, is in a U-boat brush. They yell a lot, and spit. They come from Monongahela, Pa., or Red Dust, Ark., and they talk about gut checks. By character, they mean a guy who would kill for a living.

Now, look at Walsh, by comparison. He has a face that looks out of place without a halo around it. He looks as if he should be feeding birds or reading his breviary. He's so pale you can see through him, and he has this shock of

This column appeared three days before the 1985 Super Bowl between the Miami Dolphins and the San Francisco 49ers. Jim Murray talks about how he writes about people on pgs. 111–112.

© 1986, Los Angeles Times. Distributed by Los Angeles Times Syndicate. Reprinted with permission.

fine white hair and wears sweaters and shoes to match. He looks like a bar of Ivory soap on the sidelines.

When he talks, all the sentences have verbs in them. He never raises his voice or his fists. He seems bemused by what he sees, almost as if he were watching the opera. He should have a lorgnette and be wearing a tux. He doesn't look as though he even sweats.

He distances himself from the coaching fraternity by his very aloofness. Don Shula paces up and down the sideline on his crouched legs like a caged puma. Vince Lombardi used to rant and rave like the third act of "Carmen." John Madden looked like a moving laundry bag.

Walsh permits himself an occasional move of annoyance now and then, a slight wrinkling of the brow, as if the fish hadn't been boned properly, or the wrong wine came with the salad. As if what were going on in the field were distasteful but not worth making a scene over.

He wasn't raised in the coaldust leagues of the anthracite country or the longhorn trails of Texas but in the quiche country of Northern California. Where most coaches drink beer from a bottle, Walsh prefers white wine in a goblet. He probably never ate a chicken-fried steak in his life. Most coaches play golf or bowl. He plays tennis.

Genius is a word that is bandied about too much in sports. *Genius* is a word applied to a guy who has Ruth, Gehrig, Dickey, Lazzeri, Gomez and three 20-

game winners in a lineup and beats the St. Louis Browns, 5-3. In coaching, it's a guy who has recruited every All-State football player from three states around and goes 9-2-1 and wins the Liberty Bowl.

Walsh has had *genius* applied to him more often than Albert Einstein. Typically, it embarrasses him. Probably because he's one of the few guys in the league who knows who Einstein was. Walsh's theory of football is a lot more comprehensible than Einstein's Theory of Relativity. It must be. It's understandable to pro football players, and Lord knows, there are very few college graduates among them.

Walsh's genius is certifiable in that he plots out a football game 25 moves in advance for the start of a game. Now, this smacks also of clairvoyance. Does it mean that, if play No. 12 calls for a punt and the team finds itself on play No. 12 on the other guys' 1-yard line, first-and-goal, does it punt? No, but under Walsh's system, neither does it try a line plunge. Walsh's teams abhor the expected. They're like a play by George Bernard Shaw. No one does what you think he will. Walsh would rather fail than bore.

Walsh's 49er teams are everything the game expected—except they are successful. The league figured they would be entertaining. They are. The league figured they would be competitive. They are. The league just didn't figure they would be victorious. The league thought they would be flashy—but inconsistent. That they would look good losing. Instead, they look good winning.

Everyone always knew Walsh knew something about attack football that nobody else knew. What they didn't think he knew was how to win with it.

He was like a fighter they call a crowd pleaser. Incapable of retreat. Disdainful of consequences.

That's why they left Walsh in the assistant coaches' ranks for decades. He was all right in the engine room but not on the bridge. He developed all-time quarterbacks and passing attacks for the likes of Stanford, Cal, the Raiders, Cincinnati Bengals, San Diego Chargers, Stanford again and, finally, the 49ers. He looked good on the drawing board. The word was, with the football, Bill Walsh was a great coach. Without it, he was just another guy in a headset waiting for a turnover.

The league figured the Peter Principle would work with Walsh. Like, all those pretty plays on the blackboard looked like French Impressionism—but if they promoted him, the league would draw mustaches on them.

The strategem of big business in this country is: If it isn't broken, don't fix it. Leave it be. If a guy's a good writer, you let him write. If he's a good pilot, let him fly. If he's a good accountant, let him add. If he's a good assistant, let him assist.

It was considered a gamble when the 49ers hired Walsh to do more than assist. It was like hiring St. Francis of Assisi to drive a truck. When he went 2-14 the first year, the wise guys said, "Ho!" But when he went to the Super Bowl two years later, they said, "Who?"

When he went to two Super Bowls in six years, they said: "We told you so. Genius."

Walsh is as unimpressed with the new as he is with the old assessments of him. If he wins Sunday, don't look for him to be standing in any champagne shower. For the wine connoisseur, Bill Walsh, wouldn't wash his dog in that cheap stuff, let alone his own hair.

Courtesy of Philip Taubman

"The relationship between government and the press is very intense in Washington, probably unhealthy in many ways."

PHILIP TAUBMAN

Philip Taubman sits under the trees in the backyard of his Washington, D.C., home. His collection of files from six years of reporting for *The New York Times* is packed in cardboard boxes upstairs, ready for storage. One of those files is three inches thick with the articles Taubman wrote about two former CIA agents who were illegally exporting explosives to Libya. In 1982, Taubman and Jeff Gerth won the George Polk Award for their coverage.

Taubman is on his way to Russia, where he will live with his family and work in the *Times'* Moscow bureau. He has spent several months studying Russian, and he's excited. "Going to Moscow is better than anything yet," he says. "It's a fabulous opportunity."

Taubman, 38, is maintaining a family tradition. His father, Howard, worked for *The New York Times* covering the cultural beat. When Philip was 10 years old he went with his father to Europe to cover the Brussels World's Fair. His father covered Adlai Stevenson's visit to the fair, and young Taubman went along. "One of the Brussels papers ran a photograph the next day of Adlai Stevenson and me and described me as his son, which I thought was kind of fun. I still have the picture."

After graduating from Stanford in 1970, Taubman spent seven years at *Time* magazine. He turned down a job at the *Times* right out of college. During a visit to the Stanford campus, *New York Times* columnist James Reston had offered Taubman a job on the metropolitan desk, with the understanding that in six months he probably would go to Vietnam.

"It was a very tempting offer, but I didn't take it because of a wildly romantic idea. By that time, I had met Felicity. We were not quite engaged, but we were headed in that direction. We got married soon after I graduated. And I didn't like the idea of heading off to Vietnam, 10,000 miles away.

"I was also a little concerned about going to work at a place my father was working, for fear that I would be forever viewed as having gotten the job only because of his presence and perhaps his intervention, which hadn't been a factor. I didn't want to work in his shadow."

After working at *Time,* Taubman spent a year at *Esquire* and then went to work for the *Times* in Washington, D.C. "In some ways," he says, "I've wondered how much I've missed as a journalist, not having covered zoning, school boards, and the night police beat. As a journalist, I probably have failings because I never had some of those experiences. Right away I was thrown into something that was going to be as intellectually stimulating to me as anything I'd be doing the rest of my life." ❖

from Philip Taubman

- The effect of competition among journalists for stories
- How public officials can restrain publication of a sensitive story
- How to evaluate a source's motives for talking

Beginnings

My father worked for *The New York Times* for 43 years, so I caught the disease at close quarters at home. He was a critic—music critic, drama critic and critic-at-large. So as a kid, I have wonderful, vivid memories of his career—travels with him, stories that he worked on, visits to *The New York Times*, of being imbued with the world of journalism without even knowing it.

I remember falling asleep any number of nights to the sound of him dictating stories. It's such an intoxicating business to practice, but also to observe at close hand.

I grew up in New York City, and I was editor of the Riverdale high school paper, which seemed a big deal at the time. The paper came out every two weeks, but it was like running a small-town newspaper. The editor ends up doing 90 percent of the work, everything from writing stories to writing headlines to laying out the paper to carrying it to the printer's.

WORKING FOR THE *STANFORD DAILY*

I went to Stanford in 1966 when I was 18, and the first day on campus, I headed over to the office of the student newspaper, the *Stanford Daily*.

I only took one journalism course because I thought the *Daily* experience was just as good if not better than majoring in communications. I still think that's the case. I majored in European history.

I started out as a reporter at the *Daily*. Then I became an editor, which really meant that you were just a more active reporter. I also had moments of great doubt as to whether journalism was what I wanted.

It was a very impressionable age, when you're trying to decide not only what you want to do with your life, but what values are important to you. Journalism for a while seemed to clash with a value that I considered then and still consider very important, which was trying to—it sounds like a cliché—promote social justice and to be helpful to people in need.

You have experiences throughout your career as a journalist, for example, of writing a story that hurts someone, either personally or professionally. When you first have these experiences, they're much harder on you.

There was one administrator at Stanford whom I admired a great deal. He headed a big two-year review of all aspects of the Stanford educational program. I wrote a story about the difficulties he was having implementing some of the proposals that had emerged from the various committees that studied Stanford. My piece said that maybe this man lacked the administrative ability to carry through the proposals.

After I wrote that piece, I went home in great confusion as to whether I'd done the right thing. I had great anxiety that night. Eventually, at 3 o'clock in the morning, I went over to his house and left a note for him, saying that I had completely second thoughts about this piece. I was resigning from the newspaper. I was retiring from all the stringing jobs I had at *Time* and the *Los Angeles Times*, and that I was rethinking my commitment to be a journalist.

Who knows what happened as a result of my story. He got up in the morning and there was this melodramatic note from a kid. You can only write that kind of self-important note when you're 19, 20 years old. I'm sure I looked like a fool to him. I know I looked like a fool to myself in retrospect, but so be it. And I did quit the paper and I quit the stringer jobs. I stuck with it for about three months. But then, slowly I got drawn back.

TO *TIME* MAGAZINE IN BOSTON

So many things are serendipitous, and yet, in retrospect, they build on one after the other. If I hadn't been editor of the *Stanford Daily*, I probably wouldn't have been hired by *Time* magazine when I graduated from college. And if I hadn't been hired by *Time*, what would have happened, where would I have ended up in a career? It would have been very different.

I worked as a summer intern between my junior and senior year at the San Francisco bureau of *Time*. I established myself enough with them so they were serious about offering me a job when I graduated. In the fall of 1970, I started work for *Time* in Boston as a correspondent trainee.

I still think back to that time as the richest time of my life as a journalist, just in terms of the variety of stories and the emotion and involvement that I had with what I was writing. With a certain amount of maturity has been the loss of some of the energy, enthusiasm and emotion that I brought to my work in those days.

When a lot of Americans were still being held POWs in North Vietnam, I became interested in writing about the family of one of them, Colonel Ken North. He'd been shot down over North Vietnam, and he was a prisoner for six or eight years. His wife and four children, all girls, lived on Cape Cod.

I established a relationship with them to write about what life was like for the family of a POW. A year or so after he returned to the United States, I wrote a series of files—some of which were included in stories, some of which never saw publication because of the way *Time* works—about the family and their effort to cope without a husband and a father and then their effort to readjust when he returned.

Journalists are supposed to be objective, supposed to be distanced from the stories they write, and that is important. But I don't see, in retrospect, that there was anything wrong with becoming moved and interested in their situation in a way that, when I sat down to write about it, I wrote with some real understanding of what was happening to them.

FILING STORIES FOR *TIME*

When I was at *Time*, from 1970 to 1977, there were no bylines. Reporters in the field, who were called correspondents, went out and reported a story the way any journalist would anywhere, and went back to the office and wrote what is called a file, which is the same thing as a story. Instead of that file appearing in the magazine as written by the correspondent, it would be rewritten by a staff writer in New York.

This had started when *Time* began in the '20s because they were rewriting newspapers. They took a lot of turgid stuff in newspapers and boiled it down to its essence, with a snappy style that made it much more readable than the average newspaper. This carried over into the era even when *Time* had its own core of correspondents.

They still believed that writing for space, as it's called, required somebody different from the person who was out in the field gathering the information. So every week there was a voluminous amount of material produced that either never got in the magazine or got in the magazine in a very condensed form. I would be so pleased to find that one or two pieces of information from one of my 20-page files had found its way into the magazine. It seemed to me when I left, and still does, a very frustrating system for a journalist.

The advantage was that you had a certain license to write with verve, style, feeling and emotion because the stuff wasn't going to get published the way you wrote it. The disadvantage was that a lot of times, in distilling stories, the life was taken out of them. You might spend a week working yourself very hard to file a story and see it appear in one paragraph in the magazine.

But at news magazines you're always working on very interesting stories, usually stories of national interest or impact. I spent a weekend living in a commune in Vermont, I did a story on a policeman in Waterville, Maine, who was working with a group of handicapped children in a special Boy Scout unit, I did a cover story on Edwin Land, the head of Polaroid, I did stories on Carlton Fisk, the catcher for the Red Sox, and on Jim Plunkett, who at that time was quarterback for the New England Patriots. I did stories on all kinds of things.

WRITING SPORTS IN NEW YORK

Then I moved to New York in 1973, and I become a writer in the sports section. I felt then, and I still think, that sports deserves the same serious, demanding, inquisitive kind of coverage as any subject. To write about sports simply as entertainment is wrong. It has become big business. The people involved in it, though they earn their money playing sports, are extremely interesting. There's no reason they shouldn't be written about in the same kind of depth that we write about political and religious leaders.

At a national publication you are not forced, as many sports reporters are, to root for the hometown team. And a writer in New York could do a lot of his own reporting because most of the correspondents in the field were not interested in sports. Also, most people don't realize that the back-of-the-book sections, which are everything except Nation and World and Business, don't appear every week. They rotate. So there would be weeks when you wouldn't have to be in the office, when you could be out reporting.

The first cover story I did was on Reggie Jackson, who was at that point playing for the Oakland A's. Then I did a cover piece on Jimmy Connors, and one on Charlie Finley, the owner of the A's. There's nothing like writing a *Time* cover story because there's space and the display is good. You see it all over the country. People react to it. There's a great sense of pride to have authored a *Time* cover story.

A MOVE TO WASHINGTON AND THE *TIMES*

In 1976, I came to Washington, D.C., to cover labor and some economic news. I went back to doing the same thing I'd done in Boston—writing stories and having them rewritten and condensed in New York. I quit *Time* in October 1977 and went to work for *Esquire* writing sports from January 1978 until April 1979 when the *Times* inquired whether I would be interested in being the Justice Department correspondent.

The *Times* has about 40 reporters in Washington. I was at Justice for a year, and then slowly I turned to covering intelligence issues and foreign policy. I tried to do some reading, but I really didn't know what I was doing at the beginning. It's an example of a typical practice in journalism—give somebody an assignment and they learn on the job.

If I had a beat, it was the intelligence community, but my beat didn't have a lot of press conferences. The CIA didn't do much in the way of normal public exposure. I could go a week or two without having to write a story, which gave me time to research longer stories.

Ninety-five percent of what you're writing about is classified information, and sources are more scared to talk to you than in almost any other area. They're subjected to lie detector tests regularly, and most of them are brought up in an environment where secrecy is not only stressed, but is believed in, as it should be.

You pry out information slowly. You spend a lot of time getting people to trust you, so if they do talk to you they know that they're not going to get identified in any way.

You also have to build up enough knowledge so that you can talk to people on the same intellectual plane that they're on. Until you know a good deal yourself, you're hampered in your reporting, because so many people have spent a lifetime dealing with the same issues that you may have been dealing with for two weeks.

WHY SOURCES TALK

You learn patience. I also learned about the vicissitudes of sources and the different reasons they become sources. Everybody has a different reason—bureaucratic rivalries, gaining the edge on somebody else by getting a story publicized that helps or hurts them or their rival, simply the thrill or the danger of dealing with a reporter, intellectual agendas that differ from those of their organization or their boss.

Sometimes it's personal rivalries with other officials, but sometimes it's an intellectual reason—somebody thinks that some program is good and he wants to help it—or partisan political motivations where Democrats want to hurt Republicans and vice versa. The out-of-power want to expose things about the party that's in power.

It's probably very similar to the kinds of competition you would find in government at any level. Here it just happens to have national and international ramifications.

GOVERNMENT AND THE PRESS

The relationship between government and the press is very intense in Washington, probably unhealthy in many ways. The press as the means of bringing public pressure to bear on issues plays an amazingly extensive role in policy development in Washington. If a story appears on the evening news programs or prominently in the news magazines or on the front page of *The Wall Street Journal, The Washington Post* or *The New York Times,* it creates a certain amount of interest among constituents of Congress around the country. It also exposes to public debate issues that have been debated quietly within the government.

Debates that take place quietly within the government are quite different from what takes place once an issue becomes public. The most obvious example of this is the recent hijacking of the TWA plane. The White House and the officials in it have said that they felt they had to make decisions because there was tremendous pressure every night. There were interviews with family members of the hostages, there were interviews with the hostages themselves, a tremendous focus of national attention on that issue.

And that, in a less intense and certainly less widely covered way, is what happens with a lot of issues here. When they surface in the press, they take off in Washington. You're never sure whether it's the press that's discovered them or the Congress that wants the press to discover them. But once they get going, it builds up tremendous momentum. Each of the three institutions [of government] feeds each other.

INTENSE COMPETITION FOR STORIES

What you've got then is all these press organizations competing with each other to break new ground on story X. Congress is feeling that this has become a big issue, and committees are appointed or standing committees get involved in hearings or investigations. As the investigators do their work, their information is leaked to the press, which produces more headlines.

It turns into this incredible cycle that builds and builds and almost invariably leads to the resignation—if it involves a personality—of a public official. I think sometimes the whole process is very unfair and damaging. But it happens in case after case. Sometimes because of the momentum and the demands of competition, the fairness of the coverage is sacrificed.

When it's over, nobody's interested in it again. I'm sure that this is one of the characteristics of the press that the public resents, that we become like a school of sharks where somebody's dropped a carcass and everybody's straining to attack it, and then we end up attacking each other. It becomes a very destructive process, both of journalism and certainly of some of the individuals involved.

It's a result of the intense competition. On a hot story, the networks are very concerned about whether the other guy has got the same item leading off the news that they have. *The New York Times* and *The Washington Post* are very concerned about each other's coverage, and I'm sure *The Wall Street Journal* and the *Los Angeles Times*, *Time* and *Newsweek* are always looking at each other. Everybody's racing to stay ahead. And Congress gets into the act. They love the attention they get when they become identified with a hot issue.

The initial instinct of the press to want to pursue a good story is quite proper. But what bothers me is that after a while you lose track of the story, and all kinds of crazy things are published. It's a process that I don't think does anybody much credit.

The answer is restraint, but how do you restrain highly competitive news organizations and how do you restrain Congress, which is interested in attention? The dynamic builds up and the good motivations are replaced or superceded by sheer competitive zeal.

WHEN THE GOVERNMENT INTERVENES IN A STORY

The primary issue [on the intelligence beat] is when to publish or when not to publish national security information. As a journalist your primary interest is informing your readers. And what the United States government considers classified is sometimes ludicrous. The system has run amuck. The instinct of the government is to stamp stuff "Secret."

When, for example, you do stories about the ways and means by which American intelligence agencies collect information, the government often knows you're preparing a story. You have to, at some point, call them and get their comment. And they may very well make an appeal to you, to your boss, to your editor, to the publisher of the paper not to publish.

A LISTENING POST IN CHINA

Toward the end of the Carter administration, I received in the mail a little publication produced by a group of critics of the U.S. intelligence agencies. This publication had in it an item about the establishment of a secret intelligence sharing agreement between the United States and China. The stories indicated that there had been some kind of secret agreement and that there might even have been the establishment of some kind of facility in China.

At that time, 1980, the U.S. had established diplomatic relations with China and was moving very slowly and cautiously toward the sale of military equipment, but we were far removed from an intense, close relationship. Any significant military alliance between China and the United States—not in the sense of treaties, but in the sense of cooperation—has immense implications for U.S./Soviet relations and Chinese/Soviet relations.

I found a couple of people who knew about this thing who talked about it. They shouldn't have, from the government's perspective, but they did. And I pieced together information that, in fact, the United States had built and was operating, in conjunction with the Chinese, a ground electronics surveillance station in Western China, up in the mountains. The United States built a facility not too far from the border of the Soviet Union, with panoramic access to the Soviets, beginning from their launch sites down near the Caspian Sea out over the Soviet Union.

The bureau chief agreed that it was a very important and interesting story, but he wondered whether we should publish it. About this time, [National Security Adviser Zbigniew] Brzezinski heard that we were working on it. He called the Washington bureau chief and asked him to come over to the White House and talk.

When the bureau chief came back, he said he found Brzezinski's arguments persuasive. As the bureau chief described it, Brzezinski said, "Look. The Russians may already know about this, but having it appear on the front page of the *Times* as opposed to very oblique references in a small publication and in *New York Magazine* would make it something that the Russians might have to react to. And how would they react? They'd be provoked into trying to knock this facility out of operation. It could have all kinds of ramifications."

He also argued that if the Chinese felt obliged to shut down the station because of the publicity, then the United States would lose a critical means of verifying Soviet compliance. The Bureau Chief felt that those were significant and persuasive arguments, so he said, "We won't run the story."

I disagreed with his decision, and I made that clear to him, but he runs the bureau, so I'm not going to go over his head on a decision like that. It's his call.

Then after Reagan had been sworn in, or maybe a few days before, I went back and raised the issue again. I said, "Should we have another run at this?" He said, "Sure. Let's see what we can find out now."

So I went back and did some more reporting and didn't add anything to the story, except to confirm that the place was still in operation. This time, the administration appeal came from William Casey, who had taken over as director of Central Intelligence. He came by the office and talked to the bureau chief and me and made arguments that were quite similar to those Brzezinski had made.

This time the bureau chief agreed it was time to run the story because we had waited a couple of months. All this time there was the potential that somebody else was going to get the story. And Casey said, "If that's your decision, do you mind if I go and discuss it with your editors?" The bureau chief said, "No." I didn't have any objection to that either.

So Casey went up to New York and met with the publisher of the *Times,* Punch Sulzberger. And Mr. Sulzberger decided that we shouldn't run the story for the same reasons that the bureau chief had originally decided not to run the story. Again, I disagreed. Casey agreed at the time that if anyone else was reporting the story and the fact that they were reporting it came to his attention, he would let me know.

Then my colleague, Bill Safire, who's a columnist [for *The New York Times*], wrote a piece about U.S./Chinese relations. He came darn close to publishing the fact that this facility existed. He had never talked to me about it. He had his own sources of information, but when that appeared, I went back and said, "This seems to me now to be becoming untenable, where not only *New York Magazine* published something, but here we are in our own newspaper coming right up to the edge of saying on the editorial page that there's a facility like this."

Just about the same time, Marvin Kalb of NBC got word of it. One day, I was up on the Hill covering something, and I got a call. "Come back to the office immediately. NBC news is working on this story and chances are that it's going to be on the air tonight, so we need to write our story right away." Indeed, NBC had it as the lead item on the news. We had a very detailed story about it in the following day's paper, but we did not have it first. We were scooped by Marvin.

To this day, you could argue both sides of this case with credibility. As far as I know, the facility has remained in operation, so some of the worst predictions did not come to pass, but you did not know that at the time. I think fair-minded, reasonable people can disagree on that kind of issue, and we did.

As happened in this case, if the government wanted to push it, they could go to the publisher and appeal to him. But it's Mr. Sulzberger's newspaper, and he can publish whatever he wants or not publish whatever he wants. I'm an employee of *The New York Times.* I do the best job I can, but it's their decision. If there were some grossly unfair or unethical decision, I would quit. But it's never come to that.

ETHICAL DILEMMAS

As a reporter, I've never been inclined to become very good friends with sources. I just prefer to keep a separation between my private and my professional life.

More than that is the ethical question where the *Times* is provided information because somebody is really trying to manipulate something. Somebody comes to you with a piece of information that could conceivably be very damaging to a rival. You end up publishing a story, which you've corroborated, and the rival is hurt. So the person who came to you with the information is satisfied. That's what they wanted. You've got a perfectly legitimate story but, at the same time, they're getting what they wanted, too.

Then there's the question of, what do you do when people come to you and give you information that they've obtained through questionable means? Is it appropriate to take documents somebody else has stolen from somebody? There are probably times when you wouldn't know where they got them, although you'd certainly try to find out.

If you do find out that they were stolen, what do you do? Can you use them or not? I've often wondered, do you do business with crooks? Just because information comes from a convicted felon, does it mean that you shouldn't take it? I don't know. They're not easy issues.

Generally there's a rule of thumb, I've found, which is that the dicier the subject you're writing, the more questionable your sources are. It's not unlike a prosecutor who takes a plea bargain from somebody and then uses the information to convict somebody else.

In the kind of journalism I was involved in, you're constantly dealing with shadowy figures. I don't have a particular problem with that, as long as I know who they are, what their motivation is, and as long as I do my job of checking their information thoroughly before I publish it.

SUB-CATEGORIES OF "OFF THE RECORD"

Here in Washington we've got sub-categories of "on the record" and "off the record." You've got four categories—on the record, where you attribute it to Joe Blow, Assistant Secretary of State; not for attribution, or background, where you can attribute it to a State Department official; deep background, where you can attribute it to an administration official; then, off the record, which means that you can't put it in the newspaper.

Even that is subject to some difference of opinion. A lot of reporters, myself included, feel that if you're told something off the record by one person but you hear the same thing from somebody else who does not put it off the record, then you're free to use the information.

There are many journalists, and I respect their position on this, who feel that if it's off the record, it's off the record. If you've made an agreement with one source that it's off the record, it doesn't matter that you learn it from other people.

The person who loses in all of this is the reader. It's an insidious process that has gone out of control. There's far too much unattributed stuff in the newspapers out of Washington. Often, the major front-page stories in *The New York Times* from Washington are attributed to senior administration officials or senior officials in some department. It's hard to counteract that.

It becomes particularly embarrassing these days because a lot of sources will say things on television that they don't tell you on the record when you're talking to them. You interview somebody on background during the day and you write your story, and then Tom Brokaw's interviewing the person at 7 o'clock and this very same person, whom you haven't named in the newspaper, says the same thing on the news. They're willing to talk about things on television because that's the way they reach the most people.

SYSTEMATIC ORGANIZATION

I'm very organized, reasonably systematic. In my case, some stories are daily stories, when you have to have everything in a hurry. Other stories are two- or three-week projects, and it's a different kind of work.

On a project, my tendency is to keep track of what I'm doing so I don't turn around three weeks after I've started and [find] I'm not really sure what it is I've learned, when or where it is that I learned it. You may have done a brilliant reporting job, but if you can't find it, then all your notes are worthless.

A project invariably begins to break down into different categories or subjects. I always take a manila folder for each issue. Every time I come back from an interview, I take those portions of the interview that go with one subject and put them in that folder, and another and another. As the research materials come in, they go in the various folders, so that when I begin to think about writing the piece, I've at least got my stuff organized.

I used to be extremely systematic. I used to do an outline of a story and then go through each section of the outline and note down what quotes and what pieces of information from my notes were going to go in what sections of the story. Before I sat down to write a long story, I would literally have a blueprint, where almost all the information that was going into every paragraph was figured out in advance.

My tendency now is to do a rough outline and just plunge in and write the story on the computer. Then I go back and fill in from notes what I've forgotten to use and hit "insert" and create a new paragraph or a new sentence.

USING ROUGH OUTLINES

It's really important before you start reporting to think about what you're doing, instead of heading off to interview 16 people. That is not to say that you decide before you report a story what you're going to say in it, because a lot of times you end up in a very different place than you thought you would when you started out. You try to keep an open mind.

After about a week of work or even less, I start writing rough outlines, because I have found how much you realize about your story as you're working and how much it changes as you're working on it. When a theme starts emerging, you really have to narrow your reporting.

A lot of people over-report. They call every conceivable source, gather more stuff than they're ever going to use, and they end up spending too much time reporting. You're not writing a book. I have colleagues who don't know where to draw the line. They get very far behind, they miss deadlines, they become obsessed with the reporting. Somewhere you've got to stop reporting and start writing.

You should figure out the theme of what you're writing, then step back from your material, look at what you have, where the holes are, and figure out what is going to fill those holes—get the kinds of interviews you need to fill out the material—never losing track of the outline of your story.

WRITING A FIRST DRAFT

If you're immersed in a project, by the time you sit down to write, you almost know the whole story. I usually develop a lead halfway through. You really don't need to refer to your notes that much. You've absorbed and retained it. The story has a shape to it that comes naturally, organically out of your head.

A first draft is a very good idea because it focuses your work and your reporting. Writing forces you to organize your story in a way that you could not have organized it before you sat down to write. I can think of a lot of stories where the discipline of sitting down and writing the first draft focused the reporting in very valuable ways. Often I've had to go back and do more reporting, and those last few days of reporting have been crucial because I haven't really understood what I'm doing until I sit down and try to write.

WHAT MAKES A GOOD REPORTER

The first thing is to be fair, because we're all subject to getting excited about things we work on. I get very enthusiastic when I'm working on pieces, and it's a wonderful kind of adrenaline, finding out information and getting carried along by it. You're naturally drawn toward one side of an argument or another, or one person or another. You should try to resist that and not let that seep into the story. The tough thing is to harness that energy and that commitment to reporting without letting it color what you're ultimately writing.

You've also got to be willing to go out in the middle of the night to meet people, be willing to sacrifice a certain amount of your personal time. You've got to be utterly committed to working as a reporter to do really brilliant work. If you're not working the phones at night talking to people at home, you're not going to do as good a job as you would. Another thing is patience. A lot of times I've gone out of town on stories and I get restless after a few days. I want to go home. There have been occasions when I have been straining, chomping at the bit to go home, I can't stand it. You're lonely in some city, you haven't any friends, you're sitting in a hotel room all the time.

I always think that if I reach the point where almost every instinct in my body says, "Forget it, you can't do any more," that's exactly the point at which I've got to bear down, because it's at that point that I'll probably make a breakthrough.

You also must have cleverness, in the sense that a good reporter is an actor who plays many roles, not in the sense that he misrepresents himself, [but] you play roles within your capacity as a journalist. With some people, I'm very low key and easygoing and, basically, myself. With other people, it's better to be very severe and, to some extent, intimidating. It's not easy to do if you're like me, relatively small in stature. It's much easier to intimidate somebody if you're 6-5 and 230.

You must appeal to what it is in that person that will elicit the information you're looking for. At its crassest, it boils down to going to the home of some bereaved person and trying to appeal to them to talk to you about their child or whoever it is that's just been killed. You're almost certainly not going to get that if you come up to the door and demand information. If you are patient and sympathetic, sometimes you can. There are all different kinds of colorations that you have to take on. That's what I mean when I say clever. Also, clever in the sense of figuring out different ways to collect information.

Philip Taubman   137

HOW TO FIND PEOPLE

I'm really surprised sometimes at the number of reporting steps that can be taken on stories that reporters don't take, either because they don't think of them, or they're lazy, or they're impatient. On the simplest level, it's the process of finding somebody.

There are all kinds of ways to locate people, starting with going to the post office and getting them to give you the change-of-address card or going to the tax office to see what records are filed, tracking down relatives, going back to colleges to get alumni directories. I subscribe to the notion that there is almost nothing that a good reporter can't find out if he or she really puts a mind to it and is given enough time and resources.

MISTAKES REPORTERS MAKE

The biggest failing is laziness. That's the undoing of so many journalists. At a certain point in your career, you just get tired. It's a very demanding profession, and it takes a tremendous amount of energy to keep at it in a sustained way.

A lot of people just wear out, and I can't blame them. I'm sure I'm going to wear out eventually. They take the easy way out on a story—make three or four calls and accept the story at face value rather than trying to go beyond what is easily obtainable. Lack of imagination, lack of drive, lack of commitment are at the root of a lot of sloppy journalism.

WORKING FOR *THE NEW YORK TIMES*

My reputation is as a reasonably good writer, not a wordsmith or a lyrical writer, but somebody who can write clear, well-organized stories and occasionally turn a nice phrase, somebody who is very energetic, who usually gets the story—not always.

Being a writer for *The New York Times* is just like being a writer for a little newspaper, except with a larger impact. The process itself shouldn't be that much different.

The person who covers the school board for a small-town newspaper plays a very similar role in that community to my role in the last three or four years covering the intelligence community. What they write plays a part in the decisions that are made, in the debate about the issues. People in the intelligence community, like the people on the school board, are both repelled and attracted to the reporter.

The big difference is that the *Times* and any big paper have the resources. You're allowed to take time on stories, and you're given support to do them. I set my sights on being a journalist very early, and I can't imagine doing it any place in any way better than the chance I've had at the *Times*.

WHY I'M A JOURNALIST

The reason I'm a journalist goes beyond the excitement I get out of the profession and beyond the fun I have, and beyond the money I make—I'm not going to do it for nothing, although I'd come pretty close—and beyond the ego gratification of getting bylines. I really have a simple faith in trying to conduct this business in the spirit that it was originally established in this country, and in other free societies, that the role of the press is crucial to sustaining democratic institutions, that the people have a right to know.

We in the press happen to be the group that provides the information. There's a Jefferson comment that sums it up. I can't give you the quote verbatim,* but he commented in a letter to a colleague that if, in a democracy, there are failings because the people are uninformed, the answer is not to withhold information, but to provide more of it.

Every time I get invited to some intelligence agency to talk about the role of the press, I always use this quote to counter everything they believe in, which is that secrecy is paramount. I'm very idealistic in a way about all of this. I don't think of it every day or even every week as I do my job, because I get all these other pleasures out of working as a journalist.

But ultimately, it's hard to imagine another profession where you can so directly be a participant in the preservation of a free society. The government should be working for the people and not the other way around.

---

* *Thomas Jefferson, in a letter to William Charles Jarvis on July 28, 1820: "I know no safe depository of the ultimate powers of the society but the people themselves; and if we think them not enlightened enough to exercise their control with a wholesome discretion, the remedy is not to take it from them, but to inform their discretion by education. This is the true corrective of abuses of constitutional power."*

Philip Taubman   139

U.S. and Peking join in tracking missiles in Soviet Union

Station in China replaces
Iranian post lost in '79

by Philip Taubman

WASHINGTON, June 17—The United States and China are jointly operating an electronic intelligence-gathering station in China to monitor Soviet missile tests, according to senior American officials.

The facility was opened last year in a remote, mountainous region of the Xinjiang Uighur Autonomous Region in western China, near the Soviet border. Two key Soviet missile-testing bases are at Leninsk, near the Aral Sea, and at Sary-Shagan, near Lake Balkhash.

The establishment of the listening post involved a far deeper level of military cooperation between Washington and Peking than either Government had publicly acknowledged.

Sensitive Military Relationship

In Peking yesterday, at the conclusion of talks with Chinese leaders, Secretary of State Alexander M. Haig Jr. announced that the United States had decided in principle to sell arms to China. The United States had previously sold China only nonlethal military equipment.

Operation of the facility, which was not mentioned by Mr. Haig, brought the two nations into a sensitive, secret

---

Philip Taubman talks about this story on pgs. 131–133.

Copyright © 1981 by The New York Times Company. Reprinted by permission.

military relationship during the Carter Administration.

Officials said the post has filled a "critical" vacuum created when similar stations in Iran were abandoned during the Iranian revolution two years ago. They described the facility as one of Washington's most sensitive and important intelligence operations.

Shared by the Two Nations

Intelligence collected by the station is shared by the United States and China, officials said. The facility is furnished with American equipment and is manned by Chinese technicians. Advisers from the Central Intelligence Agency periodically visit the station.

American officials sought to keep the existence of the station secret, fearing that disclosure could adversely affect relations between the Soviet Union and the United States, and heighten tensions between the Soviet Union and China. In recent days, however, information about the operation has begun circulating openly here.

Soviet leaders, American officials said, are already seriously troubled by the growing relationship between Washington and Peking. They said the Soviet Union may already know about the facility but had not felt it necessary to respond because its presence was not a public embarrassment to them.

Anatoly F. Dobrynin, the Soviet Ambassador, in a meeting with American officials at the State Department today, condemned United States plans to lift restrictions on the sale of arms to China.

Disclosure of the monitoring post, officials here said, could also unsettle internal affairs in China, where moderate leaders may be vulnerable to charges that they made secret deals with the United States.

According to information pieced together from officials in the last eight months, the idea to set up listening posts in China was first proposed to the Peking Government in 1978, before the establishment of diplomatic relations. Initially, the Chinese were reluctant to agree, apparently concerned about cooperating too closely with the United States.

The idea was pressed again after the overthrow of Shah Mohammed Riza Pahlevi in January 1979. Senator Joseph R. Biden Jr., Democrat of Delaware, raised the issue with the Chinese in April 1979 when he led a Senate delegation to Peking. At the end of the visit, Senator Biden said that Deng Xiaoping, the Chinese leader, appeared sympathetic to the introduction of United States intelligence equipment into China, provided it was operated by the Chinese.

Formal agreement between the two Governments followed later in 1979, with the Chinese insisting that their technicians man the facilities and that operations be conducted in absolute secrecy.

Surveys for two facilities were made. The Chinese eventually agreed to permit only one, officials said.

The site in western China is close to ideal, officials said, because it allows monitoring of Soviet missile tests from launch through flight over Siberia to dispersion of warheads. It does not permit monitoring of the final stages of flight, including the re-entry of the warheads.

The monitoring of missile tests is critical to the verification of Soviet compliance with key provisions of strategic arms agreements. It permits the United States, for example, to detect whether new missiles are being developed.

The performance characteristics of missiles are detected in a number of ways, including tracing the missile with radar and monitoring data transmitted by radio signals.

Test Range Over Siberia

Typically, the United States would be seeking to determine the number of warheads the missile being tested can carry, its range, and the accuracy of re-entry vehicles that carry the warheads. Analysis of the information can show whether the missile is a new or old model or a variant.

The Soviet test base at Leninsk is used for testing intercontinental ballistic missiles, officials said. The test range extends out over Siberia, with re-entry over the Kamchatka Peninsula or the western Pacific.

The base at Sary-Shagan is used for testing antiballistic missile systems, according to officials.

The listening post in China can track tests from both sites, beginning with the launch.

Since normalization of relations between the United States and China in January 1979, the two nations have moved swiftly to forge a close friendship, marked by expanding trade and military cooperation.

The operation of a joint intelligence facility targeted on the Soviet Union, however, goes beyond any declared military cooperation.

Newsday

*"A reporter, when he is really, really good, can
approach art. Why not? There is artistry in it."*

ADRIAN PERACCHIO

When Adrian Peracchio was a child, he did not know that he wanted to become an American journalist. He did not even live in America.

Peracchio emigrated to the United States from Italy just before his 18th birthday. The Vietnam draft interrupted college at Cornell University, and in the Army he learned about journalism as a writer for *Stars and Stripes*. He never returned to college.

He worked for United Press International twice—once as a stringer in Europe after the Army and once in Connecticut when he came home. After working for three New England newspapers, he was hired by *Newsday* on Long Island in 1978.

Peracchio, 40, still lives in Connecticut and he commutes to Long Island. He speaks English with broad traces of his Italian accent. With lunch he orders Campari, an Italian liqueur Peracchio uses his journalistic experiences to craft non-fiction stories with the silky language of fiction. He studies fiction for its rhythm. His stories reflect consistent, careful attention to each word.

"An editor a long time ago told me, 'There are really two kinds of good reporters,'" says Peracchio. "'There are the lawyers and the poets. The lawyers you can't read and the poets you can't trust. If you can possibly manage to take the best of both, and not the worst of each, that's the best kind of reporter to be.'

"I am probably leaning more toward the poet, but I try to keep as much of the substance of a lawyer as I can. Clearly, I don't have the temperament to just be the lawyer."

Since 1981, Peracchio has worked on long-term projects at *Newsday*, usually as the head of a team of reporters. In 1983, the Reagan administration intervened in the case of Baby Jane Doe, a baby born with severe birth disorders whose parents had decided against surgery to correct the defects. A team of 12 *Newsday* reporters coordinated by

Peracchio wrote 10 stories about the Baby Doe case over three weeks, for which they were awarded a Pulitzer Prize in 1984.

Peracchio's regular assignment is the national desk, but he often free-lances pieces to *The Newsday Magazine,* published on Sunday. For the magazine he has written articles about AIDS, about the simple lies people live by ("The Lies of Everyday People"), and in one article called "The Missing Italian Connection," he wrote about his experiences as an Italian living in America. Although he admitted in that article that he likes American pizza much better than the original Neopolitan variety, he also conceded, "I still feel more Italian than Italian-American, and probably always will." ❖

from Adrian Peracchio

- The difference between the facts and the truth
- Whether journalists can be advocates
- The difference between cynicism and skepticism in a reporter

BEGINNINGS

I fell into journalism. I've always wanted to write. I've written quite a bit. I took some fiction and poetry writing when I was in college at Cornell. I originally had a scholarship to Cornell in biochemistry. It was so boring. Instead, I fell in love with James Joyce, and once I started reading *Ulysses* and *Finnegan's Wake*, it got me pretty far away from biochemistry.

It also got me much closer to getting drafted. News did not matter to me at that time. I was more concerned with the rhythm of the last paragraph in the story "The Dead" by Joyce than I was with the geopolitics of Indochina, which caught me like a hammer blow.

I got drafted. I was sent to basic training in the Army in the swamps of Louisiana, carrying an M-16. I still at that point didn't know what the hell I was doing. I was being given orders by some redneck sergeant who I couldn't understand half the time. I had only been in this country a few years, and my English was fine, but the cadences of Southern speech were not something that came to me very easily.

I developed such a dislike for this guy who had me do push-ups every five minutes that I decided that I was going to go to officers' school. I was one out of a class of 43 officer candidates who ended up going to Germany rather than Vietnam. It was pure luck.

When I got there I found out that I was assigned to command a platoon of five-ton dump trucks. There was a man there, too, but mostly it was the trucks, and that was when I took good stock of where I was being sent.

The only way I could think of to get out of there was to become a public information officer. They needed someone who was literate, and suddenly I was convincing the colonel that I could write the best news release he could possibly get. I'd never written any before, but I faked my way through it. I was transferred to Frankfurt, which was quite a good switch from the five-ton trucks. For about six months I was a public information officer, a flak. I also realized that really was not what I wanted to do for my next two years.

HIRED BY *STARS AND STRIPES*

I made friends with one of the editors of *Stars and Stripes,* which had a 50-50 composition of civilian and military reporters. I showed him some of the short stories that I had published in some obscure literary magazine back in Ithaca. He asked me to try out a few news stories, and I did. I was in short order transferred as a reporter to the *Stars and Stripes,* covering military affairs.

Some of the stories were sort of interesting. I was able to write about the strange kind of displacement that people who were relocating out of Vietnam felt, the so-called "delayed stress syndrome" among Vietnam veterans. I saw it because usually good stories come from the particular to the general. You notice something and you start seeing whether there is a pattern.

I saw one time a man that I had trained with in officer school, and I talked to him, and I found out some of the incredible resentment that was bubbling beneath. A lot of it had to do with the system of rotation that they used in Vietnam, which was one year in and out, very little camaraderie manifesting itself among the men, essentially a lack of feeling of purpose of what everybody was doing there.

Then I started talking to other people who had returned from Vietnam, and I put together a series of stories. I developed some respect for the *Stars and Stripes* because they were willing to tackle some hard stories. That got me through my two years.

IN EUROPE FOR UPI

At the same time I had become friends through professional contact with the bureau chief of UPI in Frankfurt, and he had asked me whether I was willing to do some free-lance stringer work.

So when I got out of the Army, I traveled for about nine months through Europe, taking assignments as a stringer. I filed stories from time to time and got enough money to keep myself going. I drove straight to Sweden, and as it got colder I would go south. I got myself to

Turkey, through Greece, and eventually I sold the car and shipped myself back to the States.

DID NOT RETURN TO COLLEGE

I never felt that it was a disadvantage that I didn't finish college. I sometimes wish I had, but not for the professional training, more as an intellectual accomplishment. My academic training was essentially in literature. I took a lot of courses in politics, in government and political science and economics at Cornell because those things interested me, and those things can be very useful, very handy in understanding things.

I did not necessarily find that a lack of formal training in the craft of journalism harmed me. A lot of it I picked up on my own by reading about it and, more important, by reading the kind of journalism that I was aiming for, whether it was the [New York] *Times* or *Esquire* magazine or *The New Yorker,* and studying it.

You learn by studying the mechanics of the craft itself, whether you are reading John Hersey or Seymour Hersh. You read for structure and depth. For example, I love the stories by John McPhee in *The New Yorker* because he's able to take the most arcane subject and go into it so deeply that you are fascinated by it. It's like the exploration of a strange land.

Or you can read someone like Seymour Hersh and realize the kind of digging he had to do to obtain the kind of information that ultimately was so damaging. How did he do it? Who did he talk to? What kind of process did he go through? What kind of documentation did he use?

You also can learn a great deal by reading. Joan Didion, for example, is able to counterpoint her stories with atmospherics and the nuances of personality, of landscape, the novelistic techniques that she brings to her writing. You should also read journalists who have turned novelists, like Ward Just, who is a wonderful short story writer. He used his experiences to write short stories. This can apply to journalism.

Those things help me a great deal, but I'm just a voracious reader. It's about my only hobby.

TO *THE BRIDGEPORT POST* AND UPI

When I got back here in 1970, I was bitten by the bug. My brother was living in a suburb of Bridgeport [Conn.], so I got a job at *The Bridgeport Post,* a large but utterly undistinguished and very mediocre paper in Connecticut. Within six months I was made a city hall bureau chief, which wasn't very much of an accomplishment because there was utterly no competition. It's a place where you can get a lot of experience very quickly doing a lot of very poor stories. You do get front-page bylines. There was good, lousy dirty politics, the classic machine politics.

Within a year I was working at UPI in Bridgeport. Some nights I would crank out 20 different stories—very short, a page-and-a-half apiece—and then rewrite them for radio. The first couple of months I was the early man, and I had to trudge through the snow from my apartment to the bureau, which was in a place where hookers also seemed to hang out, so I would wave to them and open up the bureau. I remember one of them saying, "Don't bother with that guy. It's not worth it. He opens up the bureau."

There was this whole frantic race against the clock. You had to punch in the weather on this teletype at 5 o'clock in the morning to every little tiny radio station in the state. Along with that, you had to rewrite for radio very quickly all the overnight stats [statistics] that were left over by the poor wretch who was working the night shift.

The worst part was not rewrite, but the fact that—I'm basically a three- or four-finger typist and I'm also sloppy—you had to type on a teletype with a two-second delay, which means that nothing you typed would appear until two seconds later, including all your mistakes. I was in a cold sweat every morning, hoping I wouldn't screw that up.

As soon as you finished the weather, you had to send that and then rewrite about 20 stories to radio-ese. By that time, you had to start making calls to every police agency in the state to get all the facts and names and you wrote that out. I was the only person there. By 10 o'clock people were beginning to trickle in, and I was half numb.

It was pretty dreadful. But I don't really put it down. It's something that you have to go through. You realize the kind of news that has to be cranked out daily to feed this enormous maw that we all need. That only lasted about three or four months until I began to cover the legislature.

In the legislature you get to see the workings of government at close quarters, which does not necessarily endear you to it or make you any more respectful of it. In fact, it makes you sort of cynical at times, especially since you knew perfectly well that you were going to end up writing something that you knew would not necessarily be the truth.

DIFFERENCE BETWEEN THE FACTS AND THE TRUTH

You were constrained—by time, by form, by the very nature of what you were doing. That became the real frustration because I knew that I would be reporting things that were accurate, they were objective, they were balanced, and they were utterly, utterly misleading in some cases. That became one of the limitations of journalism that I could see rather clearly at that point. I'm not talking about advocacy journalism at all, not at all, because I'm very much against the notion of advocacy journalism.

What I'm talking about is the ability to be able to use your powers of observation, of analysis, to do a service to an intelligent reader who also knows that a 300-word story from UPI or AP on what is being done to a certain bill is nothing but the barest dusting of snow on the iceberg. It's not even the tip of the iceberg. There is much more to it than that. You need the wire-service story, but you need much more than that to understand what is going on.

The facts are not necessarily the truth. I'm not saying that you can necessarily get the truth, but you can discover more than simply unadorned facts. You can gather so many facts from so many different sources that you are able to put together a picture that will push the knowledge of something beyond what it is.

For example, what I am working on right now. There is a tremendous battle in the New York legislature over medical malpractice. The rates have been jacked up over 50 percent in the last year, which would mean that a neurosurgeon in New York state would be paying about $100,000 simply in insurance premiums a year, which sounds outrageous. It is, in many ways. The battle is between the medical groups and some of the trial lawyers who are representing the plaintiffs in these cases.

Stated very boldly, the way a wire service would be constrained to do the story would be precisely that—"The medical society argues that the claims or the awards be restricted in certain ways in order to reduce the rates and enable the doctors to survive in an atmosphere of rising suits. The lawyers say that is not the case, there is no crisis. The doctors are perfectly able to absorb the increases in premiums, and the victims should be given their legal prerogatives."

That is perfectly respectable. It is a good statement of what the controversy is about. It tells you absolutely *nothing* about the nature of the crisis itself. For example, the medical society will tell you that, yes, indeed, it is true that a neurosurgeon will have to pay $100,000. It fails to tell you that a good neurosurgeon in New York City or Long Island makes about $1 million a year and that that figure [$100,000], when it is taken off before taxes, is not really such a tremendous amount as it would appear.

So you have to dig beneath it. You also have to try to find out what percentage of the doctors are involved in what percentage of malpractice suits. No one is going to tell you that. For that, you have to be able to go through court records, you have to be able to dig them out and count them, and see patterns. You can say, "Is that advocacy journalism?" I don't think it is at all.

Advocacy journalism is when you take a certain political point of view. You use reporting to back up that point of view, which I think is a travesty of journalism. If you are going to be a proponent of something, don't masquerade yourself as a journalist.

WORKING AT THE BERGEN *RECORD* AND THE *BOSTON HERALD*

So I decided that I had to do something rather than simply report basically the bare bones of the surface of the news. At that point you have to decide to go one of two ways. You can go to broadcasting, but with the exception of the very small percentage of broadcast journalists who are able or who get the time, the money, and the particular freedom to do a great deal of digging, you're going to end up doing nothing but a glamorized kind of wire-service reporting.

I didn't see myself as very much of a talking head. I also like to write. I know that you can do some fine writing in broadcast as well. It takes a certain kind of skill. But it's not what I particularly wanted. I wanted to be able to use language to the fullest. It's a little bit pretentious, but nevertheless.

I decided to apply to get a job at a newspaper that would give me some freedom to expand myself, to stretch myself, to stretch whatever abilities I might have had. I settled on the Bergen (New Jersey) *Record,* which is a large daily in New Jersey, which has a rather fine reputation within the industry. The circulation was close to 200,000 on Sunday, a bit less on weekdays. They hired me at the lower level. It was known among us as the snake pit. I have never seen a place where the competition among reporters was quite that keen.

There was this group of ferrets, gnashing at each other. Many of them were from Ivy League schools, many of them were from Columbia. I was just as competitive as every other little ferret walking around. I was perhaps a little older, in my late 20s.

One story was a reconstruction of a drug deal. I was talking to smugglers. I set up a trail from the wholesaler to the retailer in Bergen County. I was able to go along on one of the deals. In one case, I was blindfolded. It was one way to find out what was done, the kind of language that was used, the techniques they were using. They in turn had to trust me.

I was at *The Record* for three years. Then I went to the *Boston Herald.* We successfully documented the fact that some state officials were giving out contracts and these officials were also closely involved with the companies that were benefiting. It was just classic dogged document hunts.

It was a great deal of sifting through reports, the filing of corporations, annual reports, ownership files, and tax records. There is a certain kind of person for whom this is the equivalent of *crème fraîche.* They just lap it up. For me, it was just a means to, "Let's get through this stuff so I can write a good paragraph about it." The actual process was sheer undiluted drudgery most of the time. But some reporters find this exciting.

Within a few months at the *Boston Herald*, it wasn't just the hand-writing on the wall, it was five-foot high graffiti in day-glo orange that I was in the wrong place.

HIRED AT *NEWSDAY* THE SECOND DAY

Newsday gave me a tryout for a week. The day after the tryout, I was offered the job. It was a good tryout. I was lucky, there was a plane crash. An engine jacket had fallen out of the plane as it was coming down and crashed in a residential neighborhood.

It was a good hard-news story with every single fact in there, tightly written. I interviewed damn near anybody who had seen just a little bit of shrapnel from the plane, including babysitters who heard this crash. I canvassed the whole neighborhood. I went over to the FAA [Federal Aviation Administration]. I rushed over to Kennedy [Airport], and I took a photographer to take a picture of the engine. I talked to former air controllers to see if this thing had happened before. Anyway, it was a classic story.

I was hired by *Newsday* at a much higher salary, and I had finally reached the top rank of papers. I started out being a local reporter. I had to go through the grind once again. I had to hunt down stories and try to develop good ones. Within three months, I was given good general assignment stories. Pretty soon I started to get national assignments.

QUALITIES OF A GOOD REPORTER

A good reporter must have a great deal of curiosity, intelligent curiosity. If you want to be a good investigative reporter, you need doggedness, you need a real ability to withstand tedium. A lot of investigative reporting is a bloody bore, and you just have to plow through moun-tains of things that seem to be meaningless and trivial and trite to get to really good stuff.

You have to have endurance more than anything else. And you need a sense of outrage, a keenly developed sense of outrage. If you don't have that, you cease to care. Maybe caring is something that you need, too, for good reporting. The very last thing that I would want in a reporter is cynicism. Skepticism, yes.

Skepticism is listening to everything and accepting very little of it until you can ascertain whether it's true or not, keeping a lot in mind. Cynicism is the foregone conclusion in your mind that everything you listen to is pure crap. I'm not saying it terribly elegantly, but cynicism is essentially a loser's game, and I think too many people in journalism effect a pose of cynicism. But it's detrimental to the readers or to the listeners.

Reporting is all work, hard work. I'm in respectful awe of really, really good reporters even if they are lousy writers because sometimes I lose patience with reporting and I want to get down to writing. My greater strength does lie in writing, organization and being able to precisely balance out the reporting with the writing.

Good writing is very important. In my own personal list, I put it at the top. I am constantly in a struggle to try to balance reporting and writing. Good writing is very hard work, but it's an excruciating kind of fun.

DEFINITION OF GOOD WRITING

Good writing is perceptiveness and sensibility applied to language—the ability to observe and to use those observations to recreate a scene, a whole landscape, an ambiance, a personality. If you're doing hard news, good writing is the ability to be able to observe enough so that you give the reader a sense of everything that you observed and reported, organized in a way that the reader has a sense that the story is not just a report filed by some bureaucrat without a sense of time, place, season or people.

Journalists have to understand the substance of a story, but they also have to give some of the texture. A reporter, when he is really, really good, can approach art. Why not? There is artistry in it.

ORGANIZING WHAT YOU WRITE

Organization is very important. I find inexperienced reporters and writers show their inexperience in their lack of organization, even more so than in the body of their writing. In journalism, organization is a tightness of reasoned argument, which is not an argument ultimately, but the selecting of exactly the right things in exactly the right places, buttressing them with the right argument. It's not at all the inverted pyramid form. An investigative story is more like a legal argument. A feature story is more like a narrative story. It's not a news story. A news story is very easy to structure.

Ultimately, writing a good news story—to make a horrible generalization—is really very simple. All you have to do is observe what you're doing, take some notes, have the right quotes, have a few facts, do some clip work, do some background. A good journeyman reporter can scratch that out in 20 minutes. That's no trick. That's like writing a memo. But it has that inevitable kind of dead, flat tone, and sometimes has to be that way.

If you're going to write a story about Bangladesh and 10,000 people are dying, that's a complicated story but still it has that basic kind of news organization. You can do it, and you can do it tightly, and many kinds of reporters can do it very well.

But it's when you go beyond that, when you try to explain after a lot of reporting, for a hypothetical example, the failure of the government to do the kind of planning that should have been done [in Bangladesh], the kind of relief work that should have been done—that's where organization comes in. That's where you really have to select everything tightly and just not waste a single bit of space. And that's where some artistry comes in, where you go a step beyond writing news.

HOW I WRITE

When I am ready to write a story, I first read everything I have. I type up every bit of notes I have. Then I have a stack of memos to myself, a distillation of all the work I have done. You are under too much time constraint to go over every slip of paper just before you write, so I use the memos. After I read through the whole thing, I start writing the way I would tell the story to someone on the phone.

The story structures itself. I check my notes to verify the actual quotes. I catalog my notes. At the front of each notebook, I list on the inside cover the date and who I talked to. In each file, I list every single phone number of the people I have talked to. I also list a description of each person I have interviewed. You can't keep that kind of information in a Rol-o-dex.

I am naturally a very messy and disorganized person. But I developed this system of organization out of desperation. I was drowning in paper. Every morning I would push aside this drowning sea on my desk. In my personal life, I am very messy. But when it comes to work I am compulsively organized.

"LOVE STORIES"

That's how I developed the article "Love Stories." Love doesn't make news. It is the drastic murders. But it is very rare in stories that we see the first manifestation of human emotion. These people stuck in my mind. What struck me was the sheer intensity of their feelings. These are people who were very private people—people who I could not have used easily—people who made lousy sources.

One of the stories had to do with two older people. One was quite personal. One interview was with this priest, a little glimpse of himself. One was a conversation with a veteran who poured his heart out to me.

Their stories at the time they told them were out of sync with what I was writing about. But I went back through my notes, which I had cataloged, to put them together. They are true. They are real. They say something important. Certain things I think of as literature rather than journalism.

COVERING THE NAPLES EARTHQUAKE

I was sent to Italy to cover the earthquake and to develop a series of stories there. It was not just straight journalism. In Italy, we used the wires [wire services] to cover the basic news, but what I was there for was to do a series of five stories about the kinds of problems that occurred and to give a picture of what it looked like.

I was in a rented Fiat in the valleys south of Naples, driving from one destroyed village to another. In each village there was the stench of death over everything. You had to wear one of those surgical masks drenched in cologne so you could stand it. There were stacks of bodies that had been dug up from the rubble.

After a while there was a sense of numbness. I didn't even know how to tell the story. It was almost too much. Then I saw this woman dressed completely in black, the way the peasants do in that area. She was sitting in a kitchen chair in the middle of all that broken masonry, and so I stopped the car, and started walking toward her, and there were fluttering leaves from her child's school notebook around her, and some crockery that was broken.

She was just sitting there with her hands in her lap just staring at nothing. I went up to her, and I asked her in Italian, "Who are you?" She didn't answer. Again I asked, "Who are you? Did you live here?" She didn't even turn to me. She kept staring.

Then she said in this empty voice that I can't forget, "Non sono nessuna."—"I am nobody," she said. "Yesterday I was a mother, a wife, and a grandmother, and today I'm nobody." It was clear what she meant. Everybody had died. It was almost like being in a strange kind of sacred place. I thought about taking photographs, and then I thought that might be desecration. I didn't take a photograph.

I got into the car and started driving away. About a mile down the road, I realized, "I have the lead." And just as I was feeling a sense of exaltation, I realized, "Oh God, what a shit." I felt like a complete vulture, like some kind of bird of prey who had come over to peck. I had an amazing feeling of revulsion about what I was doing. At the same time I knew that was the way the story should be told.

And I felt this kind of odd tension, that I was prying, that I was witnessing something that I should perhaps not have witnessed. I had intruded on a terrible kind of privacy. I call it an epiphany, and I think it was. It gave me this kind of ambivalence about what I was doing.

THE ETHICS OF PRIVACY

A lot of ethical issues have to do with privacy. I don't feel very much compunction when it comes to exposing anything that has to do with public figures. When you're talking about lawyers or politicians, they're fair game. I have absolutely no empathy. They use us, we use them. Sometimes they use us more successfully than we use them. Sometimes we use them more successfully. It's symbiosis, parasitism.

The other folks are the equivalent of the family in Beirut being shelled by both sides. They are the ants on which the warring elephants trample. I feel a great deal of ambivalence when it comes to involving private people who have never chosen to be in the limelight, who have never chosen to have their lives exposed to the kind of acid corrosion that comes from being examined by the media, by us. They never ask for it, and here they are.

Anyone who has had a private tragedy occur to them—whether a murder has occurred, or somebody has killed a member of their family—and suddenly we're on them like a pack of hyenas. Our own competitiveness makes inevitable that we're going to tear apart every single shred of privacy these people have. This is a news target, in a sense. Do we have a right to do it?

It goes against all my instincts as a newspaperman to say, "We should put limitations on ourselves. We should not go after certain things." I don't like that. I know instinctively that's bad. But I also have an incredible distaste for the kind of havoc we can create in people's lives.

I've seen this kind of helplessness in people's faces, like I'm some kind of natural disaster that has happened to them. They seem to be powerless. And I don't give them a choice. They're news. People sometimes become much more open than they realize they're being. We know it, and we certainly don't discourage it.

"DON'T EVER TRUST A WRITER"

Does it necessarily help us understand the situation better? I don't know. The writer in me tells me yes. But whatever there is in me that is ethical tells me no. The writer is a voyeur. The writer is a hell of a user. Joan Didion said something like that at the beginning of *Slouching Towards Bethlehem*—"Don't ever trust a writer." She's right. A writer will sell you down the river for a story. I've done it. I do it.

[Right now] I'm interviewing malpractice victims. I'm dragging out of their lives some of the most excruciating pain that people have gone through. Their names are public record, it's all out there. We're going

Adrian Peracchio   155

through records, we're interviewing legal and medical experts, and that's all very nice and bloodless. But what makes a story ultimately is when you finally confront the mother who has the child dragged out of her with forceps when she should have had a Caesarean and the child is now brain damaged with an IQ of 40 at age seven.

What I want from them is feelings. I don't want facts. I want more than facts. I want the kind of sleeplessness, I want to know the pain, I want to know the agony, I want to know the changes they have gone through, I want to know the sense of self they have lost. I want something that I have no right to. The writer in me tells me, "I want everything. I want it all. I want it." Then sometimes I feel like a complete shit. I really do.

I am telling you these things that are terrible about the news process, but I would never live in a society where there is no access to good press, where the press doesn't at least make an attempt to be objective, even if they don't always succeed, even though everything we do is flawed and necessarily tinged by our own experience, our own subjectivity.

COVERING BABY JANE DOE

[In 1983, a young couple in Suffolk County decided against surgery for their infant, who was suffering from a number of birth disorders. Federal authorities intervened to challenge the couple's right to make that decision. Reporters knew the names of the people involved, but never revealed them. The baby became Baby Jane Doe.]

The Baby Doe case began with one reporter who was covering courts. Kathy Kerr [the reporter] had the good news judgment to say, "This is one hell of a story. This is not just one case. This touches on major issues."

The whole issue came out as the result of a legal action. But many legal actions go on that never see the light of day. This one was news. Why? Because it was a big social-political issue. The reason why we won the Pulitzer Prize was not because we covered the legal story, but because we pointed out the ambiguities and the terrible choices that had to be made.

One of the network of informants who were sympathetic to the right-to-life movement filed a brief. She [Kathy Kerr] found the brief. She won the confidence of the couple, the hospital officials and the other people involved. She developed rapport. Then we used a computer search to dig out all the literature in scholarly journals as well as the press.

Kathy Kerr obtained a list of the cases that the Justice Department was working on to find out which ones were still being investigated. We were working 18 hours a day because the case was about to come up. I did not come into the story until a bit later. Several people were assigned to go to different parts of the country. Baby Doe was about to die any minute. There was a very definite time constraint. I coordinated the kind of reporting that would be done. People were filing reports to me. My story was the centerpiece.

In the Baby Doe case, there is no question that a couple's lives were altered beyond recognition by the intervention of public scrutiny. By the act of observing, someone changes what he observes. It's a simple physics law. We are observers, even when we try to be as objective as possible. When we focus our attention, that very act alters the event. We are *not* innocents. Even those of us who are not necessarily cynics are not innocents.

NOT NECESSARILY MY BEST

I would not necessarily consider the Baby Doe story my best story. I reported the story in three days and wrote the story in five hours on a Friday night for Sunday. It was not a story that I care intensely about, but the story had social and political significance. We decided to bring out the very human faces, the effect that this was having on people's lives. That is what made this a big story.

You are lucky to be in the hopper. It is luck. Some of the best assignments come out as a result of luck. The fact that I have won the [Pulitzer] prize did not change me. It did give me a certain kind of distinction. But we shouldn't write stories for prizes. I know that some editors do. We should write stories because they are good stories.

TIME IS AN OGRE

I would like to write fiction. I have started. But my work is too absorbing. You have no psychic stamina left. That is why there are so many divorces in our profession. It takes too much time. You are not in it for the money. It absorbs you, it drains you.

Very often I think a spouse would find it very difficult. You are married to your job. It takes you away at unpredictable times in a very, very destructive way. To become a very successful journalist, there are some trade-offs. You have to be prepared to sacrifice deep, important relationships to a business which can be something of an ogre because the news never stops.

It is the unpredictability that does you in, the lack of control. You are at the mercy of the news—a coup in Central Amercia, a plane crash in Queens. In other professions you can work long hours but you usually control them. Now I can control it. I don't have to go out on a plane crash anymore. That is a degree of control. Do I enjoy journalism? Journalism, yes. Reporting on fires, no.

Love stories

by Adrian Peracchio

The Visit. He sat on the edge of the vinyl-covered couch in the lounge of the nursing home like someone waiting for a date. He had a look of pleased expectancy and a touch of unconscious anxiety in the way he kept glancing at the clock on the wall.

There was something vaguely military in his erect bearing, the sharp creases of his tweed suit and the mirror polish on his cordovan brogans. In his hands, he held a small bouquet of violets tied with a pink ribbon and a book that he would shift from time to time so he could smooth his ginger mustache with his thumb.

"It's always like that, every day for the last two years," the nurse whispered, pointing him out. "Always a nice suit, always neat and clean. Always a book. And the violets. I don't know where he gets them. He has the nicest manners."

He rose and shook his visitor's hand with formal cordiality.

"Good, you're early," he told the visitor. "We'll have plenty of time before we see her. I don't like to keep her waiting. She's got a fiery temper, you know, just like her red hair. She's always been high-spirited and hasn't changed a bit. It's the Irish in her. Ran me ragged when we first married, but she's kept me young."

This is one story excerpted from a collection of four stories by Adrian Peracchio for a Newsday *Sunday magazine cover article. Peracchio talks about this story on pgs. 153–154.*

© *Adrian Peracchio.*

He led the way to a coffee-dispensing machine in a staff conference room and greeted a receptionist by her first name. He looked fit, and his skin had the fine, leathery wrinkles of someone who has spent a good deal of time outdoors. His easy, loping stride and the smoothness of his gestures were those of a man at least a decade younger than his 69 years.

"I know this place better than my own kitchen," he said with a wry grin, giving a sharp slap to the side of the machine to dislodge the sticking paper cup from the chute.

He had retired from his job—he said something dismissive about marketing and advertising—four years earlier. He and his wife had looked forward to it, planned for it. Years before, they had bought an oceangoing sailboat. He, an Annapolis man, had never lost his love of the sea, or the skills to sail it. She had been as enthusiastic about sailing as he. With no children and only an aging black Labrador retriever to care for, they would follow the intercoastal highway south every year on vacation and dream of the day they could close their small house on Long Island Sound and set sail for the Caribbean.

And for almost two years, they did just that. They rented their house to a young couple, packed provisions, their dog and at least three dozen of the mystery novels that she devoured daily and sailed south, living their dream. For weeks on end, they sailed along the necklace of islands to which they had flown only for a week or 10 days at a time when they were young.

"It was like a long, long honeymoon," he said. "We were like young kids again, but it was even better. We even went skinny-dipping at night, if you can believe that. We caught pompano and redfish and broiled them on the beach. We did nothing we didn't feel like doing." From a creased wallet, he carefully took out a color photograph. Framed by a tilting mast and taut rigging was a handsome woman in her late 50s, in white shorts and a blue blouse tied above a tan midriff. The background was the preternaturally turquoise water of the Caribbean and a curving scythe of white sand fringed with coconut palms. She was shielding her eyes from the sun and holding on to the mast with her other hand, smiling broadly. Her body looked taut and still supple.

One day, in the Antilles, the tremors began. They were not serious at first, but she was scared. He turned the boat around and headed north. A month later, in Puerto Rico, a doctor diagnosed Parkinson's disease. The degeneration of her nervous system was unusually accelerated and severe. Gradually, she became unable to help with the sailing. He left the boat with a broker and flew back to Long Island with her. There were complications of her disease, pneumonia. As her body failed, he did everything he could for her, carrying her in his arms from room to room, cleaning her and feeding her. "I made a game of it, but it was harder and harder," he said. One day, she had to enter a nursing home. And his daily visits to her began. They were his only goal, his only structure. The sailboat was sold at a loss. The dog had died the year before. The house was sold to pay for the medical bills, and now he lived in a small basement apartment within walking distance of the nursing home.

"She loves flowers, especially violets," he said. "She used to grow them in a little greenhouse I built for her. I don't want her to know I had to sell the house, so I have found a florist who'll grow them for me, as a favor. They make her day. You'll see. Her face just lights right up. You know, she's still a beautiful woman, even with what's happened to her."

A nurse led her down the long corridor to the recreation area in a wheelchair. The woman was not really sitting in it. She was arranged and strapped in the chair, and her limbs were splayed at odd angles. She looked not so much shrunken as imploded, as if the cytoplasm of her cells had been suddenly sucked out and the husk of her body had drooped on the bones. Thin strands of rust-streaked hair remained on her scalp. Her head nodded uncontrollably, and her face had the vacuity of a state beyond hopelessness.

He sat next to her and gently, very gently, placed the small bouquet of flowers in her hands, folding her clawed fingers over the stems. He looked up smiling, but what he saw in his visitor's eyes caused his smile to fade.

"She's not looking her best today," he said softly, turning aside from her. "Sometimes she can't sleep, you know, so they give her drugs." He looked at her again. "She's a little uneasy with strangers," he told his visitor, "so, if you don't mind. . . . " His eyes were beginning to brim with tears, but his voice was steady and cheerful, as he turned to her and said, "Dear, you'll love this. I found this new detective novel by that English fellow, the one you've always liked. It's a long one, so let me start reading. . . . "

T E N

"One of the questions I always get from young blacks is, 'Is it hard to be a black woman working for The Wall Street Journal?' *I don't think it's hard. Sometimes it puts you in a situation where everybody is not totally comfortable with who you are, but that's their problem."*

LINDA WILLIAMS

Linda Williams has spent most of her career writing about people that *The Wall Street Journal* rarely covers. She has written about a poor family in Philadelphia whose son was an innocent bystander killed in gang warfare, a story about a child prostitute who was killed in Oregon, and a story about a retarded woman whose baby died of starvation.

Williams, 34, came from a family of sharecroppers, and her first trip away from her North Carolina home was to take an internship at *The Philadelphia Inquirer* when she was in college. She worked her way through the University of North Carolina at Chapel Hill with the help of a scholarship and loans.

After college, she learned how to cover education by following integration in Raleigh, North Carolina, for the Raleigh *News & Observer.* "School board meetings went on until the middle of the night," she says. "People called you on the phone and screamed about every story."

In Raleigh, she was the only black reporter in a newsroom with 50 reporters. Soon she tired of being stereotyped. "I found myself the black reporter covering the black story regardless of whether it had merit or not—the visiting speaker who happened to be black." When the African ambassador from Ghana came to town, for example, *The News & Observer* sent Williams. "I didn't know anything about it," she says.

Williams worked at two other Southern newspapers covering education, and then she became a Ford Fellow in Educational Journalism, a program sponsored by the Ford Foundation and George Washington University to give education reporters a chance to study a single aspect of education. Williams focused on public financing for Southern schools.

This led to a job for four years at the Portland *Oregonian,* and then, in 1983, Williams went to work for *The Wall Street Journal* in Atlanta. Like most *Journal* reporters, she must cover daily business details, with an occasional chance to write a front-page feature.

"To be a good reporter at *The Wall Street Journal*," she says, "you need to be able to get an idea, focus the idea on something that's manageable and do the kind of solid, careful reporting to execute the idea. I like the idea of having an idea and executing it. One of the good things about working at the *Journal* is you have a great deal of influence over what goes in the paper in your features. The weight is on you, the responsibility is on you to come up with the ideas." ❖

- Minorities in journalism
- What it means to be a reporter at a newspaper with a special-ized audience and philosophy like *The Wall Street Journal*
- How to make business features interesting

BEGINNINGS

I grew up in Fayetteville, North Carolina. My father was in the Army. I have three brothers and three sisters and hundreds of cousins. No one in my family was a journalist. In fact, no one in my family had been to college before I went to college.

My father grew up on a rice plantation off the coast of Charleston, North Carolina, and was fortunate enough to be one of the children who got to go to high school in Charleston. He joined the Army because he didn't want to go back to the rice plantation. My mother came from generally the same sort of background. Her family were sharecroppers who moved into the city. She has worked as a maid most of her life. She still works as a maid. She's worked in hospitals, laboring, doing things like that.

My mother did not finish high school until after I graduated from high school. The people in my family read a lot, but they were not educated. As a consequence, I read a lot as a child, and a world was opened up to me that would not have ordinarily been there, given the family circumstances.

My father, through reading and intellectual pursuits, was one out-standing element of my family. I think I got my mother's real sense of outrage. She's the kind of person who counts the change in the line at the grocery store and can always tell you when there's a penny missing. And she speaks out.

I went to college on partial scholarship and loans and working. I started at the University of North Carolina at Chapel Hill in 1970. I took my first course in journalism in my sophomore year and decided that was going to be my major. Actually, I had a double major—journalism and history. I literally wandered into the school of journalism and enrolled in a journalism course.

I never worked for the campus newspaper, but I got interested in some other publications. The black students had a newspaper, *Black Ink,* and I worked on writing and editing and did the layout for that paper for a while. I worked as a volunteer newswriter briefly for WCAR, the campus radio station. It didn't seriously dawn on me that journalism could be a career until I got an internship at *The Philadelphia Inquirer.* Again, that was a case of luck.

I went into the school of journalism one morning for class, and I saw Dean Adams. He was coming out of his office with two guys. He said, "I want you to meet these people. They're from *The Philadelphia Inquirer,* and they're looking for interns." I got the interview right there.

It was a summer internship. My salary was $189 a week. I was there during the summer of 1973 for about four months. It was really frightening, being in a big city and working for a big newspaper. I hadn't ever been away from North Carolina except for traveling to see my father's family.

At the time, the *Inquirer* had an Action Line. I did that for about a month, and then I moved into the newsroom. Basically I worked a lot of nights, did a lot of accidents, homicides and near-homicides—interviewing the victims at Temple University Hospital.

I did a feature story on gangs. That seemed to be a particularly bad summer for gang warfare, the summer of '73. The *Philadelphia Daily News* was keeping a box score of the number of youths killed in gang warfare. I still think it's probably the most difficult story I've ever done in my career, interviewing the family of a kid who was killed who was an innocent bystander.

They were a poor family, and they did not have a telephone. There was no way to call and prepare them beforehand. It's my nightmare to have to confront someone who's grieving. They knew he was dead. He had been dead for a few days, but they were not interested in talking to the press. The father had been bombed in Philadelphia since they had moved there, and he was disabled. The family was living hand-to-mouth when this happened. It was very hard. I was really a tenderfoot.

So I knocked on the door and explained who I was. I explained to them that I knew it was a difficult time, but perhaps a lot of people did not know that many of the kids who were being killed were not gang members, not involved in anything illegal, and I had heard that their son was one of those kids. He had never been in trouble before.

They opened up at that point. They were fairly inarticulate people, and it was still very difficult to get the kind of things that you need for a newspaper story—to talk about their son, to talk about where they came from, how long they had been there, just who this kid was, what he was interested in.

TALKING TO PRIVATE PEOPLE

What I try to remember in talking to people like this is that they don't understand the rules. They don't always understand that everything they say is fair game, that it will be in the paper. I take a lot more time explaining what the article is about, and explaining that if there's anything they don't want in the paper, they should tell me beforehand. Whereas the kind of people that I interview on a day-to-day basis for *The Wall Street Journal*—you assume they know the rules, and I don't spend a lot of time explaining.

WORKING AT *THE NEWS & OBSERVER*

I graduated in 1974, and right after college, I went to work for *The News & Observer* in Raleigh [North Carolina] for $135 a week. They were looking for a black reporter. There weren't any black reporters there at the time. *The News & Observer* had a staff of about 50 reporters.

I started at *The News & Observer* covering education. It had not been the beat that would get you on the front page until that point, that would get you awards and attention, that upwardly mobile reporters were interested in. I really don't have a lot of fond memories of that period. I was covering education at a time when there were two very, very hot issues locally. Segregation was still an issue and an even bigger issue was the proposed merger of the Raleigh and Wake County school districts.

The Wake County school district was mostly white, growing rapidly, fairly affluent. The Raleigh school district was getting blacker at that time. It was not a majority black school system, but it was generally at what education people call the tipping point. When a school district gets about 30 percent black, the theory then was they will become a majority black within a very short period of time. I didn't feel that I was covering education. I was covering the politics of education, which is completely different. At that time, people in education were not used to much scrutiny. Education was the light feature, like covering the ball games, the PTA charity drive. Educators were not accustomed to questions about finance—what are you spending the money for?

I learned that education is covered very poorly in this country. You have to really spend some time in the classroom watching teachers in action, watching students in action before you understand what the process of education is all about.

A MOVE TO MISSISSIPPI

I went to Mississippi in the fall of 1976 and worked for the *Delta Democrat-Times*. It's a small paper, with about 40,000 circulation. I was only there a few months, and then I moved to the *South Mississippi Sun*. It had a small circulation, about 15,000 when I was there. I was there for about two years covering education and health and general assignment. Then I got a Ford Fellowship to study how schools are financed in the South.

AT *THE OREGONIAN*

In 1979, I went to the Portland *Oregonian*. I went down to Salem for 11 months and covered state government. Covering state government was boring, very boring—getting in there and talking to all the faceless gnomes. I also covered business as well as general assignment.

I did one story with another reporter about a young woman in Oregon who was killed. She had been working as a prostitute. And I think it opened a lot of people's eyes as to how police departments, in general, treat cases of teen-agers who are missing and how child prostitution was working in their community. You couldn't bring the girl back to life, but it was the kind of story that moved people emotionally and made people think.

Then the National Association of Black Journalists met in New Orleans in 1983. I wasn't really looking for a job, but I made an appointment with *The Wall Street Journal* and went for an interview. I've been in Atlanta for the *Journal* since then.

WORKING FOR *THE WALL STREET JOURNAL*

When I came to Atlanta, I was told that this is a business newspaper and that occasionally I would get to do fun things like front-page features, but I would have to cover business—companies that are publicly traded. And *The Wall Street Journal* has a particular style and a particular mode of operation.

We cover Virginia, the Carolinas, Georgia, Alabama, Mississippi and Tennessee. *Wall Street Journal* reporters also work for the Dow Jones financial wire, so you're several things in working for the *Journal*— you're a wire-service reporter, a feature writer, and a basic daily newspaper reporter who grinds it out day-to-day.

You work for an editor, but it's also a free-lance operation in some respects. The front-page feature sections are run by people in New York whom you don't know, and they really don't know that much about you. You have to submit proposals to them the way a free-lancer would to a magazine, explaining what you're going to do in some detail.

There's a lot of competition for the feature spaces in the paper, and you have to convince them that you're going to bring something to the story that no other publication is bringing to that story, and that you're going to be able to deliver it in a reasonable amount of time. The same people in New York have control over editing and timing. If you've been around long enough, you may have met them once. I have many, many masters.

We basically look at companies that are traded on the stock exchange. That's our basic, day-to-day function. But you're also looking for stories about those businesses that are interesting to business people elsewhere that say something significant about the industry, perhaps how the industry is changing or how a particular company has been able to solve a problem.

A lot of business reporting is like covering politics. There are the takeover fights and the people jostling internally for control, and the shareholders' revolts and the winners and the losers—just like politics.

HOW TO COVER BUSINESS

To get ready for this assignment, I started reading *The Wall Street Journal* regularly. I had always read the paper, but I would read the features on the front page and I rarely looked inside the paper. Someone gave me a book about how to read an annual report. I thought that was a good place to start.

I started with some basic things, like how to buy stock, what stock exchanges do. I knew that you could get a piece of a company if you had enough money, but the practicalities had never entered my mind.

You have to learn the jargon, but it's essentially like any other reporting. What you don't know, you have to find out. You have to be well read, keep your ear to the ground, look for sources in these companies and in people who make it part of their business to follow these companies—professional analysts, stockbrokers, investment bankers, and attorneys.

AN ALABAMA MEDICINE MAN

One story I wrote that was not a business story was about a man in Alabama who practices herbal medicine. He has been growing and collecting herbs from the region around southern Appalachia for about

50 years, and he's been considered something of a local expert on traditional folk practices.

I found him through a man who works at the Southern Regional Council in Mississippi. Another story led to this story. I was doing a story on why people in the South have so many kidney stones. It occurred to me after talking to some doctors about why people have kidney stones that it might be fun to find out some of the folk theories.

So I called a guy in Mississippi who runs the Center for Southern Culture and asked if he had heard any good stories about kidney stones and folk cures. He led me to a folklorist, a guy in Atlanta, who had gotten a master's in folklore. And this guy said, "Well, if anybody in the South knows about folk cures for kidney stones, it's Tommie Bass." After I talked to Bass, I felt that he was worth a story on his own— something that the *Journal* had not written about.

When I come up with a story like that, I have to sell it to my bureau chief here in Atlanta, who determines if it's something worth one of his reporters spending time on, that will have a good chance of being accepted in New York for Page 1.

The reporter writes a proposal. You write a slugline, what the story is about, why the *Journal* should be interested in it, something unusual about this person, why this person represents something significant about our culture or a culture that few people in the nation know about and are interested in reading about.

With a story like that, you're looking for color, you're looking for the kind of interviewee this person will make. Do they have good stories and anecdotes to tell? This story was not particularly scientific, but you want this person to have some credibility because there are all sorts of faddish herbs and herb shops that pop up to be the miracle cure. This seemed to be a person who had a reputation, who had been here for a number of years.

WHAT MAKES A PAGE 1 *JOURNAL* FEATURE

What makes a *Journal* feature story work are some good anecdotes, and it has to be well organized and come to the point fairly quickly. The story has to be tightly written. The *Journal* doesn't like stories that are just full of quotes. The *Journal* is looking for some evidence that you didn't just sit down and interview somebody, that you've done some homework.

Then before the story runs, you're often asked questions by editors who are satisfying themselves that you've done some substantial reporting. There's no romantic formula to writing a *Wall Street Journal* feature, but they tend to like anecdotes, and they like the reporter to come to some sort of conclusion.

FIRST FEATURE WAS THE EASIEST

In the beginning, I did a feature story about companies that market their names on various projects, logos, such as R. J. Reynolds Tobacco. Several brand names appear on all kinds of things, not just T-shirts, from caps to briefcases, even a Jeep. There's an airplane that has Campbell on the side of it. Companies advertise themselves on all kinds of things.

My bureau chief gave me the idea. It was an idea that had been in his file for a while and no one had taken it. He said, "Do you want it?" I said, "Sure." That was the easiest story I've done. It hasn't been that simple since.

The features are usually fairly complex. There are so many people involved, so many people you have to satisfy. And while you're working on features, you get calls to do other things, breaking news, and a lot of times I've just gotten bogged down in other work.

INVESTIGATING THE DELTA FOUNDATION

It takes what I consider a long time to write a feature because I've become accustomed to coming to work with a story idea and getting it down by the end of the day, or at least the end of the week. Here I've worked on a feature for six months.

That was a story about a private, non-profit community development organization in the Mississippi Delta called the Delta Foundation that I had heard about when I was in Mississippi. When I came to work for *The Wall Street Journal*, I found a number of people were unhappy with the way the organization had evolved. It's a non-profit organization designed to develop the poor areas, to bring jobs into the area.

There were a lot of questions I felt I had to follow up on, questions to explore to see if there was a legitimacy to the complaints, and it took a long time. The company wasn't cooperative, so I filed Freedom of Information requests. I'd get a response and some information would be deleted and then I had to appeal to get the information that had been deleted.

I was looking for financial information. It was a private, non-profit company, which means they didn't publish an annual report, and their financial statements are generally not available. But I knew they had to report some of this information to government agencies that funded them.

Typically, you'd get a piece of information and you'd go back to them and say, "What about this?" You look for corroborating sources and some explanation of what is written down. A lot of times what is in a document may seem clear, but it can be misinterpreted. I found that

Linda Williams 169

some of their reports on profits in the company, taken at face value, could be misleading.

FIND A WORKING LEAD

It saves you a lot of trouble to have a working lead—not precisely what you're going to say, not your conclusion, but what you're looking for. In the herbalist story, the basic premise of my story was that this is an aspect of American culture that's disappearing that still has a fairly strong hold in certain parts of the country.

That includes not only talking to Tommie Bass, but talking to his neighbors, the people who come to the shop and the botanists who had talked to him. Some medical doctors had gone down to talk to him about what he was doing, so I talked to them. And I looked in dictionaries and herb books for other evidence that other people have used these sorts of herbs, to establish the tradition.

WHAT MAKES A GOOD *JOURNAL* REPORTER

You need patience, a lot of patience. A *Wall Street Journal* reporter is very, very careful. It's a paper that has a lot of credibility, a newspaper where what you write about and what the paper publishes have enormous influence on the stock market, the economy.

It's not a paper with huge egos because there are not a lot of bylines. There's a lot of teamwork. We do a lot of round-ups, contributing to different stories. For instance, on the news desk, we could file as many as 50 short news items between two people—a company's quarterly or annual earnings, a company's dividends, a report of a decision to declare a dividend, a report of a company that decides to purchase another company, or major changes in the management of a company. These stories may be something you could take care of in a few minutes or for which you may have to do a lot of reporting.

HOW I WORK

We have rotating assignments on what we call the news desk—people who deal with day-to-day news. Usually you spend a week doing that and you have two or three weeks to work on your features. But within that two or three weeks, you may be called away to help out with the day-to-day news. If you have been following a company, you may be asked to do a story on that. You're also responding to requests from New York—round-up requests—and asked to contribute to all of the columns, the Labor Letter, the Business Bulletins, Shop Talk. We all contribute to all kinds of columns in the paper.

For instance, the Labor Letter will send out a query—"We're interested in a story on companies that are giving rewards to employees who are coming up with innovative ideas. Can you give us some examples?" So you call some companies and find some examples and send it to them. They'll do a compilation in New York to determine the trend.

You're expected to work for the wire service, you're expected to contribute to all the columns, you're expected to write for the front page, you're expected, sometimes, to come up with an idea for the special features like Heard on the Street. Then if there's something interesting about politics or a policy issue in your territory, there is an obligation to at least talk to Washington to see if you have something interesting.

HOW TO ORGANIZE TO COVER BUSINESS

We keep card files on all the important people in companies. Various source books also list security analysts, people who follow different companies. Just from prior reporting, you know if this company has been in a takeover or some kind of restructuring. You have some idea who the attorneys are, who the investment bankers are. In the business world, there also are all kinds of floaters, people who are in and out of the various deals—consultants that you just learn about from experience.

All these companies have to file public annual reports, and they also have to publish what the Securities and Exchange Commission calls a 10Q form every quarter and a 10K form at the end of the year, which is a more detailed annual report. They have to tell what their debt is, what they owe, and they have to disclose things about lawsuits that might have a significant impact on the company—business relationships among people who are principals in the company. For example, you might have a chairman who builds homes and he may have ownership in a company that sells lumber to a home builder.

That's part of the routine, reading those reports, getting them as quickly as you possibly can after they are filed. We have an office file where we keep the reports filed under the company. We have one file that has annual reports and 10Ks and 10Qs, and we have another file that has all kinds of press releases that a company has issued and reports that analysts have done on that company.

Then I have a personal file, filed under companies, and a locked file. Then I have a file for each of the features that I've done. And I have an ideas file, where I stick stuff that I may some day want to do a story about. When I need an idea, I go to that file.

GETTING BUSINESS PEOPLE TO TALK

Business people are not any more willing to talk to a reporter than politicians. Some of them are even more closed-mouthed. They give information that they are required to give by the Securities and Exchange Commission, and that's it. When you call them up to get further explanation—"Tell me the real reason you're going to sell this division. Is it really because it hasn't done well and not that you decided it was in the best interest of your shareholders?"—business people are as reluctant to talk as politicians.

Your obligation is to report what's really true. The paper is a service to investors, a service to business people, a product that's supposed to be real and useful information, not regurgitated press releases.

It's not always possible, but what helps us is we're dealing with companies that have to make a certain amount of disclosure. You take what they have to report, and you use that as a clue when you do your digging.

HOW TO MAKE BUSINESS WRITING INTERESTING

Some people think that a *Wall Street Journal* reporter writes six features for the front page. The conception is that you're strictly a business writer when you really aren't. Business is the main concern of the paper, but business is very broadly defined. Social trends and politics affect business, and in that broad definition you have a lot of latitude.

The best business stories are those that have some kind of human element: What if this happened to me and my business? What would I do? Another good business story is one that has some kind of drama. One of the best was a profile of Carl Icahn, who's considered a corporate raider. He takes over companies. This profile included a confrontation between him and an executive of another company that he wanted to take over.

Drama and personality descriptions are appealing to almost any reader, not just a person who happens to be in business. The business person reading about how a takeover artist works may be thinking how he might be able to protect himself from that. Some of the best stories are stories that can be appreciated on several levels.

You have to capture the reader. You don't particularly have a monopoly as a dispenser of information, and you have to give readers a reason to come to you to get it, rather than watching two-minute clips on television or reading other newspapers' expanded business sections.

COVERING BUSINESS CONTROVERSY

Regular readers of *The Wall Street Journal* will find that we're pretty tough on business. What *The Wall Street Journal* doesn't do is challenge the basic assumption that capitalism is good. It certainly gets into all the warts, all the problems of businesses and how things get fouled up, how business doesn't always serve the interests of the shareholders or the public.

The editorial page definitely has an ideology, and it's very clear. Frankly, I find myself not reading it very much. That's one way to deal with it—not read it.

But I can honestly say that there's no ideology that's reflected in the news pages. There are stories just recently about whether rent-to-own deals are really fair to consumers, a lot of writing about how business almost ruined the environment of the state of Louisiana, corporate cheating, and shoddy products. Those kinds of stories are in *The Wall Street Journal* frequently.

HOW TO BECOME A BUSINESS REPORTER

A good liberal arts education is the best thing for a reporter, whether or not they want to be a business reporter. There are other ways to learn about the specifics of covering business than spending four years of your life studying economics. If somebody wants to do that, that's fine. Still, any reporter has to know about the world in the broadest sense— the history of the world, the history of a nation, the history of a community. All those things will eventually come to play in any story.

For example, Coca-Cola [which is based in Atlanta] did not get to be Coca-Cola in a vacuum. It had a lot to do with the culture of the country, a lot to do with the politics of the country at a particular time—the opening up of the rest of the world diplomatically. So I think the well-educated liberal arts person is still the best reporter. The specifics you pick up later.

It also would be very difficult to walk out of college and work for *The Wall Street Journal.* Spending some time at some local newspapers, medium to small-time newspapers, covering city hall, covering education, and general assignment are the kinds of things that prepare you for any kind of sustained, in-depth, careful reporting.

ETHICAL DILEMMAS

The ethics here as a business reporter are fairly clear. You do not give out any information about a company that has not been published. You don't trade in stock in the companies that you cover. You don't do business with the companies you cover.

Public companies have so many rules—securities law as well as ethics—that withholding information can have a negative effect on a company, as well as giving it to the wrong people before it's widely disseminated. To me, in the day-to-day coverage of business, the ethics have been more clear-cut than in any other kind of reporting I've done.

REPORTING IN THE SOUTH

You have to take a little bit more time with people. That's still part of the culture. You can't just call someone and say, "I want to know blah blah blah. I've got only two minutes to do it. Tell me right away." You have to say, "Hello, how are you doing? How's the weather in Birmingham?" and you chat. You have these little social amenities. If you can't talk in person, you try to bring that kind of personal, face-to-face dynamic to a telephone conversation by spending time with them.

A second thing to remember is that the South is really not monolithic anymore. There are a lot of people who are running businesses in the South who are not Southerners. It's not a case of a guy running a business out of his back pocket. He has New York bankers and New York lawyers and even some fairly slick Atlanta bankers and lawyers.

A BETTER REPORTER THAN WRITER

There are some people who can dig up information from anywhere. If there is information to be found, they will find it. I think I'm pretty good at finding things. If something's to be discovered, I can discover it.

I'm a pretty good reporter, but I wish I were a better writer. I don't think that my writing is the kind that sets off bells. It's the kind of prose that generally needs a little polishing.

I don't like to write. I really love reporting. Writing is a tortuous ordeal for me. The writing is always tension time. I eat too much. Then I have this routine. I read a magazine article, and then I fiddle around, and then I read another magazine article. Really, I find the way to get a story done is just to sit down in a room pretty much by yourself and decide you're going to tune everything out and work at it until it's done. Sustained concentration is the only way to write.

I don't know a lot of reporters who really like to write. I think most reporters—when you talk to them and ask them what they like best about their jobs—they would say reporting.

On day-to-day news, I have never had a problem meeting a deadline. I think that's probably one of my strengths as a spot news reporter, the breaking news. It's the features where I fret.

I like finding out things, the art of discovery, the satisfaction of discovering something that's not obvious. I like the art and the satisfaction of reaching a concise, clear conclusion about what a certain set of facts means.

It's the pursuit, the chase—turning over rocks and finding out something that maybe five people in the world know, and you're one person who knows it. And not only do you know about it, but you're the person who has the ability to tell it to everybody.

It's a challenge, but not particularly enjoyable, to interview the corporate executive who has decided that there's a certain set of facts he's going to give out and he's not giving any more. It's not particularly enjoyable to interview someone in a hostile situation. And I think, for a good bit of my career, I've been in that situation, interviewing people in a hostile environment.

It's been tough. I think it's been tough being a reporter. Very.

THE REWARDS OF BEING A REPORTER

I have had stories where there was an effect, that did some good. When I was in Mississippi, there was a case of a woman who was retarded who had a baby, and the baby died of starvation. The woman was convicted of murder and spent two years in jail while the case was on appeal. I think the fact that I wrote about her and, I think for the first time, brought together all the pieces for the public that she really got a rotten deal, expedited the Supreme Court in hearing her appeal and getting her out of jail and on with her life.

I'm a fairly sensitive person, and I think that sensitivity comes from living with and being around a lot of poor people, working people. I don't start with the same assumptions about people. I've known a lot of poor people who were very smart.

I can talk to just about anybody on any level. As a black reporter, you're forced to talk to anybody on every level, whereas a lot of white reporters have been able to avoid talking to poor people, talking to black people in general, having to deal with them at all.

BEING A BLACK REPORTER AT THE *JOURNAL*

One of the questions I always get from young blacks is, "Is it hard to be a black woman working for *The Wall Street Journal?*" I would say that I don't think it's hard. Sometimes it puts you in a situation where everybody is not totally comfortable with who you are. But that's their problem. You're here, and you have a role to play.

I tell a story that I think is kind of funny. When I was working in Mississippi, doing some health stories, I had a very good telephone relationship with a local doctor who was chairman of the local heart association. I had never met him.

I happened to be at a heart association luncheon and we were introduced, and he was astounded. He blurted out, "I never knew you were a colored lady." I said, "Well, yes, I'm black, and it never occurred to me that you didn't know that or that it made a difference."

Today, to get in *The Wall Street Journal,* you have to come through me. I'm the gatekeeper.

MINORITIES IN NEWSROOMS TODAY

I think it's fairly clear that this industry is still the most segregated and, contrary to its image, fairly conservative. Everybody talks about the proliferation of chains, but there are still a lot of newspapers that are in the hands of single-family ownership. Even if they've been bought by a chain, they're still run by the same people. Like a lot of small businesses, which newspapers generally are, they've been the least susceptible to integration.

PERSONAL LIFE

I make time for myself. In general, I don't have time to go out a lot during the week. I'm too tired. You can never say for sure that you're going to be somewhere at a certain time.

Out of necessity, you have to spend a lot of time reading what other people are doing, and it's a job that never ends. I feel like I'm working all the time. You're driving down the street, and you see something that catches your eye. If it's the least bit unusual, the first thing you think of is, "Is this a story?" Even in conversations with people who are telling you something about their day or an experience they've had, those little wheels are turning in your head: "Gee, I wonder if this is a story. Has this ever happened to anybody else? Is this important?" Everything is fodder for a story.

WHO MAKES A GOOD REPORTER

I think, at heart, all reporters are reformers. We are the observers who don't exactly make things happen, but we keep exposing events. I think you shouldn't be a reporter unless you have a capability to be outraged when something is wrong. You can't change it, but you can do what some people call testify. You can tell what happened—this is the way it is, and I want to tell you about it.

Doctors may frown
but hill people say
herbalist 'gives ease'

Tommie Bass, 77, even lures
folklorists and academics
to a Leesburg, Ala., shack

by Linda Williams

LEESBURG, Ala.—Despite the spring rain soaking the nearby herb garden, visitors respectfully wait outside the two-room shack. They have come to see Tommie Bass and try some of his remedies that "give ease."

"Mr. Tommie, I got me a bad hurtin'," says one man. Another praises a liniment and wonders if Mr. Bass can send a jar of it to an arthritic aunt in Georgia. Mr. Bass serves the petitioners from a storehouse of herbs stuffed in plastic bags and mixed in pungent concoctions. The shack is his home, his office and the community's alternative drugstore.

Some call him a folk healer or a mountain medicine man. The 77-year-old Mr. Bass calls himself "a herbist." Whatever he is called, his advice is eagerly sought by neighbors. "What Mr. Tommie tells you is the true facts," says one satisfied customer.

A Fading Breed

Once a common phenomenon here in the worn hills of southern Appala-

chia, folk healers now are rare. You are more likely to find franchised herb shops that serve customers wearing gold chains and driving sports cars.

But as one of the oldest and most respected practitioners of the art, Mr. Bass is getting much attention. His encyclopedic knowledge of the local flora and its applications has brought folklorists, academics and even members of the medical establishment to the shack in the shadow of Shinbone Ridge to pick his brain.

"Tommie knows them all," says Alan Tullos, who studied Mr. Bass for a master's thesis in folklore from the University of North Carolina. Adds a Duke University botanist, Jane Philpott: "He knows some 300 plants and has a working knowledge of about 70. Most herbalists are confined to about 25."

Unlike many of the modern herb and back-to-nature faddists, Mr. Bass doesn't promise cures or push some miracle plant. While he believes he can relieve any complaint from aching joints to asthma, he doesn't do any diagnosing or consider himself a substitute for a doctor. In fact, Mr. Bass had quintuple bypass surgery last December after suffering a heart attack. "I don't knock the doctors," he says. "It's the pharmacy companies that's a-killin' us with these harsh medicines."

Folk healers in this area sprang from

the need of settlers living in poverty and isolation to make do with what they found on the land. Most of the remedies are steeped in the Anglo-Saxon traditions of those people. Mr. Bass also borrowed some from North American Indian and Southern black customs.

"Didn't have no doctors," Mr. Bass says, recalling his childhood. "But we had a cabinet full of all kinds of medicines. We doctored ourselves." Mr. Bass's remedies include yellowroot tea for ulcers; maypop, or passionflower, tea for the nerves; and rabbit-tobacco fumes for sinus trouble.

Today, modern medicine has also taken hold here in rural Cherokee County. A handful of doctors serve the population of 18,700, and a new acute-care hospital recently opened. But the county stills seems a bit removed from the modern world. Leesburg, about 20 miles from the nearest interstate highway, can be reached only by car or on foot. There is no bus or rail service. There is little industry and no institution of higher learning. Centre, the county seat with about 2,400 residents, just got its first fast-food restaurant. Respect for traditions runs deep.

"Tommie is appropriate to the culture of Cherokee County," says Dr. Clark Smeltzer Jr., a family practitioner in Centre. For the farmers and working-class people who have spent their entire lives in the valley, says Mr. Tullos, the folklorist, Mr. Bass is a "less expensive, less intimidating" alternative for relief from minor ailments.

Science remains generally skeptical of such folk cures. But botany has led to some well-known modern drugs (digitalis, the heart stimulant, is made from the dried leaves of a plant commonly known as purple foxglove), and small groups of scientists are increasingly looking at plants for clues to developing other drugs. The toxic substance in pokeweed, a plant that Mr. Bass uses

for a number of ailments, has been shown to kill cancer cells in mice, and further research is planned on its possible application to human cancers.

Mr. Bass's confidence in his remedies comes from experience and religious faith. If God created humans from the earth, he reasons, it follows that the earth is the source for nourishing and repairing the human body. "God don't make no mistakes," he says.

He started collecting herbs when he was about seven years old. His father sold furs and herbs to companies. "I learned to identify plants from looking at the drawings and photographs in fliers the companies would send Dad," Mr. Bass says. Taught to read by his mother—he has no formal education—Mr. Bass later pored over old almanacs, medical texts, pamphlets and herb books.

He was drafted in 1942 but was quickly discharged because of chronic arthritis. He claims the affliction never bothered him at home where he took a variety of herbal mixtures. In the army they gave him aspirin, which he says "did as much good as pouring water on a greased goose."

Dr. Smeltzer, who is Mr. Bass's personal physician, expresses respect for him and his work. "He came along when there were no doctors and tried some things to help people," he says. "I don't frown on what he does—and I don't encourage it."

Walking in his yard and hiking past his favorite spot on nearby Lookout Mountain, the wiry Mr. Bass discusses the herbs he is most familiar with and the medical value he believes they have:

■ Yellowroot (Xanthorhiza simplicissima) "is absolutely real stuff; now that ain't no joke." You make a tea by putting about a cup of yellowroot in half a gallon of water and boiling it for 30 minutes. "It's been used ever since time, especially by old people for the sore mouth, sore eyes and stomach trouble. More people is taking it now for ulcers than anything we know of."

■ Tea made from butterfly weed (Asclepias tuberosa) is "for side pleurisy—a hurting on your side—or getting over pneumonia, or anything bothering your chest."

■ Calamus root (Acorus calamus) is chewed and the juice swallowed "instead of Rolaids or Tums. It tastes bad, but if you eat too much or have a sour or burning stomach, it makes you feel good."

■ Catnip (Nepeta cataria) tea is "good for headaches and pacifying babies. It'll do away with the hives and if the stomach didn't digest its food, why it'll just start it to digesting."

■ Maypop, or passionflower (Passiflora incarnata) "is the finest nerve medicine. Use a handful of crushed leaves in a teacup of boiling water and sweeten to taste."

■ Rabbit tobacco (Gnaphalium obtusifolium) "is good for people who have sinus trouble and asthma. Put the plants in the sink and run hot water over it and inhale the fumes. You can't find rabbit tobacco in an herb book and I don't guess a doctor would recognize it."

Of the herbs Mr. Bass gathers, he gives away about as many as he sells. He lives simply on a few thousand dollars a year earned from odd jobs as well as selling herbs. He usually recommends that a new customer try his remedy "and if it works, you can come back and pay me." The charge is never more than two or three dollars.

On Mr. Bass's front porch sits a wooden shelf with a variety of herbs and concoctions. Above the shelf a hand-painted sign says: "Friend, if you find an item you want and I am not here, just drop the money in the cigar box. I thank you and hope to be here when you are the next time. In God we trust. How about you?"

Linda Williams

"We go into the Oval Office. We see the president. We hear pronouncements before anyone else. It's tremendous. We have enviable jobs and we're lucky."

HELEN THOMAS

Helen Thomas sits in the front row at every presidential press conference—often in a red dress. She has been kidded about the dress, but she doesn't mind. She claims the president notices red more than other colors, so it helps her do her job.

Thomas, 66, has been covering presidential politics for United Press International since 1960. She has covered six presidential administrations—from President Kennedy to President Reagan—more than any other member of the White House press. She is the senior White House correspondent, with the privilege of closing the president's press conferences with "Thank you, Mr. President."

She was covering the White House when President Kennedy was inaugurated and when he was shot. She followed President Johnson to his Texas ranch. She covered President Nixon's overtures to China and then watched him say goodbye to the White House staff the day he resigned and President Ford moved in. She wrote about the Iranian hostage crisis as it plagued President Carter, and she watched President Reagan skirmish with domestic politics.

Thomas has strong feelings about presidents and about presidents and the press. As a wire-service reporter, she writes history's first, not final, draft. But as a member of the White House press corps, she has been in the journalistic front row for more presidential events than any other American journalist.

In 1971, when she was 51, she married for the first time. Her husband, Douglas Cornell, was a reporter for the Associated Press. When Cornell was asked by *Parade* magazine what it was like being married to a journalist, he said, "Someone who hadn't been a wire-service reporter probably couldn't stand being married to someone who is as energetic and devoted to her job as Helen, but I can. I think she's a terrific reporter. I hope she never gives it up." Cornell died in 1982.

In 1975, Thomas published her recollections in a book, *Dateline: The White House.* That same year she was the first woman elected to Washington's 90-year-old Gridiron Club, which previously had limited membership to male journalists. In 1985, she was the first woman to win the National Press Club's prestigious Fourth Estate Award.

Thomas, who started at UPI in 1943 at a salary of $12 a week, usually puts in 12-hour days at the White House. She says, "UPI is my life." ❖

- The relationship of presidents with the press
- Differences between working for a newspaper and working for a wire service
- How well the American press covers the president

BEGINNINGS

I majored in English at Wayne State. We had no journalism department. But I got interested in being a newspaperwoman—I had a one-track mind—from the time I was a sophomore in high school. I worked on the school paper, saw my byline, was hooked for life. I decided then and there that that was the life for me. I loved it. Then I went to Wayne and worked on the college paper.

I've always been interested in politics. I'm from a big family. We were interested in current events of the world around us, and I think that was a stimulant. My experience on a high school paper generated so much excitement. Even that demanded the extra time and devotion. I'm sure that people going to band or music would have the same thing, but it was extra hours and you were so happy to be there.

When I left Wayne State, I came to Washington. I worked as a hostess in a restaurant after beating down the doors trying to get a job as a copygirl, which was my big goal. We were always told that you have to be persistent, that you have to start at the bottom. I knew all those things, and I was just very determined. It's never very easy to look for any job. But I was persistent. I kept reading the ads, and then there was an ad for a copygirl at the [*Washington Daily*] *News,* and I applied for the job. Nothing would stop me. This was 1943.

COPYGIRL AND THEN UPI

I got the job as a copygirl on the now-defunct *Washington Daily News* and became a cub reporter. Then I went to work for UPI writing radio news for 12 years. I went to work at 5:30 in the morning, filing a wire that went all over town, sort of a city ticker of abbreviated news so that the correspondents and others could have it.

There were other copygirls, and by this time they were drafting young men, so more opportunities opened up for women—unfortunately under those circumstances—but that's the way it was. I had become president of the Women's National Press Club and that gave me a springboard, and after 12 years of 5:30 in the morning, I finally went to the boss and said, "It's about time, isn't it, that I got into the reporting world?"

There's always been discrimination against women. There's a lot less now, but in those days there were not as many women involved in hard news, so there was a natural tendency that it's still a man's world, basically, and men talk to men, so you have that kind of obstacle. Women have made tremendous strides in all newsrooms, but we've got a long way to go.

In 1961, January, I came to the White House, but I really was covering part of the campaign in '60. Then I went to Palm Beach with the Kennedys and then just moved into the White House from there.

I love history. I'm nosey. All the excitement of life comes to journalism. You really have a ringside seat to history, especially at the White House. You're involved in the world.

COVERING THE KENNEDYS

Jackie detested the press. She detested our prying, yet she loved the pictures. They [the Kennedys] were ambivalent about wanting to show how much they enjoyed reading about their own children. They resented it, and at the same time they loved it.

Jackie used to buy all the magazines with her picture in them, and at the same time she used to call us the "harpies" because we'd be tracking her at airports and arriving at Palm Beach. Any time she sneezed we could get on the front page, there was that much interest. She made it hard for us, but it was fun because you went to very wonderful places like Palm Beach and Hyannisport. They lived the good life.

Jack Kennedy was fascinating to cover. He also had a very ambivalent attitude toward the press. He'd blow up at us one minute and had a good rapport at others. He was fascinated with the news. He was the first [president] to have live televised news conferences. He made mistakes, as all presidents do, and resented our pointing them out. But he was very witty, very warm.

COVERING LYNDON JOHNSON

Lyndon Johnson had a love-hate relationship with the press. He was fascinated with reporters. He wanted to be on the front page every day. At the same time he felt he was not getting a fair shake, at least in his own perception, especially during the Vietnam War. It was a struggle on his part to be understood, to be loved.

Johnson's relationship to the press was very personal. He knew us by our first names, he liked you when he thought you had written something favorable. He was a very generous man, and we got closer to him than to any president. We were invited to the ranch, we shared a lot of things. No one else has opened the door so wide—meet me at the ranch and so forth.

When he didn't want us around, we would have to chase him all around the Texas countryside. We had to track him a lot of times, and he'd be driving 80 miles an hour.

He was like a little boy. He wanted to be liked and he wanted you to write beautiful things, and he could not understand whenever the press was critical. Sometimes he couldn't tell the truth if his life depended on it. He thought we should be forever grateful, and we never were. Every day was a new day, and every day was a new story.

COVERING RICHARD NIXON

Nixon? Watergate. Enough said. We went five months without a news conference. He came in with a lot of baggage about the press because he felt that the press had done him in in the past. They ran the White House in such a regimented way. It was a lot harder to find out what was going on. I think [Nixon Press Secretary Ron] Ziegler did very well in the early days, and then he had to go into hiding when there were no longer any answers.

COVERING GERALD FORD

[Presidential Press Secretary] Ron Nessen was not your ace press secretary. I think President Ford was badly served. It's important to have a good press secretary. They have to be mature. They have to really understand what the world is all about, what government is all about.

COVERING JIMMY CARTER

Jimmy Carter was one of the most articulate presidents in the White House. He knew what a sentence was—a beginning, a middle, and an end. But he was an engineer-type. I don't think that he was able to communicate well or express himself well to make himself understood.

COVERING RONALD REAGAN

Ronald Reagan is the most conservative president I've ever covered. I think that Reagan doesn't hold enough news conferences, and I wish he would. We all complain about that. He should have one news conference a month. The ideal is one a week. Presidents have so much power that they should be watched, in a constant spotlight. Do presidents love us? No. Should they love us? No.

ETHICAL DILEMMAS

I hope I'm an objective reporter. I try to be. I think I have been all the years I've been with UPI—"he said," "he added"—I try to write it straight. I may be astounded at times, but you don't let that get into your copy. That's my job.

I really don't remember a time when I wondered whether I could be fair because I consider fairness the top requirement of my job. I think that journalists have to do that, they have to be that.

But I permit myself to be a human being. I don't think I've ruled myself out of the human race because I'm a reporter. I think I can be very objective about doing a story. A lawyer has to defend a criminal, right? A surgeon might even be personally involved and he has to go in and perform an operation. So as reporters, you detach yourself and try to do the fairest job possible.

That's what makes this country great, and that's what makes journalism great, is to have fairness. I believe that—well, Lincoln said it. He said, "Let the people know the facts and the country will be safe." I believe that. I believe that people don't have to have my opinion. At the same time, I permit myself to have an opinion, but not in my job.

AWE OF THE PRESIDENCY

We go into the Oval Office, we see the president, we hear pronouncements before anyone else. It's tremendous. It's a tremendous opportunity. We have enviable jobs, and we're lucky.

Who could come to the White House and not feel the sense of awe at the presidency? I have no awe of presidents. I think they're human.

Eleven

In fact, you see their foibles up so close. But what the presidency means in our national life, what it can mean, what it should mean—I stand in awe.

PRESIDENTS MUST BE ACCESSIBLE

They do have life and death power over all the world today, when you consider what nuclear power is. The president has 17 minutes to decide whether to blow up the world. This is why if they take on that job, they should be willing to be covered. They should always be responsive, tell people what they're doing. You can't have a democracy if you don't know what's going on. You can't have an informed people.

If the president is inaccessible, it makes it tough. We're not adversarial. I don't feel like I'm an adversary of government. I feel like we're all in it together. I think that I should never let them think that we're sitting back or taking it when they are not providing answers. You keep pressing them and get insulted. Sometimes they rule by ridicule or trying to subject you to ridicule with your peers. The real thing is to keep pressing them, to force them to be embarrassed, because they are public servants and they are being paid by us.

ROLE OF THE WHITE HOUSE PRESS CORPS

There is a real lack of understanding in the public eye about the role of the press. We are trying to keep people informed. They don't have to love us. They don't understand what we are trying to do. They don't like presidents questioned very strongly. But you can't do your job and worry about whether people understand you or not. You just hope the public understands that it is not personal.

I am an observer. Reporters at the White House are basically semi-watchdogs. We are self-appointed watchdogs of democracy, I believe, but I believe that our service is to keep people informed about what's going on. In such power positions someone could easily slide into rule-by-edict.

If the president's going to go into an adventure, and it isn't a question of being attacked but a real choice, people ought to be in on that, to make up their own minds about whether they want to do it. Central America certainly is a case in point. I'm not saying the president wants to go in militarily. But if he did, I think people know enough now that they would put a stop to it or they could go in, depending on their point of view. At least they'd have a say, and I think they ought to have a say.

I don't blame people for wanting to be president. I think it's a magnificent job. I think they're so lucky. But they don't go in there as children, not knowing what it's all about. They watch it, they covet it, they're bankrolled by their friends to the tune of millions of dollars, and they put their friends on the rolls. They want it, and how.

People probably think we're sitting in judgment, and in a sense we are. But at the same time, I think that if they [presidents] want that job they ought to know that they're going to be judged, so I don't have any apologies for our role.

You know, pendulums swing. When I first came to journalism, people would see you and say, "Oh, you're in newspaper work. You meet such interesting people. Isn't that wonderful?" Then there have been anti-media campaigns where your image is not so great, and people say, "Who in the hell are you? Why are you so arrogant? Why do you think you can question a president?"

And then it comes back, as in the case of Watergate, people went up to reporters and said, "You saved the country." Now there's another swing. So what? You try to do the best job you can. We should always keep trying to do our jobs better.

FAILURES OF THE PRESS

I don't think the press pushes hard enough. We should always keep demanding information. I don't think we should worry about whether we're loved or not, and I don't think we do.

We fall short because we don't ask enough questions, we don't put them on the spot enough. It isn't just asking questions—you really have to have some sort of sense that they feel the pressure to tell what's going on. A lot of times they don't. Why should they? They think that information is their private preserve. And information is everything. It's golden, and it's power, and because it is, they think that it belongs to them alone. You have to keep trying. It's not easy. There are enough people interested in suppressing the news rather than informing the people.

QUALITIES OF A GOOD REPORTER

To be a good reporter, you need lots of enthusiasm and energy and a really driving interest in the world around you. You should really be curious and you should care. Every day's an education in journalism. There's not a day that you can't learn something. It sounds like a cliché, but it's really true.

WHAT I DO

There are some great reporters, I'm not one of them, the real investigative types who uncover what people ought to know. I'm just doing the

Eleven

surface job. I don't consider myself an investigative reporter at all. I wish I was, but thank God there are a lot of people around who are good at it.

I don't think I'm a good writer at all. I always think my *raison d'être* and my forte is my sense of outrage, my enthusiasm, my energy, and my feeling that people ought to know about things—my nosiness. I have an abiding curiosity, which I think is my mainstay.

That's the most fulfilling part of the job, this sense that you're alive, you're part of what's going on. Also, you really have the orchestra seat to seeing a lot of things that other people don't see and feeling the responsibility to transmit it to them.

The way the wire service works, we have to operate on a time basis, and you go with a story and then you try to fill in the gaps on the second cycle. We really do have the ideal of truth. God knows, we don't get paid for it.

I'm sure I've made many mistakes, fortunately none fatal, but I guess I try to forget my mistakes. Sometimes you're sloppy or you go too fast. The real mistakes I've made are the stories I've known and I've put off until tomorrow. You can't do that with the wire service. Later I said, "Why in the hell didn't I write it?" You can't sit on a story. You have to just go with what you've got if you have enough because somebody's going to get it next time.

You ultimately are responsible for every story, and I always wanted to be edited and I hope I am, but so much depends on your own initiative, your own intuition, your own drive. I think reporters have a lot of independence that people in a lot of other professions don't, and I love freedom. I love the freedom to exercise, to be a person, to be self-reliant, and at the same time to be dependable.

HOW REPORTERS CONTRIBUTE

I put what we do as a really important contribution to our society. What would this country be without a free press, without people being informed of everything? We're a country of news junkies, and I'm happy about it. If you just hear a snippet on a car radio, you're informed. People in this country have to know these things, and I think they're interested.

We're more alive because of it, more aware of the world around us. That's the only way you can really make a contribution beyond your little circle. How can you participate in your society if you don't even know what's happening?

You can't have a democracy unless you have an informed people, and the media makes that kind of contribution. And we enjoy it at the same time, which is what people seem to resent the most. It's not work.

When you love your work, it's really not work. I put in 12-, 14-hour days. But I don't even think of it as long. I think of it as the day.

PERSONAL LIFE

You can't have obligations because when you're covering the White House you have to be ready to jump at any minute. News doesn't break on your time, so it is your life. You live on the fringes of the presidency, really.

It's all-consuming. But wonderful. You have your own personal life, but all bets are off when a story's breaking. You stay with the story.

That doesn't mean you don't get tired, sure. But when you really love it, and you want to be there, you're angry when you're not there. When you're not there you've missed it. Being there is everything in journalism.

You're always unhappy when you're not there at any hour. I tell my office, "Call me at any hour." And I'm very unhappy when they don't call me at 3 o'clock in the morning when something's breaking. You can always sleep tomorrow.

THE RECOGNITION FACTOR

I'm the lady in the red dress. I don't mind it. Just so they spell my name right. It's nice to be recognized. It's better than not being recognized. TV does everything. You could work for a newspaper for 50 years, and people may know your by-line but they don't know you. Once you're on TV, you have a recognition factor. Why not have an identity? I like it, I like it.

Budget negotiations break down

by Helen Thomas

```
na--w
a2420na--w
u w am-budget 1stld-writeth.     7--29 0542
^(complete writethru _ congressional reaction)<
@^BY HELEN THOMAS=
@^UPI White House Reporter=

    WASHINGTON (UPI) _ President Reagan, rejecting a budget compromise
proposed by Senate Republican leaders, Monday ruled out an oil import
fee and changes in Social Security benefits and income tax indexing.<
```

The breakdown between Reagan and the Senate leaders of his own party left those trying to negotiate a budget compromise in disarray and made it even more unlikely that a compromise can be agreed to before Friday's start of Congress's summer vacation.<

House and Senate budget leaders scrambled to meet with their colleagues to determine whether it was worth trying to formulate a budget compromise this week.<

White House chief of staff Donald Regan went to Capitol Hill to urge that Congress try another approach to a budget, but Senate budget leaders were discouraged by the president's flat rejection of their proposal.<

In a brief telephone call, Reagan told Senate Republican leader Robert Dole of his refusal to accept an every-other-year cost-of-living hike for Social Security and tax indexing and a $5-a-barrel oil import fee proposed by GOP senators.<

The items had been included in an attempt to break a 7-week-old budget deadlock.<

``The president will not support a tax increase in the form of an oil import fee; he will not support a change in Social Security COLA's (cost of living adjustments); nor will he support a change in tax indexing that protects the working American from inflation-generated tax increase,'' White House spokesman Larry Speakes said.<

Speakes said Reagan told Dole ``it's up to Congress to act'' on a 1986 federal budget before lawmakers leave Washington for summer vacation Friday.<

Speakes said even though Reagan rejected the plan _ aimed at cutting $64 billion from the fiscal 1986 deficit _ ``there still remains $59.6 billion in savings'' in the Senate proposal.<

``Deficit reduction is the No. 1 issue in America,'' Speakes said. ``The only way to have deficit reduction is to cut federal spending and to do so this year.''<

Senate Budget Committee Chairman Pete Domenici, R-N.M., said after a brief meeting with Regan that he was disappointed with the White House and predicted that rejection of the Senate plan will make it difficult to make deep cuts in the $200 billion-plus deficits predicted for each of the next few years.<

Domenici reported that Regan, despite the president's rejection of the Senate effort, offered to continue to help produce a budget.<

``We told him we appreciated it, but that we didn't need his help,'' Domenici said tersely. ``We'll just have to get on with it.''<

It was the second time in three weeks that Reagan had split with senators from his own party on the budget. The first time, he rejected the curbs in Social Security the Senate budget included.<

Asked how it felt to be rejected by the president twice, Domenici sighed: ``I'm getting used to it.''<

    <
^_____=
^upi 07-29-85 05:21 ped=

Jack Lane

"Ninety-nine out of a hundred people will not go to the film they're reading the review about. They are reading the review primarily for the experience of reading the review."

ROGER EBERT

Roger Ebert barely fits in his office at the Chicago *Sun-Times*. He is being crowded out by Mickey Mouse, Donald Duck, and Marilyn Monroe—a militia of movie memorabilia that compete with Ebert for space on, in and near his desk.

A 3″-tall red, black and yellow rubber Mickey Mouse shares his corner office window with a 4-foot poster that yells "See it! Psycho!" A larger Mickey Mouse hangs from the ceiling, along with a 6″ acrylic star on a string and a 10″ rubber monster hand.

Movie posters cover the wall, empty popcorn cans crowd the floor near the desk, and guests sit in yellow and green director's chairs. On one wall is a black-and-white picture of a marquee from the Van Nuys Drive-In: "The B.O. Invasion," All Color, Rated PG, and "Beyond Bad Breath."

Ebert has been writing for publication since he was nine. He began by publishing a neighborhood newspaper in the Illinois town where he lived. His neighborhood is now Chicago where he moves frenetically from one commitment to another, commonly dressed in his familiar faded blue jeans, Oxford shirt, v-neck sweater and well-worn tennis shoes. "This job is a lifestyle," he says, but actually he has several jobs.

Ebert, 43, spends at least 10 hours a week watching movies and more time than that writing about them. Since 1967, he has been the Chicago *Sun-Times'* film critic. He produces a column and profiles for the *Sun-Times* every week. He and his colleague, Gene Siskel at the rival *Chicago Tribune,* join each other once a week on television for "Siskel and Ebert and the Movies," the country's most widely watched movie review program. [In mid-1986, the title of the program, which was originally "At the Movies," changed to "Siskel and Ebert and the Movies" after this interview took place.] Ebert and Siskel have hosted three editions of "Saturday Night Live" on NBC. Ebert also reviews movies for WLS radio.

Ebert writes wherever he is, whenever he can, using a portable lap computer on airplanes, a personal computer at home and the newspaper computer system at the office. He has created a schedule that demands quick, efficient prose, but he always tries to remember his audience.

Film criticism should not assume too much, says Ebert. "Film reviews allow the reader to experience vicariously something the person writing the review experienced firsthand. That is an entertainment function that has nothing to do with whether or not the person reading the movie review really intends to ever go see that film."

In 1975, Roger Ebert was the first film critic in the country to win a Pulitzer Prize for journalistic criticism. ❖

from Roger Ebert

- The differences between the job of a reporter and the job of a reviewer
- A film critic's responsibilities to the public
- The differences between writing for print and writing for broadcast

Beginnings

I grew up in Urbana, Illinois, and I lived across the street from a man who worked at a newspaper. His son was a good friend of mine. He took us up to look at the paper one day, the *News-Gazette* in Champaign. I was so thrilled by that first visit to the paper that I figured that was the life for me.

Then I got a hectograph kit, where you make a flat gelatin mold and then you print on paper with purple ink in such way that it sticks to the gelatin, so you can make 20 or 30 copies of something with the hectograph. I lived on Washington Street, so when I was nine or 10 I started publishing the *Washington Street News*.

My next publication was *Ebert's Stamp News*. I was a stamp collector, and I started selling stamps through the mail. I don't know if any of my customers knew that I was 11 years old. Then in high school, I went to work for the *Echo*, which was the Urbana High School newspaper. Eventually I became editor.

At the same time, all through high school I was very active in Science Fiction Fandom, which is a subculture of science fiction fans who, in the '50s and '60s, published and distributed mimeographed fanzines to each other. So I published a fanzine called *Stymie*—I think "stymie" may be the name of a typeface.

FIRST NEWSPAPER JOB

After my sophomore year in high school, I was hired by the *News-Gazette* to be a sportswriter. I covered Urbana high school sports for the local daily. That was my first newspaper job. In the summer between my junior and senior years in high school, I went to work as a general assignment reporter for the *News-Gazette,* lowest man on the totem pole. In particular I remember the city editor, Bill Schmelzoe, who took me under his wing and let me write about some automobile crashes and some stuff at the state fair, and I covered a few speeches at the Rotary Club.

The next year, between high school and college, I was the Saturday night police reporter. I covered police and fire from 3 to midnight. I was 17 years old. The pay was very low. I think I began at a dollar an hour, but the experience was invaluable. I went to the University of Illinois right there in Champaign-Urbana, so I worked for the news-paper on and off from '58 until '66.

At the U of I my freshman year, I started a weekly newspaper called *Spectator,* which was kind of a liberal political and arts weekly, six tabloid pages once a week. That came out for a year. Then at the end of my freshman year we ran out of money for that project, and I went to work for the *Daily Illini,* the student newspaper. By my senior year, I was editor.

I majored in English my first two years in college and then I switched to journalism the second two years, so I graduated with a degree in journalism. I continued to work for the *News-Gazette,* and then I went to the University of Illinois graduate school of English starting in the fall of 1964. I spent 1965 at the University of Capetown in South Africa as a Rotary Fellow.

HIRED AT THE CHICAGO *SUN-TIMES*

When I came back I continued at the University of Illinois until the fall of '66, when I came to the University of Chicago as a Ph.D. candidate in English. I'd been working at the *News-Gazette* that whole summer. At the same time, I came here to the *Sun-Times* as a feature writer for the Sunday magazine. On April 1, 1967, I was named the film critic, and I've been a film critic ever since.

I never took a single class on film or criticism. There weren't any film classes at the University of Illinois when I was there. I went to a lot of films—the campus film society, the cinema international. I had writ-ten film reviews for the *Daily Illini.* But I didn't have it on my agenda that I was going to be a movie critic until they gave me the job. I had written about movies for the *Sun-Times,* and the previous film critic retired. Otherwise, things might have happened differently.

A CROWDED WORK WEEK

I have a schedule that makes sense to me. Mondays, Tuesdays, and
Wednesdays, there's almost always a movie at 10 a.m. at screening
rooms. Then frequently there's another movie at noon. Monday and
Tuesday I write both for Friday and for Sunday—Friday is two or three
weekend reviews and Sunday is an interview or a think piece. On
Wednesday, if I haven't already written, I write five 60-second commen-
taries for the ABC radio network, and I record them.

I also write the script for "At the Movies," and usually, two quarters
out of the year, I teach a film class on Wednesday nights at the
University of Chicago Extension. Thursday we tape "At the Movies."
Friday we usually have an "At the Movies" staff meeting, and there may
be another screening, or a movie may have opened at the theater on
Friday, or a review may have to be written for Monday's paper.

I write here on our ATEX system, which is a word processing
system. When I don't write here, I either write at home or out of town.
When I write at home, I write on my DEC Rainbow, which is a
computer. I have the Xywrite word processing program, which is
designed by the same people who made the ATEX system, so that my
home and office word processing systems are pretty much the same.
When I'm out of town or flying around—and I fly a lot—I use a Radio
Shack Model 200 and send copy back to the office by telephone.

Using a portable computer to write on an airplane is a tremen-
dously focusing way to write because you're not going anywhere and
there's nothing else to do. Part of the general disassociation that takes
place in the air anyway, that hypnosis that takes over between takeoff
and landing, helps you to write in a very clear and expressive way, as
long as you're not being annoyed by the person next to you.

This job is a lifestyle. Gene [Siskel] and myself sometimes say that
we are the only two people who really understand each other's lives,
because we both work for newspapers and we're on the same TV show.
I additionally teach and have a radio program. He has a two-year-old
daughter who keeps him pretty busy, and he's on the air live on his
local TV station more than I am.

All the pieces kind of fit in together. I don't believe that either Gene
Siskel or myself could start from scratch and reassemble the kind of
interlocking situation that we're both in right now, but it was just put
together piecemeal. I'm sure there are a lot of people who work a lot
harder than I do.

WHAT TO LOOK FOR IN A FILM

A good film critic should have a working knowledge of film, but he
should also know how to write well and entertainingly. Ninety-nine out

of a hundred people will not go to see the film they're reading the review about. They are reading the review primarily for the experience of reading the review.

Basically, what you're doing when you write film criticism for a newspaper is a combination of things. First of all, you're a reporter. You're covering what happened. You're giving some kind of accurate notion of what somebody is likely to expect to see if they go to see the same movie you saw.

You also have got to be in touch with what you felt about it, not necessarily what you thought about it, but what you felt about it. If you were excited, you have to say you were excited. If you were disgusted, you have to say you were disgusted. You've also got to be able to put the movie in some kind of context. If it's a Spielberg movie, it's this summer's Spielberg movie. Everybody's seen "E.T." and "Indiana Jones." They know about it, so you've got to know about it, too. And you should have some sort of a notion of popular culture.

I also sit through the whole movie, believe me. Eight to ten hours a week is taken up sitting and watching movies. I don't take notes. Whatever the movie has, that's what I'm looking for. It started before I did. I have no preconceived list of things. I love the introduction to a book called *On Movies* by Dwight MacDonald, in which he lists the things he looked for in a good movie when he started out as a critic in the '20s. As he grew older and wiser he realized that they were all totally irrelevant, that the only thing you should look for in a good movie is what makes it good and in a bad movie, what makes it bad.

How could you say, for example, what makes a good novel? What makes a good painting? What makes a good piece of music? It's the purpose of the critic to remain open to whatever the artist has now done, and if the artist is going to do something that corresponds to an idea that already exists in your mind, then he's not an artist anymore. He's simply a manufacturer.

I don't know what makes a good movie. I know certain kinds of things that I like to see in films. For example, I love extremely accurately observed moments of life, but on the other hand one of my favorite films is "2001," which has nothing to do with psychological accuracy about human behavior. Film criticism is totally subjective. I believe that most criticism is subjective—"This is what I feel, and here's what I feel about it, and you're welcome to have your own opinion."

WHAT A FILM CRITIC DOES (AND DOES NOT) DO

People think I get to go to the movies all day long and hang out with the stars, and basically they're right. What they don't perceive is the work involved in writing, taping, the actual work.

Then there are things that you just can't help them out with. Not a week goes by when I don't receive an unsolicited manuscript or screenplay, which I send back. I do not provide addresses of directors, producers, agents or stars. I do not forward mail.

I cannot provide a literary agency service, nor can I read or rewrite manuscripts. And people sometimes get rather irritated about that. They don't seem to understand, for example, that even if Steven Spielberg were my best friend and he were calling me up daily, asking me if I'd seen any good manuscripts or screenplays, it would be unethical for me to submit them to him. I would then be placing myself in a position of reviewing a movie that I'd had a hand in or asking him for a favor when I have to maintain arm's length from him.

YOU CAN'T LIKE EVERY MOVIE

You have to be willing to be unpopular. Occasionally you will dislike somebody's movie, but if they're any good at all they might make another movie before long that will be good. A critic who likes everything is not a critic worth having around anyway, because if he likes everything, he obviously has no standards.

A good movie will create its own enthusiasm. And I don't need to have my enthusiasm up for bad movies. In fact, my lack of enthusiasm for bad movies is all part of the process. A movie, generally speaking, creates its own feeling. People say, "Well, what if you go to the movie in a bad mood? Doesn't that influence your review?" I feel if it's a good enough movie, it will change your mood.

HOW TO DEFINE A WELL-WRITTEN REVIEW

A lot of people send me their reviews. "Please read my reviews and critique them." And I would like to write back and say, "I received your term papers. Apparently you put them in the envelope instead of your reviews. Please send me your reviews, because academic writing has so little to do with ordinary communication to human beings that if you really do have an interest in a journalism career, I would advise you to be aware of that." The games that you play in writing college term papers have nothing to do with the way people, even literate, educated people, talk to each other in the real world.

A well-written review is a review that the reader reads all the way through and is happy to keep reading until he gets to the end. I would like it if someone were to say, "I read your review and I disagreed with every word in it." But I wouldn't like it if they said, "I read your review and I don't think we saw the same movie." I would like them to have a certain feeling of recognition.

My average review will be between 18 and 22 inches in length, and I have all the time I need to write the review that I want to write. I think one of the things I had to teach myself was not to overwrite the review. People spend a quarter, and they get a paper that has 180 pages in it. If they were to read everything in that paper, they wouldn't have time to do anything else all day long.

Many critics on newspapers write in too dense or compact a style because they are aware of old cinema professors looking over their shoulders and saying, "You forgot to mention that this film has been influenced by Renoir." I try to write in a very conversational style. I'm talking to you. And I don't mean in a literary style. I mean, "I saw the movie. You're thinking of seeing the movie. Here's what I thought."

ETHICS OF BEING A FILM CRITIC

Studios and movie people do not approach critics to tell them how to review their movies. You're working with the same people month after month, year after year anyway. It's all very straightforward—"Here's the movie. You review it." Reviewing is part of the process of publicizing the film, from their point of view. It's not a case of, "Gee, I hope you like this."

I've never been offered a bribe. I've written a few screenplays over the years, but particularly since we started doing a national television show, I believe that it would be wrong for me to submit a screenplay to anyone. I wrote a screenplay for Russ Meyer, "Beyond the Valley of the Dolls," but I've never reviewed any of his films. That would be a conflict of interest. Film critics who try to sell screenplays, I feel, are treading on thin ice.

I do not give blurbs to advertisers before my review has appeared. People will sometimes call up and say, "Can we have a line for our ad?" and I don't do that. Once my review has appeared or once it has been written or broadcast or taped, then they are welcome to quote from it if they want to.

For some time I haven't accepted junkets where they pay your expenses. If I go to interview someone, it is paid for either by the Chicago *Sun-Times* or by Channel 7 here in Chicago or by both. In the early days, we took free junkets, but now we don't anymore, and I have that written into my contract, that I cannot be asked to take a junket. Even when we took free junkets, it didn't make the slightest bit of difference. For example, I remember when I went all the way to Bora Bora to visit the set of "Hurricane," which, when it came out, I picked as one of the worst movies of all time.

I know there are some papers that don't have any travel budget at all, and a film critic might never get to be on a movie set or meet anyone in the business without accepting a junket. I'm not talking for everyone. I just believe this for me. It's much simpler if I pay my own way, or if my employers pay my way.

COVERING THE STARS

I think that celebrities have changed a little bit in the 18 years I've been a movie critic. One of the reasons they've changed is that I've grown older. The first time I interviewed Robert Mitchum, I was 24, and I was utterly awestruck. I was 24 when I interviewed John Wayne for the first time. These were people who were imbedded in my consciousness from childhood and adolescence, so it was hard for me to see them as real human beings.

I talked about this, oddly enough, with Woody Allen. Woody agreed with me. It was an interesting conversation. The cut-off date is when you start your own adult life. Movie stars whom you related to primarily on the screen will always seem different to you than people who are your own age or who came along after you became an adult. So, for example, Woody Allen was saying, "I have great admiration for Robert DeNiro. I have great respect for Meryl Streep. But if I were to meet them or talk to them, we would have an ordinary conversation, two people alive at the same time talking over things."

But in "The Purple Rose of Cairo," one of his stars was Van Johnson, and he [Woody Allen] could hardly talk to Van Johnson. He had to practically have his assistant director talk to Van Johnson, because this was the guy who won the Second World War and flew down to South America and got all the pretty girls. Van Johnson was part of Woody Allen's adolescence.

It's the same with me and movie stars. The ones who were stars when I was a kid, when I was a teen-ager, I cannot really respond to except as stars. The ones who have come along since, the ones whose first and second movies I may have reviewed, I can relate to on a more ordinary basis.

HOW TO INTERVIEW A STAR

As for what questions I ask, I really don't go in with a list of questions, just as I don't go into a movie with a list of things I'm looking for. In general what I try to be is an observer. I enjoy it best when I am in a situation where it's not really an interview. There's something really happening, and I'm reporting on what's happening.

For example, getting in the back seat of a car where Robert Mitchum and his friend were going to drive to the movie location and we wound up in Ohio. Or interviewing Tony Curtis at the Cannes Film

Festival, and he's suddenly trying to pick up a girl that he saw outside his hotel window. I like the interview best in which the subject of the interview is leading his life and I'm just sitting there watching.

Groucho Marx, for example. It was terrific to be able to go to an Academy Awards party with him. I had a lot of chances, in doing Groucho Marx for *Esquire,* to talk to him, to get the answers to all the questions that I wanted. I could tell you a great deal about his mother, Minnie, and about the early days of vaudeville and about his family and his brothers. Those would be the kinds of questions that you would need for an encyclopedia interview.

But what I really wanted to do, and I was able to do it, was to go along with him to an Academy Award party with a real mixed bag of people there. Hugh Hefner was there, and Johnny Weismuller and Willie Shoemaker and Fay Wray, all kinds of Hollywood strange people, and I just listened to his one-liners and tried to duplicate his conversation and show the way his mind worked. To me, that was a lot more important than getting his specific answer to what it was like to make "Duck Soup."

You don't ordinarily get an opportunity to do something like that, but when you do, it's precious. I really feel that the difference between a feature interview, say a show business interview, and a news interview is that in the news interview what matters are specific answers to specific questions. In the feature interview, what matters is whatever happens to happen. Feature writing has much more to do with human style, and news writing has more to do with substance.

You don't really go for the stories. I'll give you an example. I'm sure that if I were to ask Clint Eastwood what he thought about "Dirty Harry," the answer I would get would be an answer he had given before. But if I can ask him those questions in a context in which he is constantly being interrupted by people with Polaroid cameras, I then begin to set up a dramatic situation in which Clint Eastwood, the professional filmmaker who is giving an interview, is at the same time involved in real-life events which are are wearing him down as a person.

Eastwood is one of the most intelligent interviews in the movie business, but by being able to spend a whole day with him out in California, I was able to see over a period of time the cumulative effect of his celebrity—the Chinese water torture of dozens and hundreds of people. Each one wants an autograph, or each one wants a Polaroid picture taken.

And then occasionally a dramatic event will occur that will tie everything together, and in this case a man wanted the barrel of his Magnum handgun to be autographed. That tied in celebrity and violence and the "Dirty Harry" character. It was just a lucky chance because then a real event was able to make the point for me.

HOW TO WRITE A CELEBRITY INTERVIEW

The way I write a celebrity interview is often structured a lot like a John O'Hara short story. There are probably greater short-story writers than John O'Hara, but he was somebody I could learn from because what he often does is start in the middle of things with dialogue. Eventually the dialogue will reveal things about the situation and about the characters that weren't known at the beginning. Themes will be set up that are disguised until another line will come along to trigger or reveal them.

Many of O'Hara's short stories are told probably with 80 or 90 percent dialogue. And many of my interviews are 80 or 90 percent dialogue. I am not really into long paragraphs where I tell what I think about Groucho Marx. At the end of the Groucho Marx piece, you can figure out by reading who the Groucho Marx was that I thought I met. But I don't want to tell you that.

I agree with something that I heard, so long ago that I can't remember who told me, that the word "said" is invisible. People never get tired of reading "he said," "she said." But if you try to find synonyms for it they will almost always call attention to themselves—"he sputtered," "she exclaimed."

What I try to do in some of my interviews is to use a lot of dialogue, to keep myself fairly well in the background, and it's almost like the fly on the wall in which you are like a playwright. You are saying what was said. You're saying what happened while it was said. And then the audience or the reader will figure out what it all means.

SHOW, DON'T TELL

I think that the very worst thing you can do in a personality interview is tell in the first paragraph what you thought about the person or what you think the piece is about. Your first paragraph is not, "John Wayne is the most heroic figure in the last 40 years of American motion pictures." Your first line should be, "Wanna play a game of chess?" Or, I often like the first line that opens totally *in medias res,* like Robert Mitchum talking to his pal about lime spray, which he thought might be an aphrodisiac for the teen-age girls that were hanging around the movie location. Just start right in the middle, and structure it only to the degree that you leave out what is irrelevant or boring.

PRINT VS. BROADCAST WRITING

The difference between writing for print and writing for broadcast is that in the newspaper, you avoid clichés or use them ironically. For broadcast, you frequently make judicious use of certain clichés because they can be heard well. They talk in radio writing about, "Will something hear?" Some words that are perfectly clear in print, when said aloud, do not really make an impression on the viewer. So you've got to write in such a way that they will be able to hear and understand what you're saying.

I'll give you an example. One of the most useful words to a movie critic is "genre." The problem with that word is that there's no word in English that I know of that says the same thing. That word just never really "hears," no matter how you pronounce it. I pronounce it, "jon-ra" because I think that comes closer to sounding like what you might picture it as being spelled like. Even then, I'm sure that every time I use that word a lot of people don't know what I'm talking about. But there's no substitute for "genre."

You have to write in shorter sentences. The viewer cannot hear a semicolon, cannot see parentheses. Conversational speech is made up of bursts of ideas, linked together by buried grammar, whereas written language is often much more logical. You can diagram sentences that are written, but it's very hard to diagram spoken sentences. You will find that they are missing parts or that they are implying parts that aren't there.

One of the things that I've sometimes seen on television, especially with print journalists trying to make a transition to television, is somebody on TV who is reading a perfectly well-written piece and it is boring. It is usually too long, and it is usually too hard to hear.

Most print journalists would probably save clippings of their newspaper articles but would not save copies of their television scripts. The reason is, in print what you're proud of is the writing. On television, what you're proud of—if you're proud of anything—is the energy or the degree of sincerity or conviction. It's more of a performance.

I had to learn that. I'm sure that when I first started out on "Sneak Previews" 10 years ago, I was very proud of some turn of phrase or some clever little word choice. People at home watching television are not really listening to the words and appreciating the words. They are getting the whole *Gestalt*.

They're getting the energy, they're getting the emotion, they're getting the body language, they're getting the facial expressions, they're getting the tone of voice, they're getting the hand movements, they're getting the other person, Siskel. All of this communicates, and at the end they will know what we think about the movie, but they will not necessarily have been listening to some wonderfully turned phrase.

THE BENEFITS OF THE PULITZER

Winning the Pulitzer Prize was kind of earth-shaking. It was just a great honor. It meant a lot to me, but it didn't mean that I had any trouble writing or getting back to my typewriter. That's pretty much second nature.

I got the award when I was 32, and I think that was an ideal age to get it because I could enjoy it for that many more years. It's the world's shortest job resume. Job resume: Winner of a Pulitzer Prize. Unless you've really got a lot of problems, the Pulitzer on your resume will get you a job on a lot of newspapers.

HOW TO BECOME A FILM CRITIC

The important thing is to realize that film critic isn't a job description. Newspaperman on the film beat is the job description. So many people who want to be film critics for newspapers or popular journalism in general know all there is to know about film and nothing about communicating. They study film and perhaps they should equally study or spend time writing journalism.

Also, get a lot of experience. When I get high school kids who write me, "I'm in high school. I want to be a film critic. What should I study in high school?" I write back, "Study typing." They think I'm being facetious, but I'm not because until you can type as fast as you can think you can never be a newspaperman.

Of course, everyone feels that the way to get into their field is the way *they* got into their field, but I believe it was useful to me that from an early age I was working for newspapers wherever and whenever I could. I believe that the best way to do something is to do it, not to theorize about it, and not even necessarily to study it.

BEGIN WITH LETTERS TO THE EDITOR

You start. You find a job. You get an internship. You write letters to the editor of every publication that you subscribe to, every week if necessary, long letters that won't get printed. Writing a letter to the editor of *The New Republic* every week is like writing for *The New Republic* every week—the only difference being that it's not printed. A lot of people can't bear the thought of writing something that won't be read, so they never keep a journal, for example, which is another good thing you can do.

My advice is to write letters to the editor, not just "I thought this was a good article," but to the editor as if it's an essay on the subject. Mail it off. That way you have at least the impression that somebody is reading it. If you do see it in print, it will really make you feel good.

The first thing I got published in the greater world was when I was about 7 or 8. It was a letter to the editor of the *Chicago Daily News* warning against people throwing away refrigerators without taking the doors off the hinges.

Roger Ebert   205

I wrote to newspapers like the *Chicago Daily News* and the local papers where I lived. And I wrote to all the science fiction magazines. I had dozens of letters printed in the science fiction magazines on esoteric and arcane topics in the late '50s. If you go back to the late '50s and look through the old files of *Amazing Stories, Fantastic Science Fiction,* and *Infinity* you'll find my name in there.

WRITE THE FIRST 500,000 WORDS

The best insight I ever got into the teaching of writing came from Daniel Curley, who I took several short-story courses from. He said, "Nobody really has any more than about 500,000 words of really bad fiction in them. After that, they get better or they quit. And the job of this course is to get rid of 20,000 of those words." I thought he was very pragmatic.

I think by the time I got to 1967 [at the *Sun-Times*], I had already written the 500,000 words. I had been working on papers for 10 years by then. I don't expect everybody to get the breaks that I got, but I believe that many, many, many tens of hundreds of thousands of words have to be written even in the practice of routine journalism before people become fluent enough to begin to find their own voice. To me, daily beat journalism, obituaries—of which I've written thousands— automobile accidents and county fairs are to a journalist what practicing the scales is to a pianist.

Clint Eastwood

**You have to make a choice.
Are you gonna showboat to the fourth wall,
or get with the program?
Carmel, Calif., 1984**

by Roger Ebert

For a man who got his start by striking matches on a hunchback and shooting three men with one bullet, Clint Eastwood has inspired an amazing amount of serious analysis. I was looking at some of the literature out on the patio behind the Hog's Breath Inn, the restaurant he owns here on a side street not far from the ocean. There was the Norman Mailer essay ("He is living proof of the maxim that the best way to get through life is cool") and the *New York Review of Books* article ("What's most distinctive about Eastwood is how effectively he struggles against absorption into mere genre, mere style"), and the *Los Angeles Times* piece on the strong women in his movies ("Eastwood may be the most important and influential feminist film-maker working in America today").

Clint Eastwood, the Man With No Name, Dirty Harry, Joe Kidd—a *feminist filmmaker?* I put the articles aside and studied the menu. It was going to be either the Eiger Sandwich or the Dirty Harry Burger, and I'd almost made up my mind when Clint Eastwood materialized at the table and sprawled in a chair. He is very low key. He sat in a corner with his back to the patio, to give himself some small measure of privacy, but before he could tell the waitress he would have an iced tea, two little girls had come up, smiling and giggling, for his autograph.

He has a system. He signed *Clint Eastwood,* and *while* he is signing it, he asks, "Who's it to?" Then they say something like "It's to my brother Billy," and he writes *To Billy* above his signature. By asking the question while he's signing his name, he saves a few seconds every time. He has been around long enough to realize that no one ever wants an autograph for themselves. They always want it for their girlfriend or their brother Billy.

"This early hour isn't so bad," he said. "I've been in here times when the autograph hounds got so thick I was driven out. I'd have to tell people I'd meet them down the street."

How does it make you feel, all the requests for autographs?

"Like the Chinese water torture. One autograph is no big deal. But they keep coming all day long, day after day, and each one is a little tug at your patience, until you feel like screaming."

... We talked some more, there under the cypress, with Eastwood occasionally sticking a spear of beach grass into his mouth, or lobbing a pebble into the distance. Both, I reflected, were cinematic activities that brought visual interest to his answers. This man was a consummate actor. Finally we stood up, shook the sand from our shoes, and returned to our back table on the patio of the Hog's Breath.

Right away, it was clear that the customers in his restaurant weren't going to give Clint Eastwood a pass. There was a slow but steady parade to his side, until it was obvious that everyone in the room was going to ask for an autograph. Frequently, the autograph seekers would interrupt Eastwood in the middle of a sentence, and when they used the standard rituals ("I hate to bother you, but ..."), he frowned, but the frown was always down at the piece of paper he was signing. He was distant, but courteous. Autographs are a fame tax the public exacts from celebrities.

"Do you mind if I take your picture?"

"Snap it."

"And now if you would sign these napkins ..."

"I'm thinking of passing a rule: Either a Polaroid *or* an autograph, not both."

... It was almost dark out now, and time to call it a day. The parade of autograph-seekers had never slowed, but now there was one more fan approaching the table, and he would bring a chill that was deeper than the night air.

This fan had been drinking. He had some story he wanted to tell Eastwood, but it was coming out in such a dis-

---

jointed way that it was hard to follow. Something about having been at the Hog's Breath before, looking for Eastwood and not finding him, and coming back tonight, because of something about a police training program, and . . .

From somewhere on his body, the man drew a .44 Magnum and held it in his hand.

There was an instant when everyone froze.

"I hope that's not loaded," Eastwood said.

"Naw," the fan said. He opened the empty chamber.

"What do you want?"

"For you to autograph the stock," the fan said, and pulled an awl from his pocket.

Eastwood looked very grim.

"I hate to autograph firearms," he said.

The guy said something about how all the boys on the force admired Eastwood so much. Eastwood frowned. But he took the awl and scratched his initials, C. E., into the wooden stock of the most powerful handgun in the world.

"Be careful where you leave that," he told the guy.

&IDEAS &ISSUES

These questions, listed by topic, are designed to compare and contrast the ideas and issues from the 12 interviewees with one another. Section I, for example, will help compare how Madeleine Blais works with how Linda Williams works. Or you can discuss the work habits of all the journalists listed at once. For quick reference, the pages where you can find the topic discussed in each interview follow the interviewee's name.

I. Work Schedule

1. How does the work schedule of a news writer differ from a feature writer? From a columnist?

2. How do some of these journalists combine the specific demands of a beat with the desire to write in-depth stories about a subject?

3. How do daily news events sometimes affect what a feature writer or a columnist covers?

4. How much control do these reporters have over what they cover and when they cover it?

5. How do deadlines affect what these reporters can cover?

II. Organization Techniques

1. How do these journalists use organization to help them write?

2. What five organizational techniques can you use that are suggested by these journalists?

3. What role does organization play in these journalists' work?

4. Which of these journalists applies the most systematic organization? Is it possible for all journalists to use this technique? Why? Why not?

5. Which aspects of systematic organization suggested by these reporters are adaptable to most journalistic assignments?

III. Research Techniques

1. What role does research play in the reporting these writers do?

2. How are research questions different for a news writer and a feature writer? For a columnist?

3. What five useful research suggestions can you use that are used by these reporters?

4. According to what these writers say, is research a separate task from reporting or is research integral to good reporting? Why?

5. Discuss how poor research can harm a good story, using an example from one of these reporters.

IV. Interviewing Techniques

1. What role does interviewing play in the reporting process for each of these writers?

2. What are the benefits and the drawbacks of using a tape recorder?

3. How do the techniques for interviewing private people differ from the techniques for interviewing public people?

4. Why is it important for reporters to adapt to each individual interviewee?

5. List five approaches suggested by these reporters that will help you to improve your interviewing technique.

V. Writing Techniques

1. List five (or more) specific suggestions from these reporters to help improve your writing.

2. How do the elements of a good news story differ from the elements of a good feature story?

3. Why do many of these writers say a working lead is important?

4. How do these writers integrate research and interviews into their stories?

5. Which of these reporters seems the most ritualistic about the writing process? Why? Do you have any writing superstitions?

VI. The Role of Editors

1. Should editors always "Do no harm," as one reporter suggests? Why? Why not?

2. How can editors interfere with a reporter's goals?

3. What role do the best editors seem to play?

VII. Characteristics of Different Beats

1. What are the differences among the specific geographic beats (Miami, the Pacific, Dallas, the South, Washington, D.C.)?

2. What are the differences among the specific subject beats (aerospace, business, labor, sports, intelligence agencies, the White House, celebrities)?

3. Are the best stories only found in the best news towns? Why? Why not?

4. Which kinds of stories can best be done in certain locations? Why?

5. How do these reporters' interests match their locations or their beats?

VIII. Criticism of Journalists and Journalism

1. What are five (or more) criticisms of the journalistic profession raised by these reporters?

2. Is their criticism justifiable? Why? Why not?

3. How do members of the press affect the events they cover?

4. What is the press's social responsibility?

5. What is the press's professional responsibility?

IX. Characteristics of a Good Reporter

1. On which characteristics of a good reporter do these journalists agree?

2. To you, which five characteristics seem most important?

3. Which characteristics of a good reporter, as described by these journalists, do you have? Which should you work to improve?

X. Role in Personal Life

1. What role does their profession play in each of these journalists' lives?
2. What choices have these journalists made about their personal lives?
3. How are the personal lives of some of these journalists enhanced by their professional responsibilities?

XI. Ethical Dilemmas

1. Is it possible to create a list of ethical principles that would cover the ethical dilemmas described by these reporters? Why? Why not?
2. Is each of the ethical dilemmas described by these reporters situational, or are there some general ethical principles that could be used to anticipate solutions to these problems before they emerge? Why?
3. Would you have made the same choice each of these journalists made when faced with the specific ethical decisions they describe? Why?

XII. Discussion of Story Sample

1. How do the elements of each story match the reporter's description of his or her approach to the story or the subject?

2. How do the reporter's biases or viewpoints about the story influence what is written?

3. Which elements of good writing do you see in each story sample? How could the writing be improved?

4. Does a writer working on a quick deadline necessarily have to write differently than a writer with no imminent deadline? Why? Why not?

5. Compare the story samples of each of these writers with what they say about writing. Which of their writing goals do they achieve?